Shaping Words to
Fit the Soul

Shaping Words to Fit the Soul

*The Southern Ritual Grounds
of Afro-Modernism*

JÜRGEN E. GRANDT

 THE OHIO STATE UNIVERSITY PRESS · COLUMBUS

Library of Congress Cataloging-in-Publication Data
Grandt, Jürgen E., 1968–
   Shaping words to fit the soul : the southern ritual grounds of Afro-modernism / Jürgen E. Grandt.
      p. cm.
   Includes bibliographical references and index.
   ISBN-13: 978-0-8142-1112-0 (cloth : alk. paper)
   ISBN-10: 0-8142-1112-7 (cloth : alk. paper)
   ISBN-13: 978-0-8142-9209-9 (cd-rom)
   1. Modernism (Literature) 2. American literature—African American authors—History and criti-
cism. 3. Douglass, Frederick, 1818–1895—Criticism and interpretation. 4. Toomer, Jean, 1894–
1967—Criticism and interpretation. 5. Wright, Richard, 1908–1960—Criticism and interpretation.
6. Jones, Tayari—Criticism and interpretation. 7. Modernism (Music) 8. Handy, W. C. (William
Christopher), 1873–1958—Criticism and interpretation. 9. Allman Brothers Band—Criticism and
interpretation. I. Title.
   PN56.M54G73 2009
   810.9'896073—dc22
                                        2009017396
This book is available in the following editions:
Cloth (ISBN 978-0-8142-1112-0)
CD-ROM (ISBN 978-0-8142-9209-9)

An earlier version of chapter 1 appeared in the fall 2001 issue of CLA Journal as "A Life and Power
Far Beyond the Letter: Life and Times of Frederick Douglass and the Authentic Blackness of Autobiography."

Cover design by James Baumann
Text design by Juliet Williams
Type set in Adobe Goudy
Printed by Thomson-Shore, Inc.

∞ The paper used in this publication meets the minimum requirements of the American National
Standard for Information Sciences—Permanence of Paper for Printed Library Materials. ANSI
Z39.48-1992.

9 8 7 6 5 4 3 2 1

For Nico

CONTENTS

ACKNOWLEDGMENTS

It may seem incongruous at first that the initial spark for what eventually became this book was somehow ignited in a pizza parlor in Bern (Switzerland, not North Carolina) and hastily jotted down on a paper napkin. Portions of the manuscript were fine-tuned on an airplane sitting on the tarmac in Glasgow (Scotland, not Alabama) waiting for takeoff to Amsterdam (the Netherlands, not Virginia), in a taxi inching through the clogged streets of downtown Dublin (Ireland, not Georgia), or during many an uncomfortable ride on the diesel-powered local train rumbling from Nuremberg to Bayreuth in Bavaria (Germany's version of the Dirty South). But in a way, these places, and many more, became *Shaping Words to Fit the Soul*'s own 'ritual grounds,' however temporarily.

Much, much more important than the places, though, are the people I was traveling to see, had just met, or whose acquaintance I made along the way. Whatever is good and useful in the following pages is in no small measure due to them:

In the U.S., I am indebted to Rolanda C. Burney, Richard Freedom Byrd-Harris, Newton "Newt" Collier, Chester J. Fontenot, Maryemma Graham, La Vinia D. Jennings, Jared S. Johnson, Joseph Johnson, Tayari Jones, John W. Lowe, Hubert H. McAlexander, Barbara McCaskill, Christian Moraru, Jed Rasula, Frank "Rat" Ratliff, Calaya M. Reid a.k.a. Grace Octavia, Roger Stolle, and Kirk West. Many, many thanks to Karen and Richard Lyle-Roken and their families, especially Robi Lyle: keep on rockin', my friend. Malcolm Litchfield, Eugene O'Connor, and particularly Sandy Crooms and Heather Lee Miller at The Ohio State University Press are simply the best in their field, but I have shared so much laughter with them that I often forget they're my editors, too. With their sharp eyes and tough questions, the two anonymous readers who perused the manuscript were instrumental in transforming this into a real book. Erika B. Vinson and my Honors students at the University of Georgia deserve credit not only for helping me hone my own critical chops, but for succeeding where others had failed: in making me *listen* to hip-hop. The completion of this project owes much to the unwavering support of DoVeanna S. Fulton Minor and R. Baxter Miller—I am inspired by their example, humbled by their generosity, and proud of their friendship: thank you both for keeping the faith.

In Germany, I want to thank Klaus Benesch, Karsten Fitz, Sascha Pöhlmann, Christoph Ribbat, Heidi Rossner-Schöpf, and Kerstin Schmidt; I, too, have always depended on the kindness of strangers, and I'm glad that these six are strangers no more.

In Namibia and Nigeria respectively, I am grateful for the help and support of Mbongeni Malaba and Wumi Raji.

In Switzerland, I have always been able to count on my posse, the families of Simone and Daniel Althaus, Sandra and Martin Kindlimann, Sibylle and Thomas Menzi, and Friederike Pohlenz and Stephan Brunner.

And finally, most importantly, I am most thankful for my parents, Yvonne and Werner: wherever I am, I always know that I am still being backed by the *best* rhythm section anyone could ever want.

Atlanta, Georgia, August 2009

INTRODUCTION

"Gone With 'What' Wind?"

Afro-Modernism's Southern Ritual Grounds

When Count Basie entered the Columbia studios on May 31, 1940, to record a composition with the title "Gone With 'What' Wind?" he certainly had not conceived it as the kind of biting satire that, for instance, Charles Mingus would perform some two decades later with the "Fables of Faubus." Basie simply remarked that the tune "was really something from Benny Goodman's book. As a matter of fact I had sat in as a guest piano player in Benny's sextet when he recorded it for Columbia back in February while we were working at the Golden Gate." And, he added casually, he had simply "dictated a few little changes here and there" (Basie 240; Sheridan 98–100). The "something" Basie appropriated for this recording session was actually a tune composed by Goodman, "Gone With What Draft?" It is safe to say that neither the Jewish New Yorker Goodman nor the midwesterner Basie intended a trenchant contestation of symbolic territory of *The Wind Done Gone* kind—even if, in what surely constitutes a case of inadvertent poetic justice, "Gone With 'What' Wind?" is a blues.[1] Yet the title of Basie's adaptation, phrased as a question, features at its core an adjective that points to a referential void. Its allusions and wider context stake out a symbolical terrain that at once clearly demarcates a southern setting and yet ultimately resists linguistic representation. Thus, "Gone With 'What' Wind?" exemplifies in some ways a paradox central to African American musics: as Nathaniel Mackey astutely points out, "Part of the genius of black music is the room it allows for a telling 'inarticulacy,' a feature consistent with its critique of a predatory coherence, a cannibalistic 'plan of living,' and the articulacy that upholds it" (252–53). The interrogatory range at the center of Basie's song title therefore also echoes Ralph Ellison's observation that "because jazz finds its very life in an endless improvisation upon traditional materials, the jazzman must lose his identity even as he finds it" (*Shadow* 267).

The music criticism of Mackey and Ellison underlies an aspect of African American cultural production that literary theories have by and large circumvented. African American literary-critical paradigms of the past three decades have tended to privilege modes of reading that draw on the 'authentic' black folkways of the rural South framed, in Robert Stepto's words, as the "*genius loci*" (67–70). Ann duCille has coined the term "Hurstonism" for these interpretive models, where "the valorization of the vernacular" leads to "an inherently exclusionary literary practice that filters a wide range of complex and often contradictory impulses and energies into a single modality consisting of the blues and the folk" (69). DuCille continues that "such evaluations often erase the contexts and complexities of a wide range of African American historical experiences and replace them with a single, monolithic, if valorized, construction: 'authentic' blacks are southern, rural, and sexually uninhibited" (71). More recently, Madhu Dubey has pointed to the still salient "romance of the residual" suffusing cultural criticism today, a romance that hinges on a reification of preindustrial, premodern (symbolic) spaces more often than not situated in the rural South (158–70). Stepto's own investigation into "the authenticating machinery" of African American narrative, Houston A. Baker's "blues matrix," Henry Louis Gates's "Signifyin(g)" and "speakerly text"—or, indeed, Toni Morrison's "ancestral South"—all look to the vernacular culture of the Black Belt for their respective readings of African American narrative.[2] Morrison—though a self-proclaimed midwestern author, perhaps the most 'southern' writer alive today—has even called her novels "village literature, fiction that is really for the village, for the tribe. Peasant literature for my people" ("Language" 26; "Seams" 59; Interview 119).

Thus, what Stepto calls the South's rural "ritual grounds" have engendered a "pregeneric myth," one that in turn generates the critical apparatuses for the investigation of the entire black American literary tradition (xv, 66–74). The "symbolic geography" he maps

> focuses on the idea that a landscape becomes symbolic in literature when it is a region in time and space offering spatial expressions of social structures and ritual grounds on the one hand, and of *communitas* and *genius loci* on the other. . . . Symbolic geography in Afro-American narratives emerges . . . as a structural topography in which seemingly permanent (to the Afro-American) social structures manifest themselves as sites for locus-specific variations upon a nearly universal race ritual. (67–68)

Defining ritual ground as "a reaction to social structure within a structural topography" that provides "the currency of exchange, as it were, within the realm of *communitas*," Stepto's critical practice delineates "a 'tribal' geography" that is almost exclusively male and southern (69, 70, 77).[3]

And so, in an ironic reversal, the *historical* southern ritual ground, with its brutally disruptive legacies of chattel slavery, ethnic cleansing, and civil war, becomes codified in literary-critical practice as the source of an identifiable and predominantly rural 'southernness,' albeit a southernness more often than not under siege or (perpetually) fading away. In the South, the guiding Morrisonian ancestor is always in danger of vanishing—but knowable and somehow stable nonetheless, for myths are by nature consolidating in that they offer tangents of identification. In the still prevailing strains of African American critical theory, Stepto's pregeneric myth has been reincarnated in poststructuralist garb. For all their ostensible celebration of destabilizing ambiguity and heterogeneous polyvalence, Henry Louis Gates's "Signifyin(g)" and Houston Baker's "blues matrix" deploy their own stabilizing mechanisms, authenticating machineries that, like all concepts of authenticity, serve to declare as much who's out as to identify who's in (McDowell, "*Changing*" 165–67). Sandra Adell points out that the critical methodologies of Gates and Baker not only "fall short of their emancipatory goal of freeing Afro-American literature from the hegemony of Eurocentric discourses" but also "bring into sharp relief what can best be described as a nostalgia for tradition. For to summon a tradition, for example, by reconstructing it, is to search for an authority, that of the tradition itself. Such an enterprise, even as it pits two or more traditions against each other, or even as it attempts to fuse traditions, is inherently conservative. Something is always conserved, something always remains the Same" (137). That "something" is, more often than not, the symbolic ritual grounds of the American South and its vernaculars.

These critical approaches become themselves stabilizing rituals, and as such echo in part the problem engendered by Stepto's wholesale adoption of Victor Turner (Stepto 67–69). For the anthropologist Turner, ritual is geared toward "the process of regenerative renewal" ("Process" 159). A society's rituals are therefore also consensus models feeding into the maintenance of "*communitas*": "bedrock *communitas*," writes Turner, is "a generic human relationship undivided by status-roles or structural oppositions, which is also vouched for by myths and histories stressing the unity and continuity of the widest group to which all belong by birth and tradition" ("Images" 233). The evolution of *communitas* becomes, "for the groups and individuals within structured systems, a means of binding diversities together and overcoming cleavages" (*Dramas* 206). The normative tendencies in *communitas* are reinforced when enacted within a specific geographic space (*Dramas* 169, 268–69). For all its attention to liminality and rupture, Turner's social drama is actually impelled by processes of assimilation and integration as the ultimate goal of ritual as a regulatory function (Rosaldo 96–97; D. Weber 530). The status of the liminal is one that, in Turner's concept, ultimately contributes to "ensuring the continuity of proved values and norms" ("Process" 163).

However, modernism's key themes of fragmentation, alienation, and epistemology complicate the demarcation of the South's rural "ritual grounds" as a repository of the "authenticating machinery" of African American narrative.[4] As Adell stipulates, "in modernism the self is separated from its world, from its true home in the world. In modernism the self is homeless and only resides in writing. As such it participates in its own displacement even as it seeks to reconcile itself with the ordinary, familial, and social order of everyday life" (139). The modernist severance of 'word' from 'world' destabilizes the southern ritual ground as *genius loci* of a "bedrock *communitas*"—and, not coincidentally, many of his theories Turner formulated in the course of studying premodern societies. It therefore follows that Stepto fashions the *genius loci* of African American cultural production into a premodernist ritual ground, for modernism's inherent eclecticism and instability disturb what he, in the 1991 afterword to the second edition of *From Behind the Veil*, calls "the dominant meta-plot of the tale": he insists that instability is always a product of the (uninformed) reader, never a quality of the text (202, 204).

What the paradigms of Turner and Stepto minimize is that rituals, as acts that seek to regulate transferences of power and shifts of identity, in and of themselves often reinforce the disruptive impulses behind any transformation as much as they are designed to contain them (Hutcheon 97; Raboteau 86–87). Art, as Walter Benjamin reminds us, has always had an intricate connection to ritual:

> The original way of embedding the artwork in the context of tradition found its expression in the cult. The earliest artworks, as we know, originated in the service of a ritual—first a magic ritual, then a religious one. It is now of decisive significance that the artwork's auratic mode of existence is never severed entirely from its ritual function. In other words, the unique value of the "authentic" artwork has its foundation in ritual, in which it had its original and earliest use value. This ritualistic basis, however it is mediated, is still discernible as a secularized ritual in even the most profane forms of aesthetic service. . . . With the secularization of art, authenticity takes the place of cult value. ("Kunstwerk" 144)[5]

Benjamin here also stresses that the "use value" of art (reconfigured in Stepto's paradigm as "the currency of exchange" within the *communitas*) has itself become highly unstable amid the social and political upheavals of modernity. Ralph Ellison grafts the implications onto southern American ritual grounds and argues that "while the myths and mysteries that form Southern mystique are *irrational* and even *primitive*, they are nevertheless real, even as works of the imagination are 'real.' Like all mysteries and their attendant myths, they imply . . . a rite. And rites are *actions*, the goal of which is the manipulation of power—in primitive religions magical power, in the South (and in the North) political power" (*Going* 572). The experience of repeated uprooting in the Middle Passage and under the peculiar institution informed virtually every ritual, religious or secular, of the slaves, rites in which they "asserted repeatedly . . . that their lives were special, their lives had dignity, their lives had meaning beyond the definitions set by slavery," as Albert Raboteau writes (231). Thus, rituals as acts that seek to negotiate shifts of power and transformations of identity, and perhaps southern rites in particular, are always also manifestations of disruption, whose fissures often bespeak a "telling inarticulacy."

In Stepo's literary-critical paradigm, however, southern ritual grounds tend to be stable: the ritual journeys of ascent from an oppressive South to a relatively free North and of immersion from northern alienation to southern *communitas* that inform black American narrative in various later amplifications are both teleological in their (symbolic) geography. Recent critical developments of Stepto's paradigm are the narratives of dispersion and recuperation charted by Judylyn Ryan along an east-west axis, which in turn inform Edward Pavlić's concept of Diasporic Modernism. In these later narrative modes, explains Pavlić, "figures attempt to expand the communal forms of the symbolic South in relation to newly imagined African cultural codes and patterns" ("'Papa'" 62). The place where the latitudinal paradigm of Stepto and the longitudinal paradigms of Ryan and Pavlić converge is the American South. But if Nathaniel Mackey is correct in arguing that the telling inarticulacy of African American texts is, at least in part, the result too of a resistance against the dominant discourse, this inarticulacy not only seeks to destabilize "predatory coherence," but can also, inadvertently, affect the ostensible stabilities of the texts' very own expressions of "communal forms"—then the black ritual grounds of the American South extend deep into the adjectival *terra incognita* of Basie's "Gone With 'What' Wind?"

The rise of modernism in western art coincided, roughly, with the Great Migration, the exodus of African Americans from the predominantly rural South to the industrial metropolises of the North. Adell's suspicions about the summoning of "tradition" notwithstanding, the massive geographical and sociocultural dislocation and modernism's centrifugal forces generated certain patterns of sensibility that distinguish Afro-modernism from much of Euro-American modernism.[6] Hugh Kenner's intriguing hypothesis that the U.S. educational system contributed to the emergence of high modernism—for Kenner, America was "the world's first classroom civilization" and *The Cantos* simply "a Penn first-year curriculum, the one Pound happened to take"—also hints at such a crucial difference (*Homemade* 160; "Poets" 115).[7] For one, the vast majority of Americans of African descent had no access to the institutions of higher learning that helped shape the aesthetic sensibilities of the Ezra Pounds and the William Carlos Williamses:

> Several hours into the academic day, the blackboard is confronting students with a dense overlay of symbols left over from previous classes. When their instructor in the heat of exposition is moved to chalk up something of his own, no more than his precursors is he likely to wipe his whole expanse clean, not wanting to turn his back to the class for too long (a principle of rhetoric, not safety). Erasing just a little, he makes his additions slantwise. And as the palimpsest builds up day-long—dia-

grams, short lists, circles with three points marked on them, bits of math, supply and demand curves, bits of Aramaic—all superimposed, all bespeaking the day's intellectual activity in that room—you feel yourself in the presence, as Beckett put it, of something you could study all your life and not understand. The blackboard with its synchronic overlay, its tough and hieroglyphic fragments of a congeries of subjects (nothing obvious goes on the blackboard; what is obvious can merely be stated)—the blackboard is our civilization's Great Smaragdine Tablet (which said "Things below are copies," and was itself one of the things below). Absence of explicit and consecutive sense, teasing intimations of domains of order that others comprehend, that I could comprehend had I world enough and time, these are elements of its daily rhetoric, as it marshals, at random, enigmatic signs. (Kenner, "Poets" 118–19)

For the budding modernist poet enrolled at Penn, at Yale, at Harvard (Quentin Compson's college), the blackboard is a two-dimensional, physical expanse upon which those cryptic signs congregate. For the African American writer—most likely barred from institutions of higher learning—the *black*board is also a symbol of black struggle in the New World, especially considering the significance of the trope of literacy in the (neo)slave narrative. How different, then, the blackboard behind the veil:

The school house was a log hut, where Colonel Wheeler used to shelter his corn. It sat in a lot behind a rail fence and thorn bushes, near the sweetest of springs. There was an entrance where a door once was, and within, a massive rickety fireplace; great chinks between the logs served as windows. Furniture was scarce. A pale blackboard crouched in the corner. My desk was made of three boards, reinforced at critical points, and my chair, borrowed from the landlady, had to be returned every night. Seats for the children—these puzzled me much. I was haunted by a New England vision of neat little desks, and chairs, but alas! the reality was rough plank benches without backs, and at times without legs. They had the one virtue of making naps dangerous—possibly fatal, for the floor was not to be trusted. (Du Bois, *Souls* 39)

The "*pale* blackboard crouch[ing] in the corner" a youthful Fisk University student teaching summer school found near the hamlet of Watertown, at the edge of the Tennessee hill country, is indicative of the ongoing struggle against racial inequality at the dawn of modernism. There is no question, given the pallor of the blackboard, of "Great Smaragdine Tablets" in this schoolroom, for any chalk marks on that particular board would be comparatively difficult to descry in the first place. Interestingly, some ten years later, that same Fisk alumnus, now Dr. William Edward Burghardt Du Bois, returned to the area, but found his little schoolhouse gone:

> In its place stood Progress; and Progress, I understand, is necessarily ugly. The crazy foundation stones still marked the former site of my poor little cabin, and not far away, on six weary boulders, perched a jaunty board house, perhaps twenty by thirty feet, with three windows and a door that locked. Some of the windowglass was broken, and part of an old iron stove lay mournfully under the house. I peeped through the window half reverently, and found things that were not familiar. The blackboard had grown by about two feet, and the seats were still without backs. (*Souls* 43)

Symbolically, then, the "meaning of progress" in education must be measured in inches per decade.[8] In this, the blackboard is Du Bois's postemancipation updating of Frederick Douglass's pen: recalling the harsh winters he experienced on the Maryland plantation where he grew up, Douglass asserts that "[m]y feet have been so cracked with the frost, that the pen with which I am writing might be laid in the gashes" (33). For Du Bois as for Douglass, the instruments of writing and literacy serve to negotiate the pain and suffering of history, and consequently to assess the progress from the past to the present (Stepto 20).

At least, that is, for Americans of African descent at the dawning of the twentieth century. Du Bois, in fact, would go on to assume a position at the University of Pennsylvania, but not even this comparatively liberal institution was exempt from the veil: given an ill-defined one-year fellowship there, Du Bois did no teaching at all because his name was soon stricken from the catalogue. As he notes dryly in his autobiography, "I did no instructing save once, to pilot a pack of idiots through the Negro slums" (197, 194–95). It was only a few years after Du Bois's brief stint at Penn that Williams and Pound enrolled there, who after all were not even a generation younger than he. But their radically different experiences, and consequently the vastly different meanings modernity and modernism came to have for these three, are instructive. For Du Bois, who had "touched the very shadow of slavery" during his first sojourn below the Mason-Dixon line, history was not in the past but very much alive, and hence crucial to understand in the forging not just of what Alain Locke would famously call the New Negro, but of a new, modern, modernist black art (*Autobiography* 114). Appropriately, the metaphor of the veil has three dimensions, while the metaphor of the blackboard has but two—not necessarily a qualitative difference, but a conceptual one to be sure.

Certainly, American high modernism was not without a concern for history. After all, Pound famously called *The Cantos* "a poem including history" (Kenner, *Pound* 362–67). But for the white American modernist, history presented options: one could select which bits and pieces of information one wanted to copy from the blackboard, "our civilization's Great Smaragdine Tablet," into one's notebook. Thus, Euro-American and European high modernism offered to many what Jed Rasula terms an "idiomatic arsenal" consisting of a myriad of "elective parts" (70). But for the black artist in the New World, the point was that he or she did not have the same *choices* as Ezra Pound, or T. S. Eliot, or H. D., or Gertrude Stein, simply because, more often than not, there was no blackboard to copy from. Even Professor Du Bois had his blackboard taken from him at Penn. And so, for the American of African descent, "the adventure of Western culture" (to use George Kent's apt phrase) and the confrontation with modernity invariably led to the American South (Kent 15). For the African American artist, confronting the rituals of the South and their legacies was not an elective; it was inescapable. Hence, the one dimension comparatively diminished in Kenner's symbol of the blackboard in the classroom—and the one salient in Du Bois's account—is the fourth: *time*. And it is this dimension that Afro-modernism is concerned with to a much greater degree than American high modernism.

Thus, Afro-modernism is really modernism with a historical conscience. The "telling inarticulacy" at the center of Basie's song title furnishes the cue to my critical investigation into the southern ritual grounds of Afro-modernism as modernism with a historical conscience. In a variety of texts and contexts, the South constitutes a symbolic territory that actually resists the very narrative strategies deployed to capture it and hence is the catalyst of an epistemological crisis as much as the foundation of any "authenticating machineries." At the same time, this stubborn resistance, the modernist alienation of word from world, prompts ever new and imaginative (re)mappings of that same territory, ontological processes of revelation within a field of tension in which narrative postures toward existence are continuously negotiated anew. In this act of (re)mapping, Afro-modernism seeks to tap not only historical consciousness—the blackboard in Ezra Pound's classroom at Penn—but a historical *conscience*—the veil that accounts for the blackboard in Du Bois's schoolhouse in Watertown, Tennessee, and its subsequent sacrifice to "Progress." Hence, Afro-modernism suggests the reconfiguration of southern ritual grounds as situated in time and *mind* rather than time and *place*.

"Modernism with a historical conscience" may sound like a contradiction in terms, but, as Adell reminds us, the Afro-modernist text in particular "is embedded in a paradox. It is a conjuring-weaving which reveals its dark shadow, the subtext of black existence and its un-said and un-sayable history" (140). Therefore, in the present study I shall follow Craig Werner's lead and use the term "Afro-modernism" less as a definition of a specific school of artists or of a peculiar set of aesthetic paradigms, than as shorthand for the various ways in which artists confront the collision and collusion of alienation, fragmentation, and epistemology in the modern world (Werner 183–88). Nevertheless, as pointed out above, I believe there are indeed certain trends and patterns that distinguish much of Afro-modernism from its Euro-American counterpart, and the concept of Afro-modernism as modernism with a historical conscience therefore seeks to do justice to artistic form as well as to cultural history.

Stepto places the beginning of Afro-modernism with the 1912 publication of James Weldon Johnson's *Autobiography of an Ex-Coloured Man* (95–97). For Houston Baker, Afro-modernism begins on September 18, 1895, the day Booker T. Washington delivered his famous address at the Atlanta Cotton States and International Exposition (Baker, *Modernism* 15–16). Alfred Appel and Jed Rasula posit the apotheosis in 1927, the year Duke Ellington's "Black and Tan Fantasy" was released, and the year placards announced Louis Armstrong as "The Master of Modernism" (Appel 206; Rasula 109–10). Werner reads the fiction of Charles Chesnutt as the first writings heralding the full complexities of what he calls African American "(post)modernism"; and when it is Zora Neale Hurston's *Their Eyes Were Watching God* that constitutes the key black modernist text for Pavlič, it is Richard Wright's *Native Son* for Yoshinobu Hakutani (Werner 17; Pavlič, "'Papa'" 61–62; Hakutani 1–6). Notable about this roll call is the fact that the artists deemed pioneers of Afro-modernism are all southerners by birth or by upbringing—with Ellington the sole but, as a native Washingtonian, also tentative exception. Certainly, the South's significance owes as much to demographics as to aesthetic principles; but because of this, too, the South appears a region central to the emergence of Afro-modernism, regardless of its definition.

Ultimately though, the genesis of Afro-modernism, Paul Gilroy states, lies in the experience of repeated uprooting and dislocation in the Middle Passage and its aftermath. As he writes in his seminal *The Black Atlantic*, it's "the relationship between masters and slaves that supplies the key to comprehending the position of blacks in the modern world" (219–20). Thus, however varied, and sometimes contradictory, the approaches that black American artists took to meet the challenges of the twentieth century, they all

shared a sense that the modern world was fragmented along axes constituted by racial conflict and could accommodate non-synchronous,
hetero-cultural modes of social life in close proximity. Their conceptions of modernity were periodised differently. They were founded on the
catastrophic rupture of the middle passage. . . . They were punctuated by
the processes of acculturation and terror that followed that catastrophe
and by the countercultural aspirations towards freedom, citizenship, and
autonomy that developed after it among slaves and their descendants.
(197)

This dialectic of terror and acculturation was being told and retold in
countless (re)incarnations of that most 'telling' of African American
rites: call and response (Floyd 94–97; Gilroy 200; Stuckey 41–48).[9] My
study does not pretend to trace a comprehensive panorama of (southern)
Afro-modernism: in literature alone, such a feat would have to tackle
at the very least the fiction of Zora Neale Hurston, Ernest Gaines, and
Alice Walker, as well as the poetry of Sterling Brown, again Walker, and
Yusef Komunyakaa—not to mention the music of, say, Ray Charles, or the
paintings of Romare Bearden. Hence, this study visits a series of southern
ritual grounds and listens to selected, specific responses to the calls of
modernity.

The first "call" will be that of the "Old South," and my cartography
of Afro-modernism begins with the 1893 *Life and Times of Frederick Douglass*. Douglass's last autobiography has been unduly dismissed or neglected
by critics because it avails itself of an expanded aesthetic of autobiography, one that the still dominating structuralist approaches fashioning
the canon of African American narrative—Stepto's latitudinal paradigm
or Gates's Signifyin(g)—cannot accommodate. The 1845 *Narrative* and
the subsequent *My Bondage and My Freedom* undoubtedly emphasize the
joint journeys from slavery to freedom and ignorance to literacy, and thus
remain fully invested in the possibilities of literary mimesis. Douglass's final
autobiography as a protomodernist text, however, becomes more and more
concerned with the fissures created by the inherent instability of all acts
of textual representation. For Douglass, the modernist alienation of word
from world can, and must, be counteracted if text is to tap what he calls
"a life and power far beyond the letter," an historical conscience (*Autobiographies* 792). Like its predecessors, *Life and Times* ultimately places this
historical conscience at the frostbitten feet of its hero. Simultaneously,
its protomodernism recognizes that there is indeed an increasing distance
between 'telling' letters on the one hand, and as of yet unarticulated lives
and powers on the other. The expanded aesthetic of *Life and Times* therefore not only negotiates a much more complex dynamic of immediacy

and distance, inside and outside, text and history, but also reinscribes its historical, southern conscience on the *international* grounds it visits.

While Douglass's final autobiography presents us with a protomodernism in which the widening gap between word and world could still be bridged, in Jean Toomer's *Cane* the axis of mimesis becomes unhinged. The novel sets out to respond to the call of "the spiritual truth" of the post-Reconstruction South as the author himself heard it in the archetypal southern small town on the threshold of modernity (qtd. in Kerman and Eldridge 95). However, the book depicts characters who are either unable to grasp fulfillment and tap a spiritual, mystic wholeness, or who are incapable of articulating comprehensibly their spiritual selves, chronicling the futile attempts of the narrative voice in its various guises to capture and reproduce Toomer's South. The modernist crisis of representation leads to a breakdown of communication caused paradoxically by language itself, the very medium of communication. The recurring shifts between levels of narrative consciousness indicate that it is ironically language itself that prevents the book's characters from shaping words to fit their souls, as it were. *Cane* thus attests to the price for which literary modernity is to be had: the fragmentation of the mimetic power of language. The novel's historical conscience, represented by the mythical character of Father John, is still 'writable' and hence communicable, but at the same time Father John is relegated to a dark cellar, ignored or misunderstood by the community aboveground—the embodiment of a historical conscience that has shifted almost completely from the realm of 'telling' to the realm of inarticulacy.

One of the rituals *Cane* deems quintessential to the Black Belt's "spiritual truth"—as did, of course, Douglass—is the ritual of song. However, the novel constantly refers to and reports on singing, but it incorporates an actual song into its narrative but once, and only fleetingly at that. In contrast, a small Mississippi farm is the setting of Richard Wright's "Long Black Song," where the Methodist hymn "When the Roll Is Called Up Yonder" serves as the catalyst that occasions both a majestic (if utopian) vision of interracial harmony and that most brutal of southern rituals, lynching. The specific rendition of the hymn that Sarah, the protagonist, hears and that triggers the tragic events was recorded by the all-white Edison Mixed Quartet: in its performance decidedly not an antiphonal liberation text in the African American tradition, the hymn nonetheless pits two distinct realms against each other, the millennial realm of the hymn's "yonder" on the one hand, and the historical exigencies of a southern territory marked by the ritual of lynching on the other. The resulting dialectic oscillates between the realities of southern violence and the ideal of southern multiculture and reveals that, contrary to Toomer's belief (and Douglass's), song and music in fact betray the African American liberation struggle, and not just in the Deep South. Wright insists that only the *writer* can give voice to a viable historical conscience.

Accordingly, the long *black* song the title announces is one that is never sung in the story. This long black song, though, resounds at one of the 'blackest' of all black southern ritual grounds—the crossroads. This is the location where, or so the legend goes, the "King of the Delta Blues Singers," Robert Johnson, traded his soul to the devil. In critical theory, too, the crossroads has become the prime metonymy for Afro-modernism—in Houston Baker's *Blues, Ideology, and Afro-American Literature* as well as Edward Pavlić's *Crossroads Modernism*. "Music," Paul Gilroy adjudges, "becomes vital at the point at which linguistic and semantic indeterminacy/polyphony arise amidst the protracted battle between masters, mistresses, and slaves. This decidedly modern conflict was the product of circumstances where language lost something of its referentiality and its privileged relationships to concepts" (*Black* 74). But because black music is also "so often the principal symbol of racial authenticity," in the third millennium "the well-policed borders of black particularity" remain just as vigilantly guarded (34, 6). Despite Wright's profound pessimism regarding the liberatory potential of music, one of the goals of *Shaping Words to Fit the Soul* is to reference sound as a figurative ritual ground capable of decolonizing visually inscribed, petrified mappings of raciological categorization; music can, however fleetingly, indeed swing open doors to spaces that allow for the possibility of combining seemingly divergent and opposite forms of human experience and expression.

Chapter 4 will therefore not only visit the actual crossroads where said tricky transaction between Johnson and the devil took place. It will also examine the figurative crossroads in the compositional practice of the "Father of the Blues," W. C. Handy, as well as in the soundscapes navigated by the flagship of southern rock, the Allman Brothers Band. Handy's blues are a product of pastiche and collage and result from the collision of what he calls "snatches of song" from a wide variety of sources; at the same time, the so-called blue notes give voice to Afro-modernism's historical conscience (Handy, *Father* 138). At the crossroads of the blues therefore meet old and new, tradition and fragmentation, history and progress, myth and commerce, authenticity and simulacrum—and, of course, black and white. Ralph Ellison knew that "Southern whites cannot walk, talk, sing, conceive of laws or justice, think of sex, love the family or freedom without responding to the presence of Negroes" (*Shadow* 163). The music of the Allman Brothers Band, steeped deeply in the history of the music as it translates Handy's compositional technique into improvised performance, traverses an intersection closely related to the racial crossroads, namely that of cultural property and cultural propriety. A close 'reading' of the Allmans' iconic song "Whipping Post" and its minstrel echoes exemplifies how blues *can* transcend raciological typology, but it cannot, ultimately, transcend history.

The final chapter journeys to a seemingly very different setting, namely the inner city of the post-Soul generation in Tayari Jones's novel *Leaving Atlanta* and on Goodie Mob's debut album, *Soul Food*. At the core of Jones's narrative that explores the effects of the infamous Atlanta Child Murders on the lives of three fifth-graders and their community is an epistemological crisis that pits word against world, language against experience, sign against referent. The crisis, fueling a profound sense of disorientation, is so great that it revises, and even partially reverses, Douglass's archetypal, protomodernist journey in which literacy figured as "the pathway from slavery to freedom" (38). Thus, both *Leaving Atlanta* and Jones's follow-up novel, *The Untelling*, navigate a landscape that overlaps with the ritual grounds of the newest of the New Souths, the "Dirty South," a landscape that, in its original mapping by Goodie Mob, also generates a deep confusion. But even in these texts, a historical conscience manifests itself by mapping symbolic ritual grounds that betray their complicity with the legacies of white supremacy and chattel slavery.

Finally, the juxtaposition of literature and hip-hop prompts a prolegomenon on the relationship between Afro-modernism's historical conscience and postmodernism. Hip-hop is perhaps the most fiercely territorial expression of contemporary black culture, but it also avails itself of postmodernist techniques. In fact, Russell Potter hears in hip-hop "one form of radical postmodernism" (9). bell hooks's essay "Postmodern Blackness" has emerged as a key text in the field—also because she recognizes hip-hop as perhaps the most vocal (and visible) manifestation of African American postmodernism. hooks applauds its subversive and potentially liberating elements, but professes to be disturbed by "postmodern critiques of the 'subject' when they surface at a historical moment when many subjugated people feel themselves coming to voice for the first time" (28). The resistance to postmodernism's assault on notions of essence and authenticity, she writes,

> is rooted in the fear that it will cause folks to lose sight of the specific history and experience of African-Americans and the unique sensibilities and culture that arise from that experience. An adequate response to this concern is to critique essentialism while emphasizing the significance of

"the authority of experience." There is a radical difference between a repudiation of the idea that there is a black "essence" and recognition of the way black identity has been specifically constituted in the experience of exile and struggle. (29)

Afro-modernism as modernism with a historical conscience anticipates in many ways hooks's concept of "the authority of experience" informing postmodern blackness. As Little Brother's provocative 2005 album *The Minstrel Show* exemplifies, thoroughly postmodernist yet socially conscious hip-hop is often born from an impulse akin to Afro-modernism's historical conscience. The group's hip-hop satire amplifies Christian Moraru's rereading of postmodernism as "memorious discourse," which does not dissolve history into poststructuralism's wall-to-wall textuality, but seeks to recover it in an act of cultural recollection (*Memorious* 21–27). Thus, Little Brother's postmodern blackness orchestrates an impulse deeply embedded in Afro-modernism's historical conscience, namely how to wrest wholeness from the pain and terrors of American history.

The starting point for the following discussions is one that may appear geographically circumscribed, but my critical practice takes to heart George Kent's counsel: "Any universalism worthy of recognition derives from its depths of exploration of the density, complexity, and variety of a people's experience—or a person's. It is achieved by going down deep—not by transcending" (11). Thus, I hope that in "going down deep," deep below the Mason-Dixon Line, we may also find out something about the world above and beyond it.

And, finally, need I add that I who speak here am bone of the bone and
flesh of the flesh of them that live within the Veil?

—W. E. B. Du Bois, *The Souls of Black Folk*

CHAPTER 1

A Life and Power Far Beyond the Letter

The Afro-Modernism of
Life and Times of Frederick Douglass

Spanning nearly half a century, the autobiographies of Frederick
Douglass narrate the tragedy of enslavement and the challenge of
emancipation. Not only did the unspeakable horrors of the Middle
Passage entail the brutal demotion to chattel: the black experience
in the New World also prefigured the quintessential modernist
predicament of alienation, fragmentation, and epistemology, com-
pounded in the slave narrative by the precarious escape from the
South to the North. However tenuous the freedom found there
was, for Douglass the autobiographer its challenges were intricately
intertwined with the problem of textual representation. Where the
slave narrative differed from what would later come to be known as

high modernism was in its struggle toward not just survival, but wholeness. Less a Prufrockian *cultivation* of the alienated, fragmented self, African American protomodernism strove continuously toward an *assertion* of the *human* self—nowhere as crucially as in that first distinct genre of southern letters, the slave narrative.

During the last few days of the year 1862, a winter storm had engulfed much of the American east coast, but on January 1, 1863, the sun rose over Boston, Massachusetts, in a cloudless sky. It was more than just New Year's Day, as the reporter for the *Liberator* observed "a feverish unrest and expectation in the countenances" of many Bostonians ("Proclamation Day" 7). Together with the rest of America, North and South, the city awaited the issuance of President Lincoln's long-anticipated Emancipation Proclamation, which had been promised for January 1. The mostly black crowd that assembled that morning at Tremont Temple listened patiently to speaker after speaker while waiting for the text of Lincoln's proclamation to be cabled to Boston. Among the many who took the rostrum was Frederick Douglass, who, the *Liberator* dutifully noted, "was well received" ("Emancipation Day" 12). Douglass, the undisputed leader of black Americans free and enslaved, had to be recalled a second time to speak to the increasingly restless crowd, as the cable from Washington had still not arrived in the evening. After word came around 10 P.M. that it was on the wire, the wait became unbearable, and eventually Judge Thomas Russell went to the telegraph office himself, even though messengers had already been stationed there in the morning. Shortly before midnight, Russell returned, triumphantly waving the text of the proclamation, which was immediately read "amid the most enthusiastic demonstrations. The scene which here ensued," the *Liberator*'s reporter emoted, "cannot be described. . . . Speeches of thrilling pathos were made. . . . No words can depict the enthusiasm of the occasion" (12).

As for Frederick Douglass himself—everything he had worked for all his life seemed to come within immediate reach: a month after the jubilations in Boston, Douglass told a New York City audience that January 1 had been "the greatest event of our nation's history, if not the greatest event of the century" ("The Proclamation" 549). However, subsequent close scrutiny of the measure's wording elicited much criticism from abolitionists, many of whom believed that Lincoln had merely sought to secure morally the position of his administration and of the Union army.[1] Douglass himself, after more careful inspection of the document, came to the conclusion that "[i]t was a measure apparently inspired by the low motive of military necessity" (*Autobiographies* 792). Nonetheless, he refused to diminish the significance of the Emancipation Proclamation. Years later, after the promise of true and full emancipation had been betrayed and Reconstruction had failed, Douglass wrote in his last autobiography:

> For my own part, I took the proclamation, first and last, for a little more than it purported, and saw in its spirit a life and power far beyond its letter. Its meaning to me was the entire abolition of slavery, wherever the evil could be reached by the Federal arm, and I saw that its moral power would extend much further. . . . It was no longer a mere strife for territory and dominion, but a contest of civilization against barbarism. (792–93)

Looking back to this crucial moment, Douglass comes to see here that language is very much about territory and dominion, but there is, Douglass insists, a spirit, a life, and a power "far beyond the letter" that reaches beyond the terrain it describes. In other words, language acquires true meaning only if it participates in and reflects the "contest of civilization against barbarism."

Thus, Douglass in his last autobiography, the 1892 edition of *Life and Times of Frederick Douglass*, becomes increasingly preoccupied with the 'telling inarticulacies' of history and the limits of textual representation. Unlike the two previous autobiographies, the 1845 *Narrative of the Life of Frederick Douglass* and the 1855 *My Bondage and My Freedom*, *Life and Times* deemphasizes what many critics fashioning the black literary canon have viewed as the most significant and distinct property of early African American narrative, namely the quest for literacy. *Life and Times* instead manifests a significant expansion of Douglass's aesthetic: in the previous autobiographies the mastery of written language itself contained a power sufficiently liberatory to represent the emergence of an authentic, human self. In fact, Douglass's famous assertion in 1845 that literacy paved "the pathway from slavery to freedom" became ten years later "the *direct* pathway from slavery to freedom" (38, 218; emphasis added). In 1892 the pathway was still "direct," the wording taken directly from *My Bondage and My Freedom*; however, that epiphany now lay half a century in the past and was greatly tempered by the failure of Reconstruction and the betrayal of full emancipation (527). History had intervened. And so *Life and Times of Frederick Douglass* became an early expression of "the quintessential modernist attempt to represent time and bid its return," as Christian Moraru puts it, in order to assess the historical legacies of chattel slavery in America (*Memorious* 41). This, then, required not only historical consciousness, but a historical *conscience*—a conscience, moreover, that was inextricably connected to the Old South. But, as Douglass's reaction to the Emancipation Proclamation indicates, said historical con-science as "a life and power far beyond the letter" just may reside in a realm of telling inarticulacy and thus complicate textual mimesis.

In contrast, the 1845 *Narrative*'s "authenticating machinery" is evi-denced primarily in the way in which Douglass balances and eventually subsumes other texts—William Lloyd Garrison's preface, for example—to create an "integrated narrative," as Robert Stepto argues (5, 17). For Henry Louis Gates, Jr., the *Narrative* constitutes "the first charting of the black hermeneutical circle" and as such revises, or signifies upon, the distinctly black trope of the talking book (*Figures* 96; *Signifying* 166–67). William Andrews's *To Tell a Free Story*, still the definitive study of the slave nar-rative, delineates the genre as a whole as follows: "Both the fugitive slave narrator and the black spiritual autobiographer trace their freedom back to an awakening of their awareness of their fundamental identity with and rightful participation in *logos*. . . . The climax of the quests of both kinds of autobiographer usually comes when they seize the opportunity to proclaim what are clearly complementary gospels of freedom" (7). For Andrews, it is *My Bondage and My Freedom* that shows Douglass at the peak of his artistic powers (239). Eric Sundquist's perceptive analysis of the revisions Douglass undertook for *My Bondage* confirms that his basic premise conjoining freedom and literacy had not changed, but that he was merely operating within what Sundquist calls a "wider circle of literacy" (*To Wake* 93, 104–6).

Exemplary of Douglass's retention of the lesson of literacy is the pas-sage in *My Bondage* that retells the fugitive's first speech in 1841 before an antislavery meeting in Nantucket: "But excited and convulsed as I was, the audience, though remarkably quiet before, became as much excited as myself. Mr. Garrison followed me, *taking me as his text;* and now, whether I had made an eloquent speech in behalf of freedom or not, his was one never to be forgotten by those who heard it" (365; emphasis added). Where the 1845 *Narrative* ends with the protagonist's emergence as a public speaker and author who professes an unquestioned faith in the equation of liberty and literacy, in *My Bondage* a decade later Douglass recognizes that the attainment of literacy alone does not necessarily guarantee personal lib-erty, as Garrison had conveniently reduced him to the object of text. From then on, he remembers, the abolitionists would introduce him as a "gradu-ate from the peculiar institution . . . *with my diploma written on my back!*" and Garrisonians cautioned that he "[b]etter have a *little* of the plantation manner of speech than not; 'tis not best that you seem too learned" (365, 367). Where ten years earlier the attainment of literacy alone afforded triumphant liberty, Douglass now insists that "still I must speak just the word that seemed to *me* the word to be spoken *by* me"— not only must he learn how to decode and deploy written language; he had to learn to craft his own language (367). Also, in describing the initial misgivings that would eventually lead to his break with Garrison, Douglass slyly equates the abolitionist leader with Mr. Plummer, the cruel overseer on Captain Anthony's Tuckahoe plantation, who "had written his character on the living parchment of most of [the slaves'] backs, and left them callous" (239), and in the 1892 *Life and Times* he dryly adds that Garrison's speech had been a "masterly effort" indeed (660). Despite the significant differences between the *Narrative* and *My Bondage*, Douglass's aesthetic of autobiography remains the same: "The essential lesson, that language is the key to 'the *white* man's power to perpetuate the enslavement of the black man,' is the same in both texts," as Sundquist concludes, observing that "[t]he language of the fathers offers two choices: capitulation and ignorance, or resistance and knowledge. Literacy is linked to the power to enslave and, alternatively, to the power to liberate and father oneself" (*To Wake* 106, 107).

In both the *Narrative* and *My Bondage and My Freedom*, Douglass is concerned with competing textual representations of the self, but both autobiographies remain fully invested in textual mimesis. What W. J. T. Mitchell has termed "the axis of representation" therefore remains intact, as a result of the superior skills of the autobiographer himself (12–13). As Erich Auerbach notes in *Mimesis*: "In the nineteenth century still, and even at the beginning of the twentieth century, there was . . . such a clearly articulable and recognized community of thinking and feeling that a writer depicting reality had at hand reliable criteria to arrange it; at least he could recognize within the turbulent contemporary background certain directions and demarcate from each other contesting convictions or forms of life with some clarity" (512). But the reliability of the axis of representation, Auerbach also recognizes, had become more and more questionable, a growing destabilization inherent in all acts of representation. For, as Mitchell continues,

> Representation is that by which we make our will known and, simultaneously, that which alienates our will from ourselves in both the aesthetic and political spheres. The problem with representation might be summarized by reversing the traditional slogan of the American Revolution: instead of "No taxation without representation," no representation without taxation. Every representation exacts some cost, in the form of lost immediacy, presence, or truth, in the form of a gap between intention and realization, original and copy. (23)

Life and Times retains its faith in the power of textual representation in the first half: the slave narrator's archetypal journey is in some ways a countermodernist one in that it is a journey toward (ideally) autonomous selfhood. But in the second half, this power is thrown into stark relief as Douglass becomes increasingly concerned with the gaps inherent in all acts of representation, with a modernist alienation of word from world. The increasing instability of the axis of representation can be counteracted only if words strive to tap "a life and power far beyond the letter," an historical conscience.

But many critics dismiss *Life and Times* on aesthetic grounds, arguing, as Albert E. Stone does, that Douglass's last autobiography was "indicative of a general loss of emotional force and economy" (76).[2] The fact alone that, unlike the *Narrative* and *My Bondage*, *Life and Times* is not a slave narrative per se as it was published first in 1881, followed eleven years later by a revised edition adding several hundred pages to the story of Frederick, the fugitive slave who availed himself of the power of literacy, raises the problem of a mimetic immediacy that is, if not lost, receding quickly. The critical dismissal of *Life and Times,* however, is perhaps at least partly a reaction to a shift in Douglass's aesthetic: while the *Narrative* and *My Bondage* undoubtedly emphasize the joint journeys from slavery to freedom and ignorance to literacy and thus reinforce mimetic immediacy, repositioned though the axis of representation is, Douglass's final autobiography begins to take stock of the 'taxes' all acts of representation accrue.[3] This shift, in turn, necessitates an attempt to tap an historical conscience.

The first edition of *Life and Times of Frederick Douglass* appeared in 1881, but despite an aggressive advertising campaign, the book was a commercial disappointment. After Douglass was appointed minister to Haiti in 1889, a rival publisher bought the plates and asked him to bring the book up to date, hoping to capitalize on the public's renewed interest in him (Quarles 337). The two versions of *Life and Times* meant far more to Douglass than merely a source of additional income. He refused to heed the advice of several close friends who urged him to write a book about John Brown or another figure of historical importance; instead, he was extremely meticulous in revising and rewriting his autobiography. Even though the first half of *Life and Times* consists largely of the exact text of *My Bondage*—which in turn incorporated several long passages from the *Narrative*—Douglass insisted on painstakingly rewriting the entire antebellum section of his earlier autobiography, making seemingly minuscule changes in syntax and diction every now and then. He also was distressed at the shoddy edition of his 1892 revision of the original *Life and Times* that was put together by his new publisher, De Wolfe, Fiske and Company of Boston, and complained about the inferior quality of the paper and binding (McFeely 311–12, 359–60; Ripley 21–29). This strongly suggests that there was more at stake for Douglass than merely a public relations campaign or financial profit. Douglass, in fact, had come to a different understanding of the text and context of his life. As he suggested in his reaction to the wording of the Emancipation Proclamation, he saw his life no longer merely as the arena for the battle over the territory of the text and the dominion of language—this had been the thrust of the *Narrative* and *My Bondage*. Now, in *Life and Times*, he saw his life embedded in the larger historical struggle of civilization against barbarity, a struggle in which meaningful texts could and should have a life and a power beyond the words of which they consist and which therefore expanded the significance of southern ritual grounds beyond the terrain of the Old South, and beyond even the territory of the United States.

As Douglass narrates his reaction to the publication of the Emancipation Proclamation, seeing "in its spirit a life and power far beyond its letter," he fashions this moment into the turning point of his last autobiography: what had heretofore been his quest to master the word now becomes the starting point of joining the text of his life to the history of his people and his times. The "strife for territory and dominion," Douglass's quest in his first two autobiographies (and the first half of *Life and Times*) to control the text of his own life, now becomes "a contest of civilization against barbarism," a contest which necessitates that he reassess, and reposition, the text of his life within a much larger context of history. Still in the same chapter, Douglass recalls Lincoln's second inauguration and quotes at length from what would turn out to be the president's last public speech:

> "With malice toward none, with charity for all, with firmness in the right as God gives us to see the right, let us strive to finish the work we are in, to bind up the nation's wounds, to care for him who shall have borne the battle, and for his widow and his orphans, to do all which may achieve and cherish a just and lasting peace among ourselves and with all nations."
>
> I know not how many times and before how many people I have quoted these solemn words of our martyred President. They struck me at the time, and have seemed to me ever since to contain more vital substance than I have ever seen compressed in a space so narrow . . . (801–2)

Thus, as with the Emancipation Proclamation, the purpose of language is to express some "vital substance" of collective historical experience. And so the rest of *Life and Times* Douglass devotes to imbuing his own text with a vital substance that has remained still mostly unwritten.

This narrative strategy constitutes an expansion of the one employed in the *Narrative* and *My Bondage*, where the individual, heroic self emerges first and foremost through the increasing control over mimesis, and the self that exists before its representation in text is but languishing in "a horrible pit" (84). Now, the memoirist is keenly aware of the limits of textual representation and the ever-widening gaps they create, something that hence requires a recalibrated aesthetic of autobiography. Douglass elucidates the challenge when, toward the end of part II (which marked the end of the 1881 version of *Life and Times*), he explains: "My part has been to tell the story of the slave. The story of the master never wanted for narrators. The masters, to tell their story, had at call all the talent and genius that wealth and influence could command. They have had their full day in court. Literature, theology, philosophy, law and learning have come willingly to their service, and, if condemned, they have not been condemned unheard" (912–13). The hallmarks of western culture—art and religion, legislation and education—are, of course, recorded and transmitted first and foremost through the written word. The story of the slave, then, is the unwritten story still, almost a generation after emancipation, and contains the historical conscience not just of the black autobiographer, but of the American experiment as a whole. Language, writing, text, is still a property of the masters and has served them well, but it is Douglass's aim to conjoin his text, which after all uses the same words and letters that the masters have been using to consolidate and maintain their power, to those without and outside of the text, as he makes clear in the very next paragraph. This passage speaks to both a modernist fragmentation and dislocation of the self as well as to a self still connected to a communal experience embedded in historical time, not in textual space:

> It will be seen in these pages that I have lived several lives in one: first, the life of slavery; secondly, the life of a fugitive from slavery; thirdly, the life of comparative freedom; fourthly, the life of conflict and battle; and, fifthly, the life of victory, if not complete, at least assured. To, [sic] those who have suffered in slavery I can say, I, too, have suffered. To those who have taken some risks and encountered hardships in the flight from bondage I can say, I, too, have endured and risked. To those who have battled for liberty, brotherhood, and citizenship I can say, I, too, have

battled. And to those who have lived to enjoy the fruits of victory I can say, I, too, live and rejoice. (913)

Thus again, *Life and Times* is concerned not only with an individual self taking shape in and through language but also with a self seeking communion with those who remain *outside* of the text, *outside* of the circle of literacy.

To be sure, this is not entirely new, as these gestures toward communion already occur in *My Bondage* and in the 1845 *Narrative* (Andrews, *To Tell* 238–39). However, these passages are few and far between and fail to constitute an overarching aesthetic of autobiography. What is new in the 1892 *Life and Times* is that Douglass recognizes that the collective story of the slave, and the story of the slave's descendants, is still not (yet) a story told in (literary) text, but is primarily a story lived in historical experience. Douglass's final autobiography thus reclaims a black humanity because it recognizes the limitations of textual representation but simultaneously strives all the more to capture a vital substance, a telling inarticulacy, of that which lies beyond the text. In this way, *Life and Times* is thoroughly *Afro*-modernist, for Afro-modernism, as Kimberly Benston has argued, "augurs a sacramentalized performance present in order to redeem, not deny, the promissory notes of historical subjectivity. The freedom it seeks dwells within, not beyond, collective resources of memory and desire," resources that, according to Douglass, are as of yet mostly unwritten. Afro-modernist artists, continues Benston, are "[a]vatars of those silenced and abjected by modernity and western modernism alike" who, precisely as the author of *Life and Times* does, "comprehend diasporic consciousness not merely as conceit but as material condition" (21).

With the failure of Reconstruction glaringly obvious and the promise of emancipation betrayed, it became increasingly pressing to tap the resources of this historical consciousness. Accordingly, the third and last part of *Life and Times*, the part added in the 1892 edition, begins on a far less positive note than that on which the previous one ended. Douglass now senses that "the spirit of slavery and rebellion increased in power and advanced towards ascendancy. . . . The sentiment that gave us a reconstructed Union on a basis of liberty for all people was blasted as a flower is blasted by a killing frost" (963). Just as Douglass decided to find in the Emancipation Proclamation a more positive spirit than the wording actually warranted, a spirit that gave it "a life and power far beyond its letter," so does he now detect the antithetical spirit of continuous injustice and oppression surviving regardless of the Thirteenth Amendment and the letter of its law. Consequently, history continues to call on his conscience: "Time and events have summoned me to stand forth both as a witness and an advocate for a people long dumb, not allowed to speak for themselves, yet much misunderstood and deeply wronged" (938). The misrepresentation of those without a text continues unabated, and the challenge of mimesis, to witness their desire for true freedom and humanity, must be met anew. What elevates *Life and Times* beyond the journalistic act of mere witnessing and turns it into a work of art is Douglass's contention that he is not only a witness but also an advocate. The act of witnessing is a passive act that does not require any particular skills because it happens in the here and now; it demands but consciousness. The act of advocating, however, requires imagination in order to chart a course into the future once the past is assessed—it requires an historical *conscience*. Douglass the advocate thus presents his membership in a community whose plight he shares and in whose history he participates. His text strives to bridge the ever-widening gaps that acts of representation produce; similarly, his act of advocating seeks to point beyond the here and now to the future and the past simultaneously.

This relationship between the text and the world, the artistic object and lived experience, is further examined in the chapter that narrates Douglass's European tour of 1886–87. His journey took him to, among other sights, Paris, Rome, and Venice, yet it was in the museum in the Italian port city of Genoa that Douglass was left with one of the deepest and most lasting impressions of his entire trip: "But of all the interesting objects collected in the Museum of Genoa, the one that touched me most was the violin that had belonged to and been played upon by Paganini, the greatest musical genius of his time. This violin is treasured in a glass case and beyond the touch of careless fingers, a thing to be seen and not to be handled" (997). Douglass here describes himself initially as the passive witness of history as he gazes upon Niccolò Paganini's violin; his role here is to see and not to handle, to witness and not to advocate. In the sentences immediately following, Douglass explains why he was so arrested by this simple instrument:

> There are some things and places made sacred by their uses and by the events with which they are associated, especially those which have in any measure changed the current of human taste, thought, and life, or which have revealed new powers and triumphs of the human soul. The pen with which Lincoln wrote the emancipation proclamation, the sword worn by Washington through the war of the Revolution, though

of the same material and form of other pens and swords, have an individual character, and stir in the minds of men peculiar sensations. So this old violin, made after the pattern of others and perhaps not more perfect in its construction and tone than hundreds seen elsewhere, detained me longer and interested me more than anything else in the Museum of Genoa. . . . So it was not this old violin, but the marvelous man behind it, the man who had played on it and played as never man played before, and thrilled the hearts of thousands by his playing, that made it a precious object in my eyes. Owing perhaps to my love of music and of the violin in particular, I would have given more for that old violin of wood, horsehair, and catgut than for any one of the long lines of pictures I saw before me. I desired it on account of the man who had played upon it—the man who revealed its powers and possibilities as they were never known before. (997–98)

The attraction emanating from all of these artifacts Douglass enumerates is not created by the objects themselves; there are, as he points out, scores of instruments like Paganini's, scores of pens like Lincoln's, and scores of swords like Washington's. But Paganini's violin is more than the sum of its parts "of wood, horsehair, and catgut"; it has accrued a special sacredness and power that is derived from historical experience. For it is the history of the Revolutionary War that makes Washington's sword different from any other, and it is the history of American chattel slavery that makes Lincoln's pen different from any other—two instruments that also had been wielded with conscience. It is history that makes these artifacts special by imbuing them with a sacredness and power, a telling inarticulacy, that distinguishes them from other objects that are otherwise identical. It is also in this same passage that Douglass underscores the subtle shift from his role of passive witness of the historical object to active advocate of the human imagination: what intrigues him most about Paganini's violin is that its owner invested it with "an individual character, and stir[red] in the minds of men peculiar sensations," and thus made it reveal "powers and possibilities as they were never known before." Is this, then, not precisely the aim of Douglass's *Life and Times?* It, too, consists of the same materials as countless other books, paper, ink, glue, and leather or cardboard, and yet it seeks to attain a character of its own and to stir the minds of men by revealing the powers and possibilities of autobiography as they were never known before.

To be sure, his violin meant as much to Paganini the musician as *Life and Times* means to Douglass the autobiographer:

This was his old violin, his favorite instrument, the companion of his toils and triumphs, the solace of his private hours, the minister to his soul in his battles with sin and sorrow. It had delighted thousands. Men had listened to it with admiration and wonder. It had filled the largest halls of Europe with a concord of sweet sounds. It had even stirred the dull hearts of the courts, kings and princes, and revealed to them their kinship to common mortals as perhaps had been done by no other instru- ment. It was with some difficulty that I moved away from this old violin of Paganini. (998)

Just like the Emancipation Proclamation, Paganini's violin becomes not only a tool of personal fulfillment and salvation, but a weapon in the struggle of civilization against barbarity. And just like Paganini's violin, the words that constitute *Life and Times of Frederick Douglass* strive to become more than their collective sum so that men will "listen to it with admiration and wonder." And as they strive to accrue a spirit and a power of their own, they anticipate Walter Benjamin's famous dictum that "[t]here is never a document of civilization that is not simultaneously one of barbarity" ("Über" 254). Douglass's book, like the old violin of Paganini, calls on a life and power far beyond the letter (or beyond the music, respectively), on the common humanity of all humankind and its historical struggle, epic and eternal, for equality and justice.

This particular relationship between the world and the text, art and history, the self and the word affords an expanded aesthetic in *Life and Times* compared with either the 1845 *Narrative* or the 1855 *My Bondage*. But the narrative aesthetic of Douglass's final autobiography uses Western European culture and history as a point of reference even more so than its predecessors. So what exactly is the function of Douglass's southern ritual grounds? Moreover, what is their relationship to historical conscience, and where exactly is that conscience to be located? This question inevitably leads back to the soil of the Old South.[4]

In the 1845 *Narrative*, Douglass sums up the two years he spent on Colonel Lloyd's plantation thus:

I was seldom whipped by my old master, and suffered little from any thing else than hunger and cold. I suffered much from hunger, but much more from cold. In hottest summer and coldest winter, I was kept almost naked—no shoes, no stockings, no jacket, no trousers, nothing on but a coarse tow linen shirt, reaching only to my knees. I had no bed. I must have perished with cold, but that, the coldest nights, I used to steal a bag which was used for carrying corn to the mill. I would crawl into this bag, and there sleep on the cold, damp, clay floor, with my head in and my feet out. My feet have been so cracked with the frost, that the pen with which I am writing might be laid in the gashes. (33)

The prolepsis at the end of the paragraph contains the autobiographer's historical conscience. Here, the pen links the text with historical experience and personal memory; the memoirist's pen literally touches a lived experience that precedes its representation in text. In Robert Stepto's brilliant reading, "[t]he pen, symbolizing the quest for literacy fulfilled, actually measures the wounds of the past, and this measuring process becomes a metaphor in and of itself for the artful composition of travail transcended" (20). But the measuring process as "a metaphor in and of itself" is not only part and parcel of the "pregeneric myth" of African American narrative. After all, Douglass's feet are more than just a myth, and the illiterate slave's feet were indeed scarred from their contact with the southern soil. Douglass retained the exact wording of the final sentence in each of his subsequent autobiographies, even though the prolepsis recurs in passages that have otherwise been substantially revised and amended (208, 520). Shrinking the axis of representation to its absolute minimum, almost collapsing it altogether, the sentence is subsequently never framed by quotation marks either, as though to try and efface that in My Bondage and My Freedom the prolepsis constitutes, in effect, the re-presentation of a representation, and in Life and Times the representation of a represented representation.

At the same time, the passage in all the autobiographies re-presents us with the persona of the lone male questing hero. It is, after all, Frederick Douglass's own superior literary skill, his individual, artful manipulation of the axis of representation, that allows him to tap historical conscience. Douglass's relationship to the slave culture of the South, on the other hand, was a rather ambivalent one, and many students of his life and writings have pointed out how suspicious and often openly dismissive of African American folk culture he was. More than in any other figure, the encounter with that culture is personified in all three autobiographies in Sandy Jenkins, the root doctor who, Douglass intimates, betrays the escape attempt that lands young Frederick and his conspirators in the Talbot County jail. Jenkins is also the most enigmatic figure, a figure Douglass never embraces but is reluctant to condemn: Douglass points out that he was "a genuine African, and had inherited some of the so-called magical powers said to be possessed by the eastern nations," calls him "an old advisor," but concedes that "he professed to believe in a system for which I have no name" (585). Quite likely, as David Van Leer argues,

Jenkins "stands as the symbol of something that Douglass cannot fully assimilate to the reconstruction of his personal history—a challenge that Douglass suspects may be even more authentically black than his own individualistic rebellion" (126). Others have contended that Douglass dismissed the notion of a distinct black culture altogether, and David F. Walker even diagnoses in Douglass a general "hopeless secret desire to be white and . . . blot out his blackness" (Moses 78–81; D. Walker 247). In any event, Douglass could not solve his conflicted stance on the South's African American rural folk and its culture (W. Martin 199–202; Warren 254–58).

Another account of the autobiographer's relationship to black slave culture occurs in chapter VI of *Life and Times*, where Douglass discusses the music of the slaves. He remembers that the Lloyds' slaves when walking home from the fields "would make the grand old woods for miles around reverberate with their wild and plaintive notes. They were indeed both merry and sad. Child as I was, these wild songs greatly depressed my spirits" (502). Douglass continues that the lyrics of these songs would be

> improvised as they went along—jargon, perhaps, to the reader, but full of meaning to the singers. I have sometimes thought that the mere hearing of these songs would have done more to impress the good people of the north with the soul-crushing character of slavery than whole volumes exposing the physical cruelties of the slave system; for the heart has no language like song. Many years ago, when recollecting my experience in this respect, I wrote of these slave songs in the following strain:
>
> "I did not, when a slave, fully understand the deep meaning of those rude and apparently incoherent songs. I was, myself, within the circle, so that I could then neither hear nor see as those without might see and hear. They breathed the prayer and complaint of souls overflowing with the bitterest anguish. They depressed my spirits and filled my heart with ineffable sadness." (502–3)

Here, then, is the *genius loci* of his people's historical conscience, and song the ritual that gives it voice. These songs, sung in the language closest to the singers' hearts, are the most authentic expressions of southern slave culture. Yet their meaning is not readily accessible, and Douglass himself confesses that he did not understand them because he was himself immersed in the very South that produced them. Interestingly, by using the metaphor of the circle, Douglass appears to privilege the position of the cultural outsider, one who has the necessary critical distance generated by the axis of representation that a participant in the culture would lack.

Only the cool, detached observer outside of the circle can assess objec-
tively and understand fully what is going on within the circle, Douglass
seems to say. The passage that Douglass says he first wrote "[m]any years
ago" is in fact taken verbatim from the 1845 *Narrative;* he also inserted
that same passage, again clearly marked as a quotation, in the 1855 *My
Bondage.* Obviously, this extended metaphor of the circle was important
enough to Douglass not only to include it in all of his autobiographies,
but to retain its original wording after almost half a century. And yet, the
interpolation of a direct quotation draws attention to the rising taxes that
textual mimesis levies. Does Douglass here deliberately propel himself out
of the circle of the southern slave community?

First of all, Douglass's contention that he did not understand the
meaning of the songs he heard as a young boy on the Lloyd plantation
must not be taken at face value. It seems highly improbable that young
Frederick was ignorant of the meanings of the songs, because he even
turns out to be an expert in using and manipulating what he calls their
mere unintelligible "jargon" when he describes how he and his comrades
were planning their escape from Mr. Freeland of St. Michaels: not only
did they infuse the spirituals they sang with "a double meaning" alluding
to their impending attempt at flight to a free state, they also had "several
words, expressive of things important to us, which we understood, but
which, even if distinctly heard by an outsider, would have conveyed no
certain meaning" (608, 609).[5] Consequently, Douglass (or, at the very
least, young Frederick) is not just most certainly to be placed *within* the
circle of slave culture, but he also turns out to be adept at deploying its
discursive rituals to his own advantage. Nevertheless, Douglass simultaneously stresses that he stands *outside* the circle as well, and it is this position
outside of the circle that affords him the capability not only of feeling
and experiencing, as he did as a young boy, but now also of assessing and
articulating, as he does as the elderly autobiographer. Douglass now has
the advantage of seeing and hearing analytically, but this refined perception comes at the necessary cost of forsaking the unmediated experience
of seeing and hearing, which is *feeling.* The passage highlights the crux at
the core of textual representation in that it "compares an unarticulated
meaning of experience and an articulable meaning of distance," as David
Van Leer points out (129). Thus, there is always something that remains
unarticulated and unwritten; what *is* being articulated is the modernist
fragmentation of the axis of representation. To put it differently, outside
the circle is literary text, and inside the circle is the *genius loci* of tribal
communitas; the former is articulable, the latter yet unwritten and, indeed,
perhaps unwritable. More than in any of his earlier autobiographies, in

Life and Times Frederick Douglass is aware of the dilemma, which Houston Baker describes as follows: "the slave narrator must also accomplish the almost unthinkable (since thought and language are inseparable) task of transmuting an authentic, unwritten self—a self that exists outside the conventional literary discourse structures of a white reading public—into a literary representation" (*Journey* 39). Therefore, continues Baker, "[t]he voice of the unwritten self, once it is subjected to the linguistic codes, literary conventions, and audience expectations of a literate population, is perhaps never again the authentic voice of black American slavery" (43).

What Douglass is wrestling with here is how to give an authentic voice to historical conscience. Paradoxically, the southern ritual grounds that indelibly marked this voice are too close to grasp, but too far away to lose. As such, this is related to an element of Benjaminian aura, namely the auratic as a "strange web of space and time: a unique appearance of distance, however close it may be" ("Kleine" 297). As Benjamin's colleague Theodor Adorno (who, of course, had his own historical conscience to wrestle with) tries to explain the paradox, "distance is the primary condition for the closeness to the content of works," because "[a]rt is actually the world once over, as like it as it is unlike it" (460, 499). Afro-modernism's historical conscience is therefore also engendered by the dialectic between closeness and distance, inside and outside, telling and inarticulacy, the concreteness of alphabetic script and the impalpability of aura. As Kimberly Benston sees it, this dialectic "acknowledges the endless reverberations of black language while imagining the proximity to this open-ended performance of a meta-linguistic realm of ineffable amplitude" (16).

When viewed chronologically, Douglass's autobiographies seem to move from an aesthetic of mimesis that recalibrates the axis of textual representation, toward an aesthetic of historical conscience straining to look and listen beyond the text itself. According to R. Baxter Miller, Douglass in the 1845 *Narrative* already "writes his way from being a copyist of the white Patriarchal script into a literary artist of African American truth" ("Rewritten" 93). *Life and Times* expands that very journey, linking the slave songs of the Old South's ritual grounds with the violin of Niccolò Paganini. And when the score of the former slave's text accords Paganini's violin a brief solo, this does not atrophy the southern ritual grounds' historical conscience, but instead makes it resound on a global scale. The careful inclusion of the metaphor of the circle suggests that Douglass was acutely aware of the losses with which textual representation taxes the autobiographer, and he decided in *Life and Times* that an authentic human self could arise only if his text were linked to a history and an experience

that lay beyond it, that would imbue it with a conscience. Nevertheless, his retention of the circle metaphor also suggests that he was just as
aware that, paradoxically, this all-important linkage to the world beyond
the text had to be instigated by the text itself—and this is the crux from
which *Life and Times*, despite its flaws, derives its power.[6]

This also presages what Christian Moraru, citing a strikingly Benjaminian dynamic, calls "the fruitful paradox of postmodern representation" where quite often "the memorious constitution of the world, the
world's intertextual 'packaging' and seemingly *distancing*, interposing textual and fictional garments actually deliver the world's living body to us,
bring it intimately *closer*" (*Memorious* 164–65). The book's intertextual
play of call and response with linguistic instability and discursive multi-
plicity is indeed compellingly postmodern, and in some aspects, *Life and
Times* prefigures not just Afro-modernism, but postmodernist discourse
as well, as does the genre of the slave narrative in general (Spaulding
12; Werner 7–11). At the same time, Douglass's autobiographical trajectory also points to a pertinent connection between Afro-modernism and
postmodern blackness that sets the latter apart from other postmodernist discourses. In postmodernism, observes Moraru, "[t]here is no 'nude,'
'given' 'reality'" (*Memorious* 171). In decisive contradistinction, Douglass
gives a powerful voice to "the authority of experience" when he places his
pen in the gashes of his feet still cracked from frostbite (hooks 29). To be
sure, today, the image of Douglass's scarred feet is delivered to us—to bell
hooks as much as to Christian Moraru—as literary text. But the point is
that Frederick Douglass's scars were *real*; they *predate* their representation
in/as text. They are a literally 'nude' reality that, at one point, *was* 'given.'
The chain of signifiers is therefore not infinite: that *chain* ends at the feet
of Frederick Douglass.[7] The former slave's feet symbolize a moral authority
that not only comments on, but seeks to redress, literally from the bottom
up, the direction of the ongoing experiment that is American democracy,
thereby rejecting the postmodernist dismantling of any and all hierarchies.
Douglass's last autobiography in particular hence prefigures the postmodernist projects of his heirs, who, as Timothy Spaulding explains, insist
"that the past history of slavery is a *knowable object*, retrievable through
written form" (123; emphasis added).

Surely, James Olney is correct, though, when he posits that "memory
at its farther reaches is more nearly akin to the inventive, shaping power
of poiesis than it is to the mechanical retrieval of a fixed content" (*Memory* 68). But if mimesis is not the "enemy" of demands that emanate from
beyond the work of art, but supposes such demands, how are they to be
met in fiction, which is much less referential still (C. Taylor 41)? Douglass

in his 1892 autobiography had started to map out the demands, but had also implied that the story of black America—exempting, possibly, his own book—had not yet been written. When no less a writer than Toni Morrison reflected back on her beginnings as a black novelist in America, she pondered, "The struggle was for writing that was indisputably black. I don't yet know quite what that is, but neither that nor the attempts to disqualify any effort to find out keeps me from trying it" and added: "I can say that my narrative project is as difficult today as it was thirty years ago" (Afterword 1774, 1776). Thus, Morrison at the end of the twentieth century, and into the twenty-first, is facing much the same challenge that Douglass had wrestled with over one hundred years earlier: how to infuse the African American text with a life and power far beyond the letter, how to tap the historical conscience of the black experience in the New World. And it is a challenge that has continually revisited the ritual grounds of the American South.

CHAPTER 2

Shaping Words to Fit the Soul

*Afro-Modernism and the Breakdown of Coummunication
in Jean Toomer's Cane*

In Frederick Douglass's autobiographies, the figurative circle of the author's southern ritual grounds remains intact to the last, and the famous passage introducing the motif is retained verbatim in all the different versions of Douglass's life. As such, the passage also evokes the literal circle of the ring shout, perhaps the most significant of slave culture rituals, which one antebellum eyewitness described thus:

> [T]he true "shout" takes place on Sundays or on "praise" nights through the week, and either in the praise-house or in some cabin in which a regular religious meeting has been held. . . .

[A]ll stand up in the middle of the floor, and when the "sperichil" is struck, begin first walking and by-and-by shuffling round, one after the other, in a ring. The foot is hardly taken from the floor, and the progression is mostly due to a jerking, hitching motion, which agitates the entire shouter, and soon brings out streams of perspiration. Sometimes they dance silently, sometimes as they shuffle they sing the chorus of the spiritual, and sometimes the song itself is also sung by the dancers. But most frequently a band, composed of some of the best singers and of tired shouters, stand at the side of the room to "base" the others, singing the body of the song and clapping their hands together or on the knees. Song and dance alike are extremely energetic, and often, when the shout lasts into the middle of the night, the monotonous thud, thud, thud of the feet prevents sleep within half a mile of the praise-house. (qtd. in Allen, Ware, and Garrison xiii–xiv)

Scholars agree that the ring shout derives directly from African rituals (Floyd 19–40; Raboteau 68–74). Mostly, but not exclusively, a worship ritual, variants of the ring shout have been prevalent in all black diasporic cultures. Whether religious or secular, the ring shout in the New World is, according to DoVeanna Fulton, an "oral and dance ritual that functions as a vehicle to collapse time and space dimensions so that participants experience and are sustained by history"—an expression, in other words, of an historical conscience (*Speaking* 119). The performance of circle rituals by the slaves, maintains historian Sterling Stuckey, "was so consistent and profound that one could argue that it was what gave form and meaning to black religion and art" (11). Yet like any ritual, the ring shout as practiced in the black diaspora indicates displacement even as it sustains a continuous identity across time and space. The ring shout in the American South evinces the brutal effects of dislocation in the Middle Passage and of the implementation of the peculiar institution: the distinctive "thud thud thud" of the dancers' shuffling movements was produced by feet whose soles may very well have been scarred from frostbite, as Frederick Douglass's were. Although the ring shout retained its basic African elements, it also transformed itself under the pressures of enslavement, most notably as a result of the Christianization of the slaves and the frequent injunctions against dancing (Floyd 35–36; Raboteau 74–75; Rosenbaum 18–25, 56–58).

This dialectic between retention and displacement is also at the center of the figurative ring that circumscribes Jean Toomer's *Cane*. What Douglass had located within the circle, the Toomer of the early 1920s often referred to as "the spiritual truth" of the South's rural black folk, and, equipped with the latest tools of the literary avant-garde, he set out to capture that spirit in what would remain his only published novel (qtd. in Kerman and Eldridge 95). The 1923 book is, as Paul Anderson notes, "at once ancestralist and ultramodernist" (73): on the one hand, *Cane*'s 'ancestralism' is very much concerned with what's inside the circle, with what Ralph Ellison would come to call "*the 'Blackness of Blackness'*" (*Invisible* 9). On the other hand, the novel's 'ultramodernism' renders this circle visible only as fragments. Where the figurative ring remains intact in Douglass's *proto*modernism, the segments of the triptych that is *Cane* are interlinked by three arcs—the pieces of a broken circle. The ritual of call and response, so central to the ring shout, appears irrevocably disrupted.

The transition from Douglass's circle to Toomer's arcs thus also exemplifies the rise of modernism in western art. In the Pound era, writes Hugh Kenner, the arts were "all simultaneously released from the mimetic" (*Pound* 245). "The long tradition of mimesis," he elaborates, "uses words to imitate actions and speeches; but confronted by a world of matter and motion, from which actions and speeches have departed, mimesis can only imitate (1) old poems, or (2) the movements of the mind transposing and reconstituting what is seen" (*Homemade* 78). Auerbach grumbled from his exile in Istanbul that with the rise of modernism, "in all nooks and crannies of the earth crises of adaptation developed; they increased and massed together; they led to shocks that we have still not overcome" (511). Where Douglass remained confident that text, his text at least, was still capable of representing a "vital substance," the crisis of mimesis that resulted in the modernist movement of the early twentieth century was a reflection of the white westerner's sense that things were indeed falling apart, that the center could no longer hold.

The Great War that broke out in 1914, which would radically transform both Ezra Pound's New World and Erich Auerbach's Old, fueling the emergence of high modernism, also had its impact on black America: it was in many ways American military involvement overseas and its socioeconomic ramifications at home that were among the catalysts for what came to be the Harlem Renaissance. But what for the white western writer, including Auerbach, was often an anxiety over the fate of mimesis, over cultural and aesthetic fragmentation, was for the African American writer an opportunity, too, to explore what a black American literature was to look like in the first place. And it was then, during this first major and sustained flowering of black American art, that the role, function, and value of the South and its various ritual grounds were being reassessed. For the African American artist, it was not so much that things were falling apart as that they were in flux. The Great Migration from South to

North, from country to city, from the field to the factory, not only offered to but demanded of the black artist an inquiry of where the center was, or had been, in the first place. The dialogue between modernism and blackness—in Alain Locke's words, "a significant and satisfying new phase of group development, and with it a spiritual Coming of Age"—we know today as the Harlem Renaissance (51).

In literature, the beginning of the Harlem Renaissance is often dated to the year 1923, the year that saw the publication of a slender volume by the enigmatic Jean Toomer, titled *Cane*. Henry Louis Gates has lauded the book as "that blackest of black traces . . . imprinted on the New Negro Renaissance" (*Figures* 211). And yet, a vexing aspect of the novel is that *Cane*, perhaps more than any other work of the Harlem Renaissance, attests to the price for which literary modernity can be had: the fragmentation of the mimetic power of language.[1] Toomer's text encircles its southern ritual ground, but is never able to penetrate to its center and preserve and store its spirit in its own language.

In the concluding section of *Cane*, the author's fictional alter ego Kabnis describes the act of artistic creation as "shapin words t fit m soul" (111). Initially, Toomer himself was confident that he had managed to shape words so as to make them fit the vivid and stimulating impressions that his first trip into the deep South, this "land of the gret [sic] passions," had left on his soul ("The South" 233). Back in Washington shortly after his return from the small town of Sparta, Georgia, where he had substituted for two months as principal of a black school, he effused, brimming with confidence, "My seed was planted in the cane- and cotton-fields, and in the souls of black and white people in the small southern town. My seed was planted in *myself* down there. Roots have grown and strengthened. They have extended out. I spring up in Washington" (qtd. in D. Turner, *Cane* 148).

However, after Boni & Liveright published *Cane* in 1923, Toomer admitted that, as with Kabnis, the shaping of words had not been that easy at all. The book, he wrote, "was born in an agony of internal tightness, conflict, and chaos"; it "was somehow distilled from the most terrible strain I have ever known. . . . The feelings were in me, deep and mobile enough. But the creations of the forms were very difficult" (qtd. in D. Turner, *Cane* 156). He had also begun to doubt whether the shape of the words really did fit his soul. In a poem Toomer included in the cover letter of the manuscript he sent to Horace Liveright, he wrote of *Cane*, "And when I look for the power and the beauty / I thought I'd caught, they too seem to thin out / and and [sic] elude me. / Next time, perhaps . . . " (qtd. in D. Turner, *Cane* 154). But as it turned out, there would not be a next time. With the publication date of *Cane* approaching, Toomer underwent a drastic reassessment of himself and his art. "The forming of a man is more important than the forming of a book," he insisted, and began to withdraw into the mysticism of would-be *staretz* Georges Gurdjieff (qtd. in Kerman and Eldridge 110). Furthermore, he thought of himself now no longer as an African American, but as a member of a new 'American' race, a self-definition that confused and sometimes angered his friends as well as his publisher, as he steadfastly refused to promote *Cane* as the work of a black author (D. Lewis 70–74; Michaels 52–54, 62). Toomer was frustrated over what he felt was a misrepresentation of his new self and his book: "My writing, namely, the very thing that should have made me understood, was being so presented and interpreted that I was now much more misunderstood in this respect than at any other time of my life. . . . The label 'Negro' was of no more consequence than any other" (*Wayward* 133). For the rest of his life, Toomer would be devoted to explaining his newfound self and trying to clear up the misunderstanding.

He continued to write, but never again would he reach the power and the beauty that is in *Cane*. He would strain to explain himself and his work to America—and arguably to himself, too. Toomer's literary career after *Cane* can be viewed as a breakdown of communication, a failure to communicate successfully what kind of text he was forming, and what kind of man he had formed. Much of what he wrote remained unpublished in his lifetime; his fiction was largely limp and didactic, his philosophical writings highly abstract and vapid (Kerman and Eldridge 378–79). However, this breakdown of communication was already foreshadowed in his greatest work. In *Cane*, Toomer said he attempted to "drive straight for my own spiritual reality, and for the spiritual truth of the South" (qtd. in Kerman and Eldridge 95). Yet the book depicts characters who are either unable to grasp fulfillment and tap a spiritual, mystic wholeness, or who are incapable of articulating comprehensibly their spiritual selves.[2] A close textual analysis and examination of the recurring shifts between levels of narrative consciousness reveals that more than anything else, it is language itself that prevents the book's characters from shaping words to fit their souls. Language distances not only the characters from each other but also, by extension, the narrative voice from its subject matter, the South. *Cane* consistently employs a narrative voice that observes "the spiritual truth of the South" from the vantage point of the outsider; sometimes the voice employs a first-person narrator, sometimes an omniscient one, but there is always a perceptible distance between the observer and the observed. The space between is filled with words, but this process inevitably leads to a breakdown of communication caused by language itself, the very medium of communication. *Cane* the book thus chronicles the attempts of the narrative voice in its various guises to capture the southern ritual grounds it visits and how it is ironically defeated by the very medium with which it seeks to survey the terrain, dramatizing instead the telling inarticulacy of Afro-modernism.

According to his own estimate, Toomer came closest to capturing the power and the beauty of the South in "Fern" in the first section of *Cane*. He judged it to be one of "those pieces that come nearest to the old Negro, to the spirit saturate with folk-song" (qtd. in Kerman and Eldridge 98).[3] The plot of "Fern" is very basic and simple. The first-person narrator, evidently a newcomer to the small Georgia town of Sempter (the fictional counterpart to the Sparta Toomer visited), is captivated by the strange magic of Fern, her eyes, and her singing. Fern has had many men, but none of them could give her anything she needed or wanted. Seeing her sitting on her porch, the narrator asks her to join him for a walk. "I felt strange, as I always do in Georgia, particularly at dusk," he continues; "I felt that things unseen to men were tangibly immediate. It would not have surprised me had I had a vision. . . . When one is on the soil of one's ancestors, most anything can come to one" (19). They embrace in a cane field, but Fern extricates herself quickly and, shaking with torment and anguish, breaks out in song. Shortly thereafter, the narrator returns north, yet he is still haunted by the strange eyes of Fern. Like many of the other women in the first section of *Cane*, Fern—beautiful, sensuous, and strong, yet also misunderstood, vulnerable, and marginalized—is fashioned into a symbol of the folk culture of the (semi)rural black South (McKay 90–91).

The narrator's failure to understand fully the magic of Fern is ultimately a breakdown of communication and a failure of language. The text shifts restlessly between different levels of narrative consciousness in its attempt to penetrate to Fern's spiritual truth. These various levels of narrative consciousness can be roughly divided into four categories:

{I}   First person (the narrative "I")
{II} Second person (the "you" as reader—or the observer of the observer)
{III} Third person ("one," "they," or "everyone")
{IV} The collective human mind (the omniscient observer of all observers)

The differentiation among these four levels is not always clear, because the language has a very lithe quality that flows almost effortlessly in and out of any given level. However, at the very least fifteen shifts of narrative consciousness occur in the first eleven sentences alone. The sequence of shifts is indicated by Arabic numerals below:

> Face flowed into her eyes. Flowed in soft cream foam and plaintive rip-
> ples, in such a way that [1] wherever your glance may momentarily have
> rested, it immediately thereafter wavered in the direction of her eyes.
> [2] The soft suggestion of down slightly darkened, like the shadow of
> a bird's wing might, the creamy brown color of her upper lip. [3] Why,
> after noticing it, you sought her eyes, [4] I cannot tell you. [5] Her nose
> was aquiline, Semitic. [6] If you have heard a Jewish cantor sing, if he
> has touched you and made your own sorrow seem trivial when compared
> with his, you will know [7] my feeling when I follow the curves of her
> profile, like mobile rivers, to their common delta. [8] They were strange
> eyes. In this, that they sought nothing—that is, nothing that was obvi-
> ous and tangible [9] and that one could see, and [10] they gave the
> impression that nothing was to be denied. When a woman seeks, [11]
> you will have observed, [12] her eyes deny. Fern's eyes desired nothing
> [13] that you could give her; [14] there was no reason why they should
> withhold. [15] Men saw her eyes and fooled themselves. (16)

In its relentless shifting between levels of narrative consciousness, the text appears to encircle Fern, but is nevertheless unable to penetrate to her essence. Separately as well as in concert, the four approaches, indicated by Roman numerals below, still fail to capture her spiritual self:

> {IV:} Face flowed into her eyes. Flowed in soft cream foam and plaintive
> ripples, in such a way that {II:} wherever your glance may momentarily
> have rested, it immediately thereafter wavered in the direction of her
> eyes. {IV:} The soft suggestion of down slightly darkened, like the shadow
> of a bird's wing might, the creamy brown color of her upper lip. {II:} Why,
> after noticing it, you sought her eyes, {I:} I cannot tell you. {IV:} Her
> nose was aquiline, Semitic. {II:} If you have heard a Jewish cantor sing,
> if he has touched you and made your own sorrow seem trivial when com-
> pared with his, you will know {I:} my feeling when I follow the curves
> of her profile, like mobile rivers, to their common delta. {IV:} They were
> strange eyes. In this, that they sought nothing—that is, nothing that was
> obvious and tangible {III:} and that one could see, and {IV:} they gave
> the impression that nothing was to be denied. When a woman seeks, {II:}
> you will have observed, {IV:} her eyes deny. Fern's eyes desired nothing
> {II:} that you could give her; {IV:} there was no reason why they should
> withhold. {III:} Men saw her eyes and fooled themselves.

Clearly, the narrating "I" of level I does not understand Fern. Level II provides no better inroad into the mystery and magic of Fern, for although we notice, hear, and observe, and even perhaps relate to the narrator's feelings, we still cannot comprehend. Level III seemingly opens the pool of epistemological resources, yet we still merely see, but do not understand. And finally, level IV appears to be the most promising: here, the observer seems to have knowledge of the fundamental rules that govern human behavior, such as, "When a woman seeks . . . her eyes deny." But even on level IV, the words that strive to bridge meaningfully the gap between the narrator-observer and Fern's soul fall short and fail to let us see behind her eyes.

Having already encircled Fern with language on all four sides, the narrator begins to engage in speculation in the story's second section: "Her eyes, if it were sunset, rested idly where the sun, molten and glorious, was pouring down between the fringe of pines. Or maybe they gazed at the gray cabin on the knoll from which an evening folk-song was coming." This is followed by even more "[p]erhaps" and "[l]ike as not" (17). Then, the "I" implores the reader to aid him in his speculation: "Besides, picture if you can. . . . Or, suppose. . . . Your thoughts can help me, and I would like to know" (17, 18). For him, however, language remains the only tool with which he feels he can reach her: "Something I must do for her. There was myself. What could I do for her? Talk, of course. Push back the fringe of pines upon new horizons" (18). But here his privileging language fails him. Talk, language, may be able to "[p]ush back the fringe of pines upon new horizons," but he can reach Fern only by removing the linguistic barrier, all the well-shaped words, from the space between his soul and the southern landscape, just as Fern does: "Like her face, the whole countryside seemed to flow into her eyes. Flowed into them with the soft listless cadence of Georgia's South" (17). Fern—who speaks only once throughout the story—is at one with the spiritual truth of the South because she is capable of a direct experience, untainted by language, of the southern landscape. The one time Fern speaks, she asks the narrator as they walk to the cane field, "'Doesn't it make you mad?' She meant the row of petty gossiping people" (19). She expresses her contempt here at being circumscribed by the language of others, an irony of which the narrator, who has been doing just that, is not aware.

Thus, it is ultimately language itself that separates the narrator from Fern, man from woman, human beings from nature, knowledge from understanding, one soul from the other, and the modernist text from the South. Ironically, it is language that is responsible for the breakdown of communication. It is significant that in the only passage in which the first-person narrator is able to communicate meaningfully with Fern, his message is transmitted in nonverbal fashion:

> "Let's take a walk," I at last ventured. The suggestion, coming after so long an isolation, was novel enough, I guess, to surprise. But it wasn't that. Something told me that men before me had said just that as a prelude to offering their bodies. I tried to tell her with my eyes. I think she understood. The thing from her that made my throat catch, vanished. Its passing left her visible in a way I'd thought, but never seen. (18–19)

Here, he finally connects with her by 'telling' her with his eyes and breaking through the barrier of language—he comes to see her in a new light. Nonverbal communication opens new vistas of recognition, but the narrator, using words as his means of communication, obfuscates as much as he reveals. We are not told (and perhaps we cannot be told) in precisely what new way Fern is now visible to him, except that her new visibility is the result of an imaginative leap. In the climactic moment of his interaction with Fern, he loses again whatever precarious connection to her spirit he might have had:

> From force of habit, I suppose, I held Fern in my arms—that is, without at first noticing it. Then my mind came back to her. Her eyes, unusually weird and open, held me. Held God. He flowed in as I've seen the countryside flow in. Seen men. I must have done something—what, I don't know; in the confusion of my emotion. She sprang up. Rushed some distance from me. Fell to her knees, and began swaying, swaying. Her body was tortured with something it could not let out. Like boiling sap it flooded arms and fingers till she shook them as if they burned her. It found her throat, and spattered inarticulately in plaintive, convulsive sounds, mingled with calls to Jesus Christ. And then she sang, brokenly. A Jewish cantor singing with a broken voice. A child's voice, uncertain, or an old man's. Dusk hid her; I could hear only her song. (19)

In this crucial moment, "[t]he narrator leaves blank the place where he touches Fern, leaves 'unreadable' his relation to her, making it uncertain whether his relation is one of liberatory breakthrough or patriarchal reenclosure," Laura Doyle argues (98). His relation to Fern is partly 'unreadable' because her spiritual essence is, if occasionally visible, then decidedly 'unwritable.' Nellie McKay sees this "[a]s a metaphor for the relationship between the poet and the folk culture, the narrative point[ing] to the problems that those like Jean Toomer, removed in time and place from it, face in accurately trying to record and interpret it" (111). The educated observer-narrator relies on well-shaped words to tap the soul of the southern folk, but the only possible way for Fern to communicate her spiritual essence is through nonverbal means, through trying to 'tell' with her eyes and with her song.

This, then, calls for a reconsideration of how close "Fern" actually comes "to the old Negro, to the spirit saturate with folk-song." Toomer's own assessment anticipates Stephen Henderson's condition of "saturation," a condition in which "personally and communally recognized meanings . . . are more felt than named" (43). As a critical concept, saturation is "chiefly the communication of 'Blackness' and fidelity to the observed or intuited truth of the Black Experience in the United States" (10). Henderson's theory links saturation as "a sign, like the mathematical symbol for infinity, or the term 'Soul,'" with the concreteness of poetic structure, that is, the inner mechanics of a poem, so that black poetics demarcate a "Soul-Field" of "the complex galaxy of personal, social, institutional, historical, religious, and mythical meanings that affect everything we say or do as Black people sharing a common heritage" (68, 41, 28–30). As Kimberly Benston points out, though, in the attempt to link saturation with structure, saturation "becomes suspended in the space of its own tautology, allowing only the choice between a hypertrophied (*sated*) and an empty (*satired*) blackness: the blacker you are . . . the blacker you are" (Benston 15; Baker, *Blues* 81–83). Fern, the southern earth mother, embodies this Hendersonian "Soul-Field," but she, too, simply *is*; her essence defies linguistic description. This tautology at the core of saturation as well as of "Fern" recalls Walter Benjamin's concept of aura: aura is a "halo of breath" ("*Hauchkreis*") and is predicated in "the Here and Now of the work of art—its unique presence at the place where it is located" ("Kleine" 376; "Kunstwerk" 139). The aura's "Here and Now" is also characterized by a "vulnerable" core of its "genuineness," and this genuineness in turn contains "the essence of everything that can be handed down from its origin, from its material duration to its historical testimony" ("Kunstwerk" 140).[4] Just as Benjamin pits nebulous aura against the material conditions of technological reproducibility, so does the Hendersonian Soul-Field pit saturation against poetic structure. Both issue the same demands that Fern does: the mystery of (black) art must be accepted a priori and can only be experienced directly, because its auratic "halo of breath" ultimately defies linguistic representation and empirical analysis.

The breakdown of communication caused by the inability of language to capture and transmit "aura" is a recurring theme that appears in all segments of the book. Most of the middle section is set in Washington,

D.C.—at the time still very much a southern city—in the urban counterpart to the sleepy, semirural Sempter, Georgia. "Avey" is in many ways
a companion piece to "Fern" in that it tells of a male narrator's futile
attempt to connect with a seemingly indifferent woman. The narrator
here is much more assertive and aggressive, trying to impose his understanding of love onto her, but he too fails: "I talked. I knew damn well
I could beat her at that. Her eyes were soft and misty, the curves of her
lips were wistful, and her smile seemed indulgent of the irrelevance of my
remarks. I gave up at last and let her love me, silently, in her own way"
(46). But Avey's way has no need for words—just like Fern, she speaks
only once in the entire story—and it is a way that remains unacceptable
and perhaps even inaccessible to him: "I wanted to talk. To explain what
I meant to her. Avey was as silent as those great trees whose tops we
looked down on" (46). They eventually go their separate ways, but after a
number of years have gone by, he accidentally meets her in the street one
day and asks her to accompany him to Soldier's Home, a park "to which
I always go when I want the simple beauty of another's soul" (47). He
explains how he feels about their relationship, what Avey should do to
make something of herself, and "I talked, beautifully I thought, about an
art that would be born" (49). But Avey falls asleep during the monologue,
and the narrator comes to realize that, just like his fellow soul-searcher
does in "Fern," nothing ever happens to Avey either, not even himself.[5]
It is again language that fails to capture and convey the spirit, and again
language is the barrier between the narrator and Avey. The narrator leaves
Avey as an "[o]rphan woman" at the end of the story, and so words have
both literally and metaphorically orphaned her from the text into the
simple but indescribable beauty of her soul (49).

Thus, there are no fulfilling relationships between men and women in
Cane, as language always interpolates. For instance, when Tom in "Blood
Burning Moon" tries to tell Louisa that he loves her, he discovers that
feelings, emotions, 'spiritual truth,' cannot be conveyed in language, for
"words is like th spots on dice: no matter how y fumbles em, there's times
when they jes wont come. I dunno why. Seems like the love I feels fo
yo done stole m tongue" (32). The language of Toomer's male narrator-observers fails to capture the female spirit.[6] Language prevents all of
these characters from either attaining or sharing spiritual reality and truth.
Ironically, they are all frustrated by language itself in their effort to communicate the ineffable, to shape into words the inarticulable.

It is the last section of Cane where the breakdown of communication
is dramatized most significantly, where the use of language carries the most
compelling ramifications for the (male modernist) artist and his endeavor.

The title character of "Kabnis" is a transplanted northerner and would-be writer who teaches at a rural school for blacks in Georgia. Unable to sleep during a hot and humid night, he finds that his thoughts begin to wander:

> Near me. Now. Whoever you are, my warm glowing sweetheart, do not think that the face that rests beside you is the real Kabnis. Ralph Kabnis is a dream. And dreams are faces with large eyes and weak chins and broad brows that get smashed by fists of square faces. The body of the world is bull-necked. A dream is a soft face that fits uncertainly upon it . . . God, if I could put that in words. Give what I know a bull-neck and a heaving body, all would go well with me, wouldn't it, sweetheart? If I could feel that I came to the South to face it. If I, the dream (not what is weak and afraid in me) could become the face of the South. How my lips would sing for it, my songs being the lips of its soul. (83–84)

Kabnis is unsure of his identity, which he thinks of as an amorphous dream. If he had the right words, he could personalize his identity, give it a body and a shape; and if, like Fern, he could let the southern ritual grounds flow into his eyes, he would attain some spiritual truth. Kabnis fails to put the aura of the landscape in which he moves into words, and as a result, he will not attain the spiritual wholeness he longs for, and he will never be able to sing the songs of the South. Kabnis, who never sings and in fact does not like the spirituals and folk songs of the local black peasantry, chooses instead to repudiate what he sees after he has left his bed to get a breath of fresh air:

> Kabnis is about to shake his fists heavenward. He looks up, and the night's beauty strikes him dumb. He falls to his knees. Sharp stones cut through his thin pajamas. The shock sends a shiver over him. He quivers. Tears mist his eyes. He writhes. "God Almighty, dear God, dear Jesus, do not torture me with beauty. Take it away. Give me an ugly world. Ha, ugly. Stinking like unwashed niggers. Dear Jesus, do not chain me to myself and set these hills and valleys, heaving with folk-songs, so close to me that I cannot reach them. There is a radiant beauty in the night that touches and . . . tortures me. Ugh. Hell. Get up, you damn fool. Look around. Whats beautiful there? Hog pens and chicken yards. Dirty red mud. Stinking outhouse. Whats beauty anyway but ugliness if it hurts you?" (85)

Again, the auratic beauty of the Georgia night is impossible to put into words, and so Kabnis uses language to detach himself emotionally from the beauty. Unable to communicate beauty and unwilling to accept the insufficiency of words to tap spiritual truth, Kabnis verbally fashions the beautiful into the ugly.

Unlike Kabnis, Lewis, another of Toomer's wandering observer-artists and himself a writer, is the only outsider in the book who manages to connect to the beauty and the power, the South's spiritual truth.[7] Both men encounter Father John, an old black man who has been relegated to a dark cellar and who mumbles incomprehensibly every now and then, and their reactions to him exemplify their differing notions as to how history and blackness, the pain and the beauty, are encountered and negotiated. Lewis tries not to explain verbally but to connect spiritually:

> Lewis, seated now so that his eyes rest upon the old man, merges with his source and lets the pain and beauty of the South meet him there. White faces, pain-pollen, settle downward through a cane-sweet mist and touch the ovaries of yellow flowers. Cotton-bolls bloom, droop. Black roots twist in a parched red soil beneath a blazing sky. Magnolias, fragrant, a trifle futile, lovely, far off . . . His eyelids close. A force begins to heave and rise . . . (107)

Lewis also understands that the old man, as the "flesh and spirit of the past," is the very embodiment of historical conscience (109). He accepts the past with all its beauty and pain, and this acceptance, an acknowledgment of historical conscience, unencumbered by language, endows him with a spiritual force. At the same time, Father John is also a personification of telling inarticulacy, a "mute John the Baptist of a new religion—or a tongue-tied shadow of an old," who will not and cannot shape his "force" into easily decoded words (106). It is, significantly, the only instance in *Cane* where one individual meaningfully connects with another, and it is also a nonverbal event. Kabnis, on the other hand, rejects Father John, saying that "he aint my past" (108). Later, Kabnis angrily clarifies his position to Lewis in a long-winded invective that ironically serves only to foreground the insufficiency of words:

> Y misapprehended me. Y understand what that means, dont y? All right then, y misapprehended me. I didnt say [I was born into a family of] preachers. I said orators. ORATORS. Born one and I'll die one. You understand me, Lewis. . . . I've been shapin words after a design that branded here. Know whats here? M soul. Ever heard o that? Th hell y have. Been shapin words t fit m soul. . . . I've been shapin words; ah, but sometimes theyre beautiful and golden an have a taste that makes them fine t roll over with y tongue. . . . Those words I was tellin y about, they

wont fit in th mold thats branded on m soul. Rhyme, y see? Poet, too. Bad rhyme, bad poet. . . . Th form thats burned int my soul is some twisted awful thing that crept in from a dream, a godam nightmare, an wont stay still unless I feed it. An it lives on words. Not beautiful words. God Almighty no. Misshapen, split-gut, tortured, twisted words. . . . White folks feed it cause their looks are words. Niggers, black niggers feed it cause theyre evil an their looks are words. Yallar niggers feed it. This whole damn bloated purple country feeds it cause its goin down t hell in a holy avalanche of words. I want t feed th soul—I know what that is; th preachers dont—but I've got t feed it. I wish t God some lynchin white man ud stick his knife through it an pin it to a tree. (111)

Kabnis's tragedy is that the beautiful, golden, tasty words he has been shaping—perhaps the words of traditional romantic poetry—are incapable of expressing his spiritual reality as they stand between himself and his soul. But the contorted impressions on his soul do feed on language, they cry for expression, yet Kabnis cannot find the right shape for his words (Hutchinson, "Jean" 240). R. Baxter Miller points out that passages such as these "represent the artist's profound tension in dramatic fiction, his narrative encounter with himself" ("Blacks" 37). Ironically, Kabnis the *artiste manqué* approaches momentary greatness in his dramatic description of the tension within himself, and *Cane* as a whole dramatizes Toomer's own negotiation of modernism's fundamental crux: how to shape words to fit one's soul, how to overcome the breakdown of communication and give voice to a telling inarticulacy, how to extend Frederick Douglass's project and transfer historical conscience into literary language.

The ending of "Kabnis" is therefore fittingly ambiguous: the protagonist ascends to the rays of the morning sun, the "[g]old glowing child" that "sends a birth-song slanting down gray dust streets and sleepy windows of the southern town" (117). But he leaves behind the cellar where Lewis, his foil, was able to connect, as the only one of Toomer's artist-types, to the beauty and pain of the South's historical conscience. In Lewis, Toomer presents us with a potentially positive outcome of the artist's narrative encounter with himself, but significantly, Lewis exits the text before the end of *Cane* as he "finds himself completely cut out" (110). Once Lewis has tapped spiritual reality and acknowledged Father John as the embodiment of historical conscience, the narrative orphans him from the text "out into the night," just like Avey and many other of Toomer's female characters (111). Paradoxically, it also orphans him from language in that Lewis never actually writes anything (for all we know) and, expelled from the narrative, his text, too, remains unreadable.

Not even Lewis, it seems, can shape words to fit the soul in the way that Frederick Douglass's pen fit in the gashes of his frostbitten feet. Apropos the American modernist enterprise, Hugh Kenner notes that "[t]he quest for the one true sentence leads to wordlessness"—which is precisely the destination Toomer maps for Lewis's journey (Kenner, *Homemade* 155). Once again, words separate the artist from his subject. Jean Toomer and his observer-artists all try to shape the words to fit the soul, yet in this painful process they come to foreground the fundamental artistic tension of writing the unwritable.

Cane thus dramatizes how literary language in and of itself seems incapable of rendering spiritual essence and auratic Soul-Field. The constant shifts between levels of narrative consciousness in "Fern" and other stories, as well as between various literary forms, poetic, dramatic, and narrative, do nothing to avert the breakdown of communication. The structure of the work is as fragmented and modernist as the language that the various narrator-observers employ to communicate spiritual truth. Each of the three sections of the book is prefaced by an arc; combined, the three arcs form a fractional circle. The circular progression of the book's structure—incomplete and disrupted as it is—leads us back to the beginning, the very first word of the epigraph, "Oracular" (1, 39, 81). We, as well as the author himself, have not so much driven *at* but driven *around* the spiritual truth of the South. But the text does not aid us in capturing it. In *Cane*'s version of American modernism, language itself becomes a ritual, the "focus of ritual distraction from engulfments that will not submit to being ritualized," as Kenner puts it (*Homemade* 152).

Toomer himself envisioned a different circle in the book: "From the point of view of the spiritual entity behind the work, the curve really starts with Bona and Paul (awakening), plunges into Kabnis, emerges in Karintha etc. swings upward into Theatre and Box Seat, and ends (pauses) in Harvest Song. Whew!" (qtd. in D. Turner, *Cane* 152). However, if one views "Harvest Song" as the completion of the circle, the spirit of the South, its aura, still remains elusive in the end:

> I am a reaper. (Eoho!) All my oats are cradled. But I am too fatigued to bind them. And I hunger. I crack a grain. It has no taste to it. My throat is dry . . .

> O my brothers, I beat my palms, still soft, against the stubble of my harvesting. (You beat your soft palms, too.) My pain is sweet. Sweeter than the oats or wheat or corn. It will not bring me knowledge of my hunger. (71)

As Robert Jones points out, the poem "describes an artist's inability to transform the raw materials of his labor into art. . . . Although the poet/reaper has successfully cradled the fruits of his labor, when he cracks a grain from the store of his oats, he cannot taste its inner essence" ("Jean" 261). Cracking the grain to still the hunger, shaping the word to fit the soul, cannot connect with the spirit. "The American harvest," Darwin Turner observes, "is sterile" ("Jean" 193). Even in Toomer's own tracing of the figurative ring, the circle remains broken. Where Douglass was still able to tap that which lies within the circle, even though he situated himself outside of it, now the tune has changed: Toomer's narrator-observers have journeyed inside the circle, and still they cannot hear or see as those *of* the circle might see and hear. And in the rare instances when they can see and hear, as Lewis does, they cannot produce a text that represents this experience.

That language itself poses an insurmountable obstacle in representing the southern ritual grounds' aura does not mean that *Cane* is without history, or without historical conscience. Barbara Foley's research has unearthed how many of the novel's locales and characters find their historical analogues in Sparta and vicinity. Foley makes a strong case for the novel's title as also a veiled allusion to John Cain, one of the leaders of an 1863 slave uprising ("Jean" 755–56). And while Toomer had only a superficial grasp of the economics of Hancock County, he was very much aware of the politics, and the violence, of Jim Crow. The stories of racial violence that Layman shares with Kabnis allude to the brutal 1918 lynching of Mary Turner farther south in Valdosta, and especially to the notorious "Death Farm" in neighboring Jasper County: just a short time before Toomer's arrival in Sparta, a series of grisly killings took place on the Monticello farm of John S. Williams. Williams, who was under federal investigation for debt peonage, ordered his foreman to murder the laborers, carrying out at least one of the killings himself, in order to cover up what amounted to conditions of chattel slavery on his farm. The bodies of the men, most of them chained together, were tied to bags of rocks and dumped in the Alvovy, Yellow, and South rivers. The case gained national notoriety, and Williams eventually became the only white southerner between Reconstruction and 1966 to serve prison time for the murder of an African American (Foley, "'In'" 187–93).

The mythical Father John, though, the very personification of historical conscience, does not really have an historical prototype. But this character is not just Toomer's rejoinder to defenses of white supremacy that often cited the Old Testament myth of Cain but is also his retort to the accommodationist, Washingtonian politics of racial 'uplift' of

Sparta's CME Ebenezer Church and the influence it wielded over the Sparta Agricultural and Industrial Institute, where Toomer briefly taught (Foley, "Jean" 760–67; Scruggs 276–91). As Foley concludes, *Cane's* refusal of these references to lynching and the politics of white supremacy "to be completely subordinated to Toomer's mythifying imagination shows the irrepressibility of history" ("'In'" 194). While the Soul-Field of *Fern* is indeed unwritable, historical conscience is not to be equated with aura. History is still writable, even if it has become oblique and rendered almost obscured by *Cane's* preoccupation with the auratic. Nor does Afro-modernism's historical conscience necessarily require concrete historicity: the character of Father John is, unlike Douglass's feet, a fiction, a literary construct. If historical conscience defies the writing skills of the many artist-types who populate the novel, it certainly didn't those of the Jean Toomer who put Father John in *Cane*.

Even so, Father John, the personification of historical conscience, has been driven underground, his message indecipherable to all but Lewis and Carrie, the young woman who feeds the basement's denizen. The black coal in the bucket that Kabnis swings "carelessly" upstairs to Halsey's workshop at the end of the novel is "dead," Booker T. Washington's ideology of racial uplift compromised by its alienation from historical conscience (117). *Cane* is therefore itself a breakdown of communication, and there is a pervasive sense of failure in the book. Its southern ritual grounds, Darwin Turner states, constitute "a landscape conceived and designed by a man who struggled for greatness but believed that he had experienced only failure; a man who wished to guide, to teach, to lead" (Introduction x). In trying to guide us and himself to the South's spiritual truth and to the historical conscience of black America in the new American Century, Toomer found only words whose shape did not, and perhaps could not, fit the spirit of which he had caught a glimpse. Words, the novel discovers, are in and of themselves soulless—yet this same discovery ultimately transforms the geographical territory of the South into a figurative ritual ground manifesting the need to reimagine the human condition in a world that challenges the very humanity of not just its inhabitants, but its visitors, too. The banishment of the historical conscience into the cellars of the South is the price the novel pays so that it can become a modernist masterpiece that records the fragmentation of the human existence in the modern world.

However, critic Bowie Duncan has asserted that Toomer's novel "speaks of a reality like itself, something to be experienced without absolute finality" (328). On another level, the book is not simply about the breakdown of communication or the shortcomings of language. In preventing us from experiencing aura through words, *Cane* asks us to search for alternative channels of communication, and the most potent of these channels is the human imagination. *Cane* is a bold attempt to incite the imagination through language; it is a most powerful testimony to the realization that while it may no longer be possible for us to understand and communicate with our spiritual, inner selves and those of others, it is still very much possible to *imagine*. J. Martin Favor brings the paradox to a point when he argues that "[t]he South in *Cane* is as symbolic of death as it is a marker of wholly desirable black identity. But perhaps this is precisely Toomer's point in writing a swan song for the folk; if nothing else, it points out the visceral necessity of imagining alternative categories and authenticities" (66–67).

And yet, the fact remains that *Cane* dramatizes the impossibility of transforming aura into text and calls attention to the inarticulacy, telling though it may be, of historical conscience. It exudes a sense of nostalgia often found in Afro-modernist texts, a nostalgia for the perceived possibility of an earlier world in which, says Sandra Adell, "understanding was at once aesthetic, political, social, and religious, for it took place through the authentic procedures that allowed the self to be one with myth. There was an immediacy in premodern symbolic meanings" where "[t]he self, the 'I,' was not isolated or distinguishable from the objective meaning of the world, the cosmos, and the social" (139). Toomer's wandering narrator-observers clearly seek communion with the myths of the southern ritual grounds, but, unable to shape the words to fit their souls, they can only give voice to a quintessentially modernist yearning for 'authenticity' (Baker, *Modernism* 100–102; Duvall 11).

The one alternative channel of communication the novel offers up as capable of giving voice to the "truth" of the South is song. Throughout *Cane*, African American spirituals and folk songs are one of the few communicative modes that speak directly from and to the spirit, that transmit the aura of the southern ritual grounds, and the author himself referred to his book as "a swan song" (qtd. in D. Turner, *Cane* 156). Curiously, while the text itself abounds with references to song and singing wafting across the southern landscape, it doesn't really incorporate actual music. It's as though the language of Toomer's modernism itself denies a satisfactory reconciliation between vernacular song and literary text. In "Fern," for example, in the very text Toomer himself thought to be approaching the spiritual truth of the southern ritual grounds "saturate with folk-song," only the *act* of singing is described; we never actually 'hear' (that is, read) Fern's song. Significantly, the narrator cannot discern any words in her song other than Christ's name, an inability to decode that echoes the ostensibly unintelligible "jargon" of the songs young Frederick Douglass and his fellow slaves sang. Fern and the narrator operate on two different levels of communication: while he translates his perceptions into and communicates with language, she communicates directly from her spiritual self through song. The two communicative strands never meet, and so, when he finally leaves the South and Fern behind, he recognizes that "[n]othing ever really happened. Nothing ever came to Fern, not even I" (19). Language, the narrator's story, and *Cane's* "Fern" have separated them forever. Also, the four poems that frame the short story are not folk songs or spirituals themselves, but again only report the act of singing, as for example "Song of the Son," which celebrates yet does not quote directly "[a]n everlasting song, a singing tree, / Caroling softly songs of slavery, / What they were, and what they are to me" (14). Telling as it is, the inarticulacy persists here, too.

Only once does *Cane* report an actual spiritual, "My Lord, What a Mourning," namely at the end of act 2 in "Kabnis":

A false dusk has come early. The countryside is ashen, chill. Cabins and roads and canebrakes whisper. The church choir, dipping into a long silence, sings:

> My Lord, what a mourning,
> My Lord, what a mourning,
> My Lord, what a mourning,
> When the stars begin to fall.

Softly luminous over the hills and valleys, the faint spray of a scattered star . . . (93)

The level of narrative consciousness here is that of level IV, and it seems as though the omniscient observer of all observers is the only one who notices the congregation's song. Running after Kabnis, neither Halsey nor Layman appears to hear it, and act 3 opens with "[a] splotchy figure driv[ing] forward along the cane- and corn-stalk hemmed-in road. A scarecrow replica of Kabnis, awkwardly animate. Fantastically plastered with red Georgia mud"—the ironic foil of Fern, the southern earth-mother figure (93). Nor does the spiritual foreshadow the ending, for while we hear "the sinner mourn," no "trumpet sound[s] to wake the nations underground," as the original lyrics assure.[8] Father John, that "mute John the Baptist of a new religion—or a tongue-tied shadow of an old" and the personification of historical conscience, only ever utters one intelligible word in his rare ramblings, "sin" (106). Accordingly, the omniscient narrator interpolates at this point to confirm that Father John's true message, unlike his preaching in the rice fields, cannot really be spoken. While the narrative voice implores him at first to "speak," it corrects itself immediately: "(Speak, Father!) Suppose your eyes could see, old man. (The years hold hands. O *Sing!*) Suppose your lips . . . " (106; emphasis added). Even when Father John finally speaks to denounce "th sin th white folks 'mitted when they made th Bible lie," Kabnis mocks him contemptuously (117). But Father John never does sing. The telling inarticulacy of *Cane* therefore suggests that Afro-modernism's historical conscience could be retrieved from the cellars of the South and reinvigorated by *song*.

I'm gonna pack my suitcase, moving on down the line.
Aaah, I'm gonna pack my suitcase and move on down the line,
Where there ain't nobody worrying, and there ain't nobody crying.

—John Peter Chapman, a.k.a. Memphis Slim,
"Every Day I Have the Blues," as sung by Joe Williams

CHAPTER 3

Roll Call

Richard Wright's "Long Black Song"
and the Betrayal of Music

For Jean Toomer, it was the spirituals—what W. E. B. Du Bois had famously called "the sorrow songs"—that resonated with the spirit of the black experience in the New World, a spirit imperiled by the onslaught of modernity and urbanization. Strangely enough, although they have every reason to, Toomer's Sempterites do not sing the blues. The closest they come is in "Blood-Burning Moon," the story of an interracial love triangle that ends in tragedy. Louisa finds herself caught between Tom Burwell, the black field hand, and Bob Stone, scion of a prominent white family in town. The lyrics she sings at the opening of the story echo the AAB form of the classic blues stanza: "Red nigger moon. Sinner! / Blood-burning moon. Sinner! / Come out that fact'ry door" (*Cane* 31). However, Louisa's song is not concerned with the personal dramas of the individual blues singer, as it becomes the collective lamentation of black Sempter, a sorrow song that provides the soundtrack to the tragic violence unfolding in the story (33, 37).

Perhaps this is so because the sorrow songs are steeped in, to quote Du Bois again, "our spiritual strivings" and thus relate more closely to the mysticism that suffuses *Cane* than the thoroughly and often raunchily secular blues would (*Souls* 1). Perhaps this is the case also because the blues are a product of the very modernity that Toomer felt assaulted the soul of Sempter, Georgia. Coincidentally, the novel's most blueslike song not only references "that fact'ry door" but scores the murder of Tom at the hands of a white mob in the "factory town" district of Sempter, in an empty cotton mill modeled after Sparta's Montour Village (Toomer, *Cane* 36; Foley, "Jean" 750). Generally, *Cane* at least is surprisingly silent as far as actual song is concerned; music and singing are reported on by Toomer's various poems and narrator-observers, but they do not resonate in an unmediated fashion in and from the book. Even "Harvest Song," for instance, is only purported to be a song when in fact it is a self-conscious exercise in modernist poetics—much like Louisa's song.

Still, "Blood-Burning Moon," the song, becomes the soundtrack to one of the most vicious rituals of the American South: lynching. Most rituals, according to Victor Turner, seek to regulate the symbolic cycle of birth, death, and rebirth. Toomer's story is a stark reminder that the Turnerian "process of regenerative renewal" in Sempter's apartheid society claims victims for whom there is no rebirth, symbolic or otherwise ("Process" 158–61). After Tom Burwell cuts Bob Stone in a knife fight over Louisa, the black field hand is lynched in order to ritualistically resurrect white supremacy. That the deadly ritual occurs to the sounds of "Blood-Burning Moon" turns this chapter of *Cane* into a prelude of sorts to the famous Richard Wright short story "Long Black Song."

Richard Wright is an author in whose work music is rarely referenced, Ralph Ellison's famous review notwithstanding. Unlike Toomer, Wright is a writer more often associated with naturalism and realism than with modernism. As Craig Werner has pointed out, however, Wright's early work especially evinces a literary voice striving to reconcile modernism and social commitment (204). Apropos of *Native Son*, Werner diagnoses that "[b]oth Wright and Bigger inhabit a world that offers no vocabulary capable of expressing the particular Afro-American experience of the modernist situation. Nonetheless, both struggle to articulate their experience despite profound problems regarding their relationship to their audience, both real and potential" (197). This struggle Wright himself elucidates in "How Bigger Was Born." Presaging Mackey's telling inarticulacy, Wright confesses that for him as a writer, "[a]lways there is something that is just beyond the tip of the tongue that could explain it all," and that this is the fundamental challenge that links his task as author with Bigger's struggle for survival (vii). Not only was *Native Son* an attempt "to develop the dim negative which had been implanted in my mind in the South"—and Bigger, of course, hails from Mississippi as well—but "certain modern experiences" made the author himself feel acutely "estranged from the civilization in which I lived, and more than ever resolved toward the task of creating with words a scheme of images and symbols whose direction could enlist the sympathies, loyalties, and yearnings of the millions of Bigger Thomases in every land and race" (xvi, xix).

One earlier attempt at creating with words a reconciliation of modernist estrangement and spiritual yearning, and one among the very few in Wright's work to enlist music in the process, is the short story "Long Black Song." The middle selection of the five stories that make up the amended *Uncle Tom's Children*, "Long Black Song" is narrated from the point of view of Sarah and is set, like all the other tales, in Wright's home state. The modernist dialectic of alienation and yearning is amplified, indeed counted off, by music, as the Methodist hymn "When the Roll Is Called Up Yonder" pits two distinct realms against each other, the millennial realm of the hymn's "yonder" on the one hand and the real exigencies of a southern territory marked by the ritual of lynching on the other.

The beginning of the story finds Sarah and her little daughter, Ruth, alone on the small farm her husband has worked so hard to call his own. Silas has been away from their home in the northern hill country for a week to purchase provisions in Coldwater, at the northern tip of the Delta. Sarah's loneliness is exacerbated by the absence of her secret love, Tom (the namesake of Tom Burwell from "Blood-Burning Moon"), who has gone off to fight in the Great War. Now with Silas away too, she feels lonely, a loneliness that seems to arise out of the very landscape she inhabits: "Sky sang a red song. Fields whispered a green prayer. And song and prayer were dying in silence and shadow. Never in all her life had she been so much alone as she was now" (128). Into Sarah's evening loneliness drives a black car with a young white man behind the wheel. The man—who from the start impresses Sarah as comporting himself "jus lika lil boy"—sells graphophone clocks to help finance his college education and proceeds to demonstrate the high-tech pparatus for her (133).[1] The music, the southern night, the young man's seeming innocence, and her loneliness all conspire to awaken in Sarah a strong sexual desire of which the salesman only too gladly takes advantage. Afterward, the young man leaves behind the graphophone clock, promising to lower the price from the usual fifty dollars to forty and hoping to collect the down payment of ten dollars from Silas the next morning. Later that night, Silas returns and discovers what has transpired in his absence. Enraged, he throws the contraption out of the window and threatens to beat her. Sarah, sensing an escalation of violence, seeks to head off the salesman and warn him, but fails; Silas flogs him and his companion with the whip he had meant for her and then shoots one of them fatally. Knowing that the whites will return to avenge the killing, he sends his wife and child away but resolves to stay behind and take his stand. The futility of Silas's resistance fulfills itself in the most southern of violent rituals, the regulatory killing of the black male in order to ensure white supremacy. In the lynching that ensues, Silas involves a white posse in a prolonged shootout before being burned alive in his home when the whites set fire to it, while Sarah and Ruth escape across the hill into the southern landscape.[2]

The ritual of lynching is provoked by the troika of southern violence, namely love (or sex), ownership, and race. All three elements hark back to Reconstruction as well as to the peculiar institution suggested by Wright's symbolism: the graphophone clock and its 'special' low price of forty dollars sound the twentieth-century echo of the broken promise of forty acres and a mule, and Silas's use of the rawhide whip, the symbol of white ownership and control of black bodies, is all the more unforgivable in the eyes of the white South because it turns its political economy on its head.[3] What is unusual in Wright's short story is how sound and setting conspire to orchestrate the southern ritual of lynching.

The title itself, "Long Black Song," already impresses the importance of music in the tale to follow, and from the very beginning, sound plays a crucial role. The story's epigraph consists of a verse from a harmless lullaby Sarah intones to mollify her restless child: "*Go t sleep, baby / Papas gone t town*" (125). The opening scene shows Sarah and Ruth inside their home, the waning sun "a big ball of red dying between the branches of trees," while Sarah's baby beats a broken eight-day clock with a stick. The sound of "Bang! Bang! Bang!" will reverberate throughout the first section in Sarah's worries about Tom fighting the war, in her memories of their lovemaking, and in the backfiring exhaust of the salesman's car (126–31). Significantly, the eleventh, final "*bangbangbang*" occurs not during the climactic gun battle and crackling fire at the end, but during the copulating of Sarah and the salesman: the eleventh tolling of the same sound here foreshadows the eruption of violence—in bitterly ironic contrast to the ceasefire that effectively ended World War I, "the war to end all wars," at 11:00 A.M. on November 11, 1918 (137; Pitt 268–71; Sollors 122).

Also from the very beginning, sound and music are linked inextricably to the southern landscape drenched in desire: Sarah "saw green fields
wrapped in the thickening gloom. It was as if they had left the earth,
those fields, and were floating slowly skyward. The afterglow lingered, red,
dying, somehow tenderly sad. And far away, in front of her, earth and sky
met in a soft swoon of shadow. A cricket chirped, sharp and lonely; and it
seemed she could hear it chirping long after it had stopped. . . . Sky sang
a red song. Fields whispered a green prayer" (127–28). Desire, sound, and
the distinct landscape all merge in the character of Sarah, turning her into
another earth-mother figure, the literary descendant of Toomer's Fern and
the personification of Stephen Henderson's "Soul-Field."[4] The linkage
becomes particularly explicit when the young salesman demonstrates the
graphophone clock:

"Just listen to this," he said.
      There was a sharp, scratching noise; then she moved nervously, her
body caught in the ringing coils of music.
      When the trumpet of the lord shall sound . . .
      She rose on circling waves of white bright days and dark black
nights.
      . . . and time shall be no more . . .
      Higher and higher she mounted.
      And the morning breaks . . .
      Earth fell far behind, forgotten.
      . . . eternal, bright and fair . . .
      Echo after echo sounded.
      When the saved of the earth shall gather . . .
      Her blood surged like the long gladness of summer.
      . . . over on the other shore . . .
      Her blood ebbed like the deep dream of sleep in winter.
      And when the roll is called up yonder . . .
      She gave up, holding her breath.
      I'll be there . . .
      A lump filled her throat. She leaned her back against a post, trem-
bling, feeling the rise and fall of days and nights, of summer and winter;
surging, ebbing, leaping about her, beyond her, far out over the fields to
where earth and sky lay folded in darkness. (132–33)

To be sure, a desire for spiritual deliverance is there, but, given the imagery with which Wright describes Sarah's rapture, a significant part of it
remains sexual: "she wanted to take the box into her arms and kiss it"

even before the music starts (132). Again, it is the southern landscape itself—or Sarah's mnemonic perception thereof—that acts in concert with the music. Wright's use of setting, Joyce Joyce points out, "both reflects the sensuality of Sarah's character and serves—through repetition—as a rhythmic chord that echoes her arousal until the end of the sex act" (381).

The irony here is that Sarah's carnal longings are prodded by a religious hymn, namely "When the Roll Is Called Up Yonder," and sound figures as the ironic catalyst for the entire plot.[5] "When the Roll Is Called Up Yonder" is a Methodist hymn, penned in 1893 by James M. Black. Black, a white Sunday school teacher in Williamsport, Pennsylvania, was calling roll one day only to discover that one of his charges, the daughter of a notorious drunkard, was absent, and Black wrote the hymn to express his hope that she would be present "when the roll is called up yonder." Before 1919 the only commercial recording of "When the Roll Is Called Up Yonder" on disc was released in Thomas Edison's Diamond Disc series as 80276-R in 1915 and was carried in the company's catalogue until 1929, attesting to the song's popularity (Frow 47; Kenney 7).[6] The hymn was performed by the "Edison Mixed Quartet" of tenor John Young and baritone Frederick Wheeler, two veteran recording artists, and the soprano and contralto, respectively, of Florence Hinkel and Margaret Keyes, plus a small orchestra. The disc's other side contained a version of "Abide With Me," written by Elizabeth Spencer and Thomas Chalmers. The Edison Quartet was all-white—as were, presumably, the musicians—and their rendition of Black's hymn doesn't really qualify as a Du Boisian sorrow song (*Inventing*). Moreover, the sheet music for Black's song was marketed almost exclusively to whites: Tabernacle Publishing, who owned the rights to "When the Roll," also bought the rights to "Leave It There," a hymn composed by noted tunesmith Charles A. Tindley, Jr., best known for "We'll Understand It Better By and By." The music of Black's and Tindley's hymns was so similar that Tabernacle was concerned about legal action and so decided to purchase "Leave It There," licensing it for sale to a black target audience, while "When the Roll" continued to be marketed mostly to whites (Young 459).

Literary critics often gloss or misrepresent the recording Sarah is hearing as a "spiritual," but it is significant that this particular song is *not* shaped by black performance practices (Hurd 49; McCarthy 735). Joyce Joyce calls it "music that has the power and intensity of the Negro spiritual" (382). Its *effect* on Sarah may be the same, but listening to the original Edison recording, it is difficult to hear that kind of rousing "power and intensity" in the conservative arrangement or the studiedly calibrated voices of the singers. Nor can it, in its *performance*, be considered one of the black tradition's "liberation texts that are multi-valenced," as DoVe-anna Fulton defines them ("Singing"). In what Craig Werner calls the gospel impulse, the descent of the spirit occurs within the antiphonal, syndetic context of a collective and a singer, in which meaning arises from a communal process—call and response (218–22).[7] This is clearly not the case in "Long Black Song," on the contrary: Sarah lives on an isolated farm, and she and her husband rarely interact with members of a larger black community. Like Frederick Douglass's circle and Jean Toomer's arcs, "the ringing coils of music" that ensnare Sarah appear to echo the ancient African rite of the ring shout, but the music's "circling waves of white bright days and dark black nights" that she rides to inevitable disaster indicate that she hears what she *wants* to hear, not what she experiences as a member of the ring's collective.[8]

Even so, clearly there are calls and there are responses in Wright's short story. The quasi call and response between white hymn and black character is the most significant because it informs the story on multiple levels. First, Sarah responds to the music as she recognizes her existence, her dreams and desires, refractured in it. Music, in other words, opens up a territory that welcomes both the white Yankee preacher Black (the irony of his name is palpable) and the black farmer's wife from Mississippi. This figurative territory where what appear to be experiential opposites meet, this soundscape, is tied inextricably to the southern landscape. The result-ing dialectic highlights the paradoxical juxtaposition of the realities of southern violence with the ideal of southern multiculture: the playing of the hymn results in the sexual assault on Sarah and the lynching of Silas. And yet, it is while Sarah is anticipating the murder of her husband that her epiphany counters the reality of the southern ritual ground with its *ideal*, an ideal awakened by the sound recording. On the one hand, there is "that long river of blood" running from the South's past into its present and future (153). On the other hand, there is Sarah's realization that

[s]omehow, men, black men and white men, land and houses, green cornfields and grey skies, gladness and dreams, were all part of that which made life good. Yes, somehow they were linked, like the spokes in a spinning wagon wheel. She felt they were. She knew they were. She felt it when she breathed and knew it when she looked. But she could not say how; she could not put her finger on it and when she thought hard about it it became all mixed up, like milk spilling suddenly. Or else it knotted in her throat and chest in a hard aching lump, like the one she felt now. (154)

Clearly, Sarah here is wrestling with a telling inarticulacy not unlike Fern's "convulsive" spatter (Toomer, *Cane* 19). The passage is also reminiscent of Louisa's musings on her black and white lovers in "Blood-Burning Moon": "Separately, there was no unusual significance to either one. But for some reason, they jumbled when her eyes gazed vacantly at the rising moon. And from the jumble came the stir that was strangely within her. Her lips trembled. The slow rhythm of her song grew agitant and restless" (31). Wright's Sarah, though, is envisioning an ideal South triggered by the gospel impulse, an impulse marked by "its refusal to accept oppositional thought, its complex sense of presence, its belief in salvation," according to Werner (222). But following the narrative device of ironic inversion and juxtaposition that characterizes the entire text, the image of harmony Sarah conjures up is succeeded immediately by the lynching of Silas.[9] Once again, the southern ritual ground recedes before the narrative mode it has engendered itself.

Sarah escapes the lynch mob also because, as a literary descendant of Fern, she functions as southern earth-mother figure. The question of ownership of her body is contested between white and black, and the modernist fracturing of the oppressive, fatal realities of the South into glimpses of utopia also entails the collision of two distinct versions of time and history linked to a dialectic of presence and absence. Accordingly, the Methodist hymn that prompts both Sarah's sexual arousal and, ultimately, her fantasy of racial harmony incorporates and orchestrates a dialectic of time and space. As southern earth mother, Sarah embodies the ritual ground she inhabits. Thus she also embodies the dialectic of absence and presence, because her character represents and acts out the conflicting impulses reverberating in the landscape around her. The short story is therefore not so much about love, or sex, as it is about ownership: who 'owns' time and history, and with it definitions of and access to progress and modernity.

Sarah and her family live, in a sense, outside of time. Their lives are governed by the cycle of the seasons and by the cycle of the sun. The white salesman is incredulous at Sarah's disinterest in having the old eight-day clock repaired, but she simply keeps informing him, "Mistah, we don need no clock. . . . We jus don need no time, Mistah" (131). He, in turn, exclaims, "I dont see how in the world anybody can live without time" (131). Thus, the hymn's dialectic of absence and presence extends into the collision of different conceptions of time: living according to the cycles of nature, Sarah lives outside of history—that is, over yonder, outside of man-made time. She is also the only protagonist in *Uncle Tom's Children* who is not embedded in a larger black community. Arriving in this separate little world as the privileged representative (and a literate one—after all, he is an aspiring college student) of the white South, the salesman makes a pitch that seeks to bind Sarah and her family into a southern concept of time and history. His sales ploy, given the symbolic price of forty dollars, consolidates their status as objects to be regulated and defined by 'white' history: "'But you need a clock,' the white man insisted. 'Thats what Im out here for. Im selling clocks and graphophones. The clocks are made right into the graphophones, a nice sort of combination, hunh? You can have music and time all at once. Ill show you . . . '" (131). And show her he does. The graphophone clock is also a symbol of modernity, hastening the collision between the cyclical time of nature and the 'mechanical' time of progress—but this New South, at least, isn't so new as it symbolically enlists modernity in reinforcing the same historical hierarchy of white dominance.

So, rather than "a nice sort of combination," music (figurative space, or absence) and the South (historical exigencies, or presence) collude to produce tragedy. The first verse of "When the Roll Is Called Up Yonder," the only one Wright quotes in the short story, links music to a realm beyond time and space:

When the trumpet of the Lord shall sound and time shall be no more,
And the morning breaks eternal, bright, and fair;
When the saved of earth shall gather over on the other shore
And the roll is called up yonder, I'll be there.

From the outset, the southern setting in which the song reverberates ironically denies the promise of salvation. The "eternal, bright, and fair" morning with which the hymn announces the hereafter is juxtaposed by the passage of time during which the graphophone plays (actual, mechanical time, in other words), for at the end of the song "[i]t was dark now" (133). Likewise, the tale is populated not by "the saved of the earth," but by the ones condemned in and by southern history. The only gathering to occur "[o]n that bright and cloudless morning" of Silas's judgment day is the second coming of the white South in the shape of the lynch mob; and for Sarah, "over on the other shore" or "up yonder" is but the hill across which she flees. Thus, there are two contesting realms propelling the hymn's promise of redemption as well as the short story's action: there is the figurative setting of the hymn that lies outside of history, "when time shall be no more," a setting therefore characterized by its absence. Then there is the setting in which Wright's characters move, a distinctly southern landscape that reaffirms its presence over Sarah's ahistorical vision by playing out one of the most brutal historical legacies of the Old South, lynching.

Similarly, the third verse of the hymn, significantly omitted from Wright's text, delineates the earthly life from which "His chosen ones" shall be redeemed:

> Let us labor for the Master from the dawn till setting sun,
> Let us talk of all His wondrous love and care;
> Then when all of life is over, and our work on earth is done,
> And the roll is called up yonder, I'll be there.

For this, the earthly presence, the hymn preaches unquestioning sub-mission to higher authority—God, Master, Massa—and counsels meek endurance of present toils. The text of Wright's story renders this last verse absent, but it is disastrously portentous in that its counsel has been internalized by both Sarah and Silas. That the story omits the last stanza of "When the Roll Is Called Up Yonder," one requesting submission and obedience, only reaffirms that the antiphonal play between the hymn and the black couple is in fact a call and response between presence and absence: the presence of the graphophone calls and gives voice, in music, to Sarah's dreams and desires, which she otherwise could not articulate. Sarah's reaction to the absence of articulate expression in her mind is to respond with her body to the seductive music. Though she initially seeks to ward off the advances of the salesman, she gives in eventually and submits, thereby enacting the hymn's last stanza, which is missing from Wright's text, but certainly not from the graphophone demonstration earlier. Moreover, the fulfillment made present by the hymn in the first stanza is a presence in sound only, and hence an absence as far as Sarah is concerned, an absence that she fills with her body aroused to presence by the salesman: her lover Tom's absence "had left an empty black hole in her heart, a black hole that Silas had come in and filled. But not quite. Silas had not quite filled that hole. No; days and nights were not as they were before" (129).

A similar dialectic adheres to the character of Silas. His business trip to Coldwater has been very successful: he has acquired ten more acres of land, which will necessitate hiring a farm hand to tend to his expanding property. To Sarah's surprised question, he responds, "Sho, hire some-body! Whut yuh think? Ain tha the way the white folks do? Ef yuhs gonna git anywheres yuhs gotta do just like they do" (140). In insisting on forging a separate existence and economic independence, he lives out a Washingtonian philosophy (McCarthy 735–36). But, just as Booker T.

Washington's metaphorical bucket ironically becomes in Wright's story the bucket in the well behind Silas's house that is the site of the white salesman's violent sexual advances to Sarah—the Washingtonian bucket brings water to quell the white man's thirst, and when Sarah hears him drink in the dark, she hears "the faint, soft music of water going down a dry throat, the music of water in a silent night" (135)—so does the black farmer discover that his strivings for a separate existence are futile:

> From sunup t sundown Ah works mah guts out t pay them white trash bastards whut Ah owe em, n then Ah comes n fins they been in mah house! Ah cant go into their houses, n yuh know Gawddam well Ah cant! They don have no mercy on no black folks; wes just like dirt under their feet! Fer ten years Ah slaves lika dog t git mah farm free, givin ever penny Ah kin t em, n then Ah comes n fins they been in mah house. . . . Ef yuh wans t eat at mah table yuhs gonna keep them white trash bastards out, yuh hear? (143)

As Silas is about to discover, it is impossible to keep the white South out of his little world and to render it absent, partly because it has always been present in the ideology he himself embraces. He symbolically rejects the white version of southern history when he throws the graphophone clock out into the yard, destroying it. Instead, he is determined to write his *own* history, defend his own place in time with his life. Tragically, Silas never fully realizes that the white South has always already been figuratively present because of his unwavering adherence to a southern agrarian work ethic, "labor[ing] for the Master from the dawn till setting sun" (Fabre 159; Gardner 428). As Sarah muses, "Always he had said he was as good as any white man. He had worked hard and saved his money and bought a farm so he could grow his own crops like white men" (147). The white South's physical absence is negated by its overwhelming ideological presence, rendering the struggle for black (economic) separatism futile:

> The white folks ain never gimme a chance! They ain never give no black man a chance! There ain nothing in yo whole life yuh kin keep from em! They take yo lan! They take yo women! N then they take yo life! . . . Ahm gonna be hard like they is! So hep me, Gawd, Ah'm gonna be *hard!* When they come fer me Ah'm gonna *be* here! N when they git me outta here theys gonna *know* Ahm gone! Ef Gawd lets me live Ahm gonna make em *feel* it!. . . . But, Lawd, Ah don wanna be this way! It don mean nothin! Yuh die ef yuh fight! Yuh die ef yuh don fight! Either way yuh die n it don mean nothin . . . (152–53)

The "long river of blood" coursing through and in southern time is therefore seemingly inescapable and exacts two more victims, one white, the other black. The fact that the violence cuts both ways, across the deep racial divide, exposes that the dominant, white southern version of time and history that is being enforced is not without fatal consequences for the master, either.[10] Just as Bigger Thomas would later only be able to 'write' himself into history by killing Mary Dalton before dying himself, so does the dialectic of presence and absence accelerated by "When the Roll Is Called Up Yonder" find its bitterly tragic finale in the fate of Silas, who is rendered 'absent' by the mob because he insists on making his presence known by erasing the life of one of them.

Even so, the dialectic of presence and absence put into motion by the Methodist hymn suggests that music has the power to occasion a momentary suspension of historical time, allowing for the conjuring up of spaces, and visions thereof, where seeming experiential opposites can find a home. Interestingly, the hymn's arrangement on the original Edison recording also calls attention to a different world arising out of the suspension of time: at the end of each chorus section, the 2/4 time signature is arrested briefly in a fermata on the word "yonder." But just as in Sarah's rapture and subsequent vision, the suspension of time on the recording is a momentary one, too. And so, as Silas discovers with deadly consequences, one cannot remove oneself permanently from history; the return into historical time is all the more painful. As Jean Toomer himself pointed out,

> Music is an almost instantaneous evocator of the inner-experiences not being had, not being thought of as possible, until the music begins. Add music, and you can instantly transport yourself, through inner-experience, into a different world. . . . Music, however, though able to transport you into a different world, cannot keep you in that different world—no, not even if you yourself are a musician. Once it is over for the time being, you slide back into this world. ("Music" 276)

The two different worlds in "Long Black Song," Sarah's fantasy of a South of racial harmony and the reality of a South whose sociopolitical economy of white dominance is enforced by lynching, look to be anything but syndetic. That Wright appears to give Sarah's vision the moral privilege is brought out once again by the setting. Sarah witnesses the killing from an elevated position, standing on the slope of a hill behind the house. From her vantage point, the participants of the senseless violence about to enfold look like "dolls" and "toy men" enacting a brutal game "in the valley below" (149). At the end, Sarah turns away from the carnage, and the story releases her and Ruth "over yonder" across the hill into an uncertain future that, at best, entails temporary refuge at her Aunt Peel's.

Thus, in "Long Black Song" music is rendered as not only inefficient, but treacherous. The lyrics of "When the Roll Is Called Up Yonder" act as cynical betrayal of the dreams and desires of Sarah and sound the prelude to the lynching of Silas. The Methodist hymn therefore functions in opposition to the long *black* song of liberty and self-determination and mocks the betrayed ideals of the Declaration of Independence, the Constitution, and the Emancipation Proclamation. Significantly, Wright's short story does not posit black music as a corrective to the false illusions conjured up by the strains of the all-white Edison Mixed Quartet. There is, in other words, no long *black* song being *sung*. Music, like narrative, entails the embellishment of time passing by, but in Wright's southern ritual grounds black music is unable to furnish a counterweight to a passage of time chronologized by whites—just as the lullaby Sarah sings to Ruth at the very beginning fails to have the desired effect, too, for Ruth isn't mollified until she gets to hit the old clock with a stick. The notable absence of black music in "Long Black Song" and the story's strategic placement within *Uncle Tom's Children* suggests that music does not constitute a sufficiently effective tool of nascent black revolutionary appropriation of and participation in history. Hence, that this particular rendition of "When the Roll Is Called Up Yonder" is 'white' music makes the reneging on its own promises all the more cynical, not to mention historically accurate, but the betrayal owes its tragic outcome less to the ethnic makeup of the Edison Mixed Quartet than to the nature of music itself.

"Long Black Song" is the middle selection of the amended collection. As several critics have pointed out, *Uncle Tom's Children* traces a rising narrative arc of black revolutionary self-assertion, from Big Boy's escape from the lynch mob in "Big Boy Leaves Home" to Johnny-Boy's mother's taking a stand in "Bright and Morning Star." "Fire and Cloud," the selection immediately following "Long Black Song," in a way narrates the realization of Sarah's vision. At the end, Reverend Taylor is leading a crowd of black and white protesters in a march on city hall, putting into action what seemed like naive utopia with Sarah, namely the recognition that in these southern ritual grounds, white and black indeed "were linked, like the spokes in a spinning wagon wheel" (155). However, music here does not serve to accelerate the plot as it does in "Long Black Song." During the tense moments right before the black protesters are joined by the town's poor whites, a "fat black woman started singing: '*So the sign of the fire by night / N the sign of the cloud by day / A-hoverin oer / Jus befo / As we journey on our way*" (218). The racially mixed crowd picks up the song, and the story ends with Taylor proudly looking onto a "sea of black and white faces. The song swelled louder and vibrated through him. This is the way! he thought" (220). And while the singing, especially its call-and-response structure and its black southern vernacular, clearly classifies this as a sorrow song, neither the song itself nor its performance stirs up any social commitment, let alone revolutionary action. The poor whites of the town have already been sensitized before the march to their economic lot under the corrupt town leadership. The song's "fire by night" refers to the flogging of Taylor the previous night, "the sign of the cloud" to the racially mixed crowd of protesters marching toward city hall. And so, the singing of the song at the end of "Fire and Cloud" actually mirrors the status of music in "Long Black Song": in both cases, music, white and black music, is at best merely an echo, a sound mirror of things as they are. In "Long Black Song," the music echoes the dreams and wishes of the protagonist; in "Fire and Cloud" music echoes the plight of Taylor and his comrades. That one is a sorrow song and the other one isn't is less significant than the fact that the crowd's song in the latter story cannot betray them because it doesn't promise anything, because it merely accompanies the absence becoming presence but doesn't predict it.

Thus, for Wright, music always reneges eventually on the transcendence it promises. Music betrays Sarah and ultimately Silas not necessarily because it gives voice to a utopian impulse for racial harmony, but because it promises the impending realization of said impulse, conjuring up the presence of an absence. In *Uncle Tom's Children*, "Long Black Song" and "Fire and Cloud" represent the twin uses of music as either a device of structural irony or descriptive commentary. The strains of "Dis train boun fo Glory" which the first selection opens leads to Big Boy being released into, at best, an uncertain future in Chicago. The pacifist sentiment of the hymn that gives "Down By the Riverside" its title is undercut by the protagonist's murder—where else—down by the riverside. And in the last story, the one Wright added for the second edition, published in 1940, "Bright and Morning Star," music conspires with religion to effect a detrimental passivity on the part of Americans of African descent that serves only to stabilize the sociopolitical status quo. Sue "jus cant seem t fergit them ol songs, no mattah how hard Ah tries" and feels guilty about singing them. True, these sorrow songs do have "their deep meaning," and they do provide a "spell of peace." But, again, that peace is illusory, crumbling under the weight of white racism. The sorrow songs' "deep meaning" appears to have no meaningful effect other than enhancing

Sue's endurance: "The days crowded with trouble had enhanced her faith and she had grown to love hardship with a bitter pride; she had obeyed the laws of the white folks with a soft smile of secret knowing" (223–24). In keeping with Wright's dalliance with communism, Sue's self-sacrifice is made possible only by her repudiation of the passivity and acceptance preached by the sorrow songs (as Wright hears them) that have accompanied her life. And then, of course, there is the biting cynicism of the collection's epigraph, the first two verses from the Irving Caesar, Sammy Lerner, and Gerald Marks smash hit "Is It True What They Say About Dixie?"

Thus, the only transcendence music by itself offers Wright's characters is a false one, one that lulls them into dangerous, deadly passivity, objectionable escapism, or treacherous fantasy. Other than that, music remains merely descriptive. To be sure, Wright did recognize in African American music from the South a social function. As he wrote in his "Blueprint for Negro Writing," it was

> in a folklore moulded out of rigorous and inhuman conditions of life that the Negro achieved his most indigenous and complex expression. Blues, spirituals, and folk tales recounted from mouth to mouth; the whispered words of a black mother to her black daughter on the ways of men; the confidential wisdom of a black father to his black son; the swapping of sex experiences on street corners from boy to boy in the deepest vernacular; work songs sung under blazing suns—all these formed the channels through which the racial wisdom flowed. (1382)

However, black music is primarily a channel for intraracial communication and is in and of itself no viable tool for social activism and transcendence of the inhuman conditions that have characterized black life in the South. As the "Blueprint" makes clear, only "a [black] nationalism carrying the highest possible pitch of social consciousness . . . a nationalism that knows its origins, its limitations; that knows its ultimate aims are unrealizable within the framework of capitalist America; a nationalism whose reason for being lies . . . in the consciousness of the interdependence of people in modern society" can effect change and transcendence (1383–84). Music, in Wright's estimation, cannot reach this necessary "highest possible *pitch*," as his use of it in his own fiction makes clear. And the role of music would remain the same throughout Wright's oeuvre.

Once music, African American music, has traveled upstream from the semirural settings of *Uncle Tom's Children*'s Mississippi to the urban jungle of *Native Son*'s Chicago, it continues to function as a means not of transcendence, but merely of escapism. The spiritual Bigger's mother sings, as well as "Steal Away," emanating from a storefront church, even Mary's reverence for "Swing Low, Sweet Chariot," all figure as but a veiled continuation of subjugation in the novel's universe (Cataliotti 127–38). The ineffectiveness of the sorrow songs is also shared by secular black musics: the real-life Bigger Thomases, too, on whom Wright modeled his composite protagonist, "projected their hurts and longings into more naive and mundane forms—blues, jazz, swing—and, without intellectual guidance, tried to build up a compensatory nourishment for themselves" ("How" xiii).

Even after Wright abjured communist ideology, in his fiction music stayed merely descriptive at best, downright fatal at worst. Music, for Wright, could not redeem the blood-drenched southern ritual grounds, let alone change them. The chant of "We Shall Overcome" that was growing louder and louder all over the South Wright heard all right in his European exile, but was unable to translate into his fiction. When he returned with *The Long Dream* to the same grounds and rituals he had visited in *Uncle Tom's Children*, music faded still more into the background. The bildungsroman evinces the same dual purposes for music as his previous fiction. Secular music figures as mere sound mirror, "the sensual despair of the beating music" providing the eroticized soundtrack to Jack and Mack's despicable minstrel show or to Fishbelly's sexual education on Clintonville's King Street (153). Again, religious music figures as sarcastic, even bitter, commentary on a plot that inverts the message of the songs—further evidence, as Paul Gilroy points out, that for Clintonville's chronicler, "the decisive break in western consciousness which modernity identifies was defined by the collapse of a religious understanding of the world" (*Black* 160). The black sorrow songs (or white hymns) in *The Long Dream* still merely replicated what he in his "Blueprint" two decades earlier had dismissed as an "archaic morphology of Christian salvation" serving as delusional "denial" and "an antidote for suffering" (1382). The spirituals sung at the funeral of Fishbelly's murdered father, for example, function as a prelude not to a journey *"nearer my home today / Than I have ever been before,"* but to Fishbelly's impending flight from Clintonville and exile in France (322). The music of the South was therefore merely the sound mirror of brutal, unrelenting violence and of fervent hopes; the music of the South was only sounding out what Wright had elsewhere called a "paradoxical cleavage" between what is and what ought to be (*Twelve* 127). Music, to him, never ceased to be simply part of a superstructure that failed to make pertinent contributions to the struggle for black self-determination. Black sacred music in particular was woefully ineffective at best in his view; he simply could not conceive of the spirituals as also an expression and a practice of social activism, the way literature could be (Fulton, "Singing"; Reagon 4).[11]

Wright's take on the sorrow songs coincides with Toomer's in that they fail to effect change in a meaningful way. Where Wright differs is that as far as he his concerned, there is no reason to listen to them in the first place. Only the Afro-modernist text can give voice to viable historical conscience, one that also warns of the betrayal of music. Song, even black song, may contain some kind of historical *consciousness*, but it is dim, self-defeating, or treacherous. At best, (black) song is harmlessly mimetic of social reality, but does not transpose into the key of a *conscience* that can effect meaningful social change. Wright would have been incredulous at Frederick Douglass's assertion that Niccolò Paganini's violin was just as effective a weapon in the struggle between civilization and barbarity as the freedom fighter's pen. Only the literary artist's words have a chance to achieve victory in that battle: "I would hurl words into this darkness and wait for an echo, and if an echo sounded, no matter how faintly, I would send other words to tell, to march, to fight, to create a sense of the hunger for life that gnaws in us all, to keep alive in our hearts a sense of the inexpressibly human" (453). This is how *Black Boy* ends, on May Day of 1936, in Chicago, Illinois. But instead of a spiritual, or instead of the blues that the thousands of black women and men had brought to the Windy City from Wright's home state, the final epiphany in his autobiography that prompts him to pick up his pen comes as hears the strains of the *Internationale* (450–51). Once again, its sounds and lyrics of revolution and solidarity only amplify the betrayal of music, for the *Internationale* is sung at the very moment Wright breaks with the Communist Party after he comes to see its hypocrisy.

No wonder, either, that no blues were wafting through the open window of his tiny rented room that night, for to Wright's ears they too were infected with the self-defeating pathology of the sorrow songs. To be sure, Ralph Ellison famously used *Native Son* and *Black Boy* as a springboard to define blues as "an impulse to keep the painful details and episodes of a brutal experience alive in one's aching consciousness, to finger its jagged grain, and to transcend it, not by the consolation of philosophy but by squeezing from it a near-tragic, near-comic lyricism. As a form, the blues is an autobiographical chronicle of personal catastrophe expressed lyrically" (*Shadow* 129). Wright himself reacted with gratitude to his friend's essay, but also with surprise: the blues, he informed Ellison, simply had not been on his mind as the primary template for his writing (Rowley 311, 566). And indeed, what Ellison heard, and what he delineated, was a blues *sensibility* rather than blues music as a structural device—in fact, Ellison himself would later qualify Wright's knowledge of black music as rather limited indeed, and, he couldn't help but snipe, Wright "didn't even know how to dance" (*Going* 667). Wright's prose fiction, as well as his autobiography, is almost completely devoid of explicit references to blues, although he would write lyrics as well as liner notes and essays on the art form, even taking guitar lessons at one point (Dick 393, 399; Fabre 237; Rowley 227, 256–57). His own blues lyrics exhibit a stilted affectation and artificiality that suggest a certain aesthetic distance from the form (Dick 400–5; Oliver 8–13). For example, he agreed to write the introduction to British scholar Paul Oliver's *Blues Fell this Morning*.[12] In his exile in Paris, Wright showed that he understood the music as a thoroughly Afro-modernist product with a dash of surrealism: "The blues are fantastically paradoxical" because "[m]illions in this our twentieth century have danced with abandonment and sensuous joys to jigs that had their birth in suffering." Echoing the three key themes that constitute modernism, the blues for Wright are "those starkly brutal, haunting folk songs created by millions of nameless and illiterate American Negroes in their confused wanderings over the American southland and in their intrusion into the northern American industrial cities" (xiii). But Wright's central definition of the blues is but a liberal (and uninspired) paraphrase of Ellison:

> Yet the most astonishing aspect of the blues is that, though replete with a sense of defeat and down-heartedness, they are not intrinsically pessimistic; their burden of woe and melancholy is dialectically redeemed through sheer force of sensuality, into an almost exultant affirmation of life, of love, of sex, of movement, of hope. No matter how repressive was the American environment, the Negro never lost faith in or doubted his deeply endemic capacity to live. All blues are a lusty, lyrical realism charged with taut sensibility. (xv)

Where Wright claimed to hear dialectical redemption in black music, in his own fiction it never figures as more than a prop for structural irony. In blues, Wright heard a decidedly modernist sensibility arising out of their "ability to take seemingly unrelated images and symbols and link them together into a meaningful whole"; blues, to him, were therefore "our 'spirituals' of the city pavement" (qtd. in Dick 406; Wright, *Twelve* 128). But precisely because they were "the spirituals of the city"—elsewhere, Wright commented that "Protestant ministers have put to religious use the sexual power of convulsive songs and have channeled aphrodisiac music into the spirituals"—they were also characterized by "a submerged theme of guilt" stemming, perhaps, "from the burden of renounced rebellious impulses" leading to "a certain degree of passivity, almost masochistic in quality and seemingly allied to sex in origin" ("Jazz" 242; Foreword xiv). Thus, concludes Craig Werner, "[d]espite his sensitivity to the ironies and ambiguities of modernist writing, Wright seems almost entirely deaf to the double-meanings of Afro-American song" (206).

The blues' alleged passive masochism of sexual origin explains Sarah's submission to the white salesman after "When the Roll Is Called Up Yonder" has conjured up the guilty pleasure of her liaison with Tom and thus quashed her impulses to resist the advances of the white man. That black blues music should have the identical effects as a white religious hymn is but one of many idiosyncrasies in "Long Black Song," and many readers have pointed out the story's thematic and structural inconsistencies.[13] Wright himself freely admitted that his effort "did not catch the experience I was looking for," namely to find an answer to the question "What quality of will must a Negro possess to live and die with dignity in a country that denied his humanity?" (Black 402). For critic Myles Hurd, the problems arise from Wright's inability to connect the literary techniques of high modernism with African American expressiveness, resulting in "a specific source of bitonality in the work—i.e. Wright's reliance on 'white techniques' to articulate 'black themes'" (48). However, as Hurd's own terminology already suggests, the "problematic disharmonies between technique and theme" owe as much to the author's desire to replicate high modernist techniques as to his inability to hear in music a *viable* revolutionary protest against white southern violence and its most terrifying ritual, lynching (56).

In a way, therefore, precisely because "Long Black Song" contains no long black song per se, Richard Wright's modernism remains bifurcated. The short story's long *black* song is a song without music, namely, the black experience in the New World. In both secular and religious black music—Afro-America's historical conscience (and therefore America's as well)—Wright heard but guilt, repression, passivity, and even dangerous self-deception. In other words, black music expressed a stasis that rendered it impractical as a means of protest, let alone of revolutionary struggle. Ironically, it was the midwesterner Langston Hughes who heard in music, in black *southern* music, something very different, who heard in it the potential to which Wright seemed deaf:

When I get to be a composer
I'm gonna write me some music
About daybreak in Alabama

And I'm gonna put the purtiest songs in it
Rising out of the ground like swamp mist
And falling out of the heaven like soft dew. (lines 1–6)

The multicultural ideal "Daybreak in Alabama" goes on to forecast a southern ideal in which "white hands / And black hands and brown and yellow hands / And red clay earth hands" are "touching everybody with kind fingers / And touching each other natural as dew" is an ideal borne out of the *process* of embellishing time passing by, not an ideal vanquished in the collision between cyclical time and mechanical time (15–19). This ideal South, Hughes's speaker dreams, will resonate "In that dawn of music when I / Get to be a composer / And write about daybreak / In Alabama"—a dawn, in other words, where linear time (the speaker's composition will be written at some point in the future) cooperates with cyclical time (dawn, daybreak, and the poem's own circular structure) (20–23). In Hughes's Alabama, presence and absence, cyclical and linear time, collaborate, they don't collide. The collision at the center of Wright's Mississippi, however, creates not hope, just paradox. The disruption brought into the peacefully agrarian idyll by modernity in the shape of the graphophone clock engenders both: the majesty of Sarah's vision and the tragedy of Silas's lynching.

"Richard Wright," sniped Margaret Walker with deliberate ambiguity, "came out of hell" (13). But "Long Black Song" limns the setting as a symbolic ritual ground that contains damnation and redemption, joy and terror, heroes and cowards, life and death. Sarah, perhaps, could not really have received her own vision; she certainly could not articulate it. But Richard Wright, who came from hell and told about it, *could*. The tensions within "Long Black Song" are thus very much the author's own: as George Kent has pointed out, Wright's "personal tension springs from a stubborn self conscious of victimization but obsessed with its right to a full engagement of universal forces and to reaping the fruits due from the engagement. This right may be called the heritage of man" (76). And both sides of this consciousness and conscience arise out of the same ritual ground, the "fantastical paradox" that was the South—and still is. What Wright's "Long Black Song" and Hughes's "Daybreak in Alabama" intone in unison, as disparate as they otherwise are, is that the song of Sarah's majestic vision has not yet been performed. They suggest therefore a shift of focus, from literary text to musical performance, in order to elucidate the full potential of Afro-modernism's historical conscience.

CHAPTER 4

Blues and the Abstract Truth

The Southern Groove Continuum
from W. C. Handy to the Allman Brothers Band

Blues as, among other things, urbanized, secularized "'spirituals' of
the city pavements" were very much what composer-arranger and
reedist Oliver Nelson tapped for his classic 1961 album *The Blues
and the Abstract Truth*, recorded barely four months after Richard
Wright's death (Wright, *Twelve* 128). The stately "Yearnin'" combines gutbucket blues with an 'amen' cadenza; it is escorted by the
tongue-in-cheek hillbilly joviality of "Hoe-Down"; the bebop flag-
waver "Butch and Butch"; the minor vamp of the famous "Stolen
Moments"; the displaced intervals, magnified by the contrasting
solo voices of studied Nelson and atonal Eric Dolphy, of "Teenie's
Blues"; and the harmonically advanced, cerebral "Cascades." "The

blues, which is a twelve-bar form[,] and the form and chord structure *I've Got Rhythm*, being 32 measures in length, was my material for all of the compositions on this album," writes Nelson in the liner notes; "[t]he augmentation of the forms themselves comes from thematic motifs and melodic ideas" (2). Blues, then, together with the widely popular chord progression of the George and Ira Gershwin standard, furnishes the concrete musical *form* of the concept album. Thus, Nelson's album manages to succeed in what "Long Black Song" struggles to accomplish, namely, to borrow Myles Hurd's terminology again, an organic fusion of 'white forms' and 'black expression' (48). The blues' abstract truth is the modernist eclecticism borne out of the blues itself, an eclecticism Wright would surely have recognized. And so, *The Blues and the Abstract Truth* very much occupies the crossroads where the blues meets the Great American Songbook.

The Crossroads. Ground zero of the Delta blues—and, by extension, of all of popular American music. Here, or so the story goes, is where the legendary Robert Johnson traded his soul to the devil for virtuoso guitar skills and went on to become the "King of the Delta Blues Singers."[1] Not too long ago, the city of Clarksdale, Mississippi, designated the intersection of Highways 161 and 49, State Street and Delta Avenue, respectively, the mythical ritual ground where said transaction took place, and erected a black metal marker adorned with two oversized blue guitars to mark the spot. A fairly busy intersection—busy, that is, by Delta standards—it is flanked by a DoubleQuick gas station, the Clarksdale Minimart, and the H-Town Car Wash. The gleaming new green and white Church's Chicken fast-food drive-thru next to DoubleQuick seems to do much brisker business than the fading, ramshackle building of Abe's Bar-B-Q, proudly proclaiming its existence since 1924, right across State Street behind Delta Donuts, with a prime view of the intersection. Yet none of the automobiles traversing the crossroads will blast "Hellhound on My Trail" from its stereo; instead, one is much more likely to hear the booming bass lines and sampled drum parts of Ludacris, Lil Jon—or, maybe, Memphis Bleek.

Knowledgeable locals, however, will tell the inquisitive visitor that back in the 1930s, Highways 61 and 49 intersected not here, but at what today is Dr. Martin Luther King, Jr., Drive and East Tallahatchie Street.[2] Located right across the railway tracks from the center of Clarksdale, a few blocks east of the cemetery on Sunflower Street, whose headstones on Memorial Day are adorned with almost as many little flags brandishing the Stars and Bars as the Stars and Stripes, this juncture's forlorn aura belies its proximity to downtown—or what passes for downtown—and appears much more conducive to a demonic midnight rendezvous. Separated by the tracks and West Tallahatchie from an empty parking lot, an unmarked juke joint, Goon's Furniture & Package Store, the aptly named Ricos [sic] Fisherman's Shack, and the one-story brick building housing Southern Style Hot Wings and the Word of God Christian Ministry (presumably ministering to those leery of any chance encounters at this particular crossroads) that occupy the northeastern corner seem to do even less business than Abe's down the road. But in the 1930s, King Drive was 4th Street and the main drag of black Clarksdale, the nearby train station a busy railway hub (Evans 40–41; White 5; Wilkins, Stackhouse, and Kenibrew 206, 228–29). One would think that businessmen intent on conducting a very tricky transaction would prefer a location other than the busiest intersection of south Clarksdale, teeming with life at all hours.

No wonder, then, that there is a third, much more plausible, location: Luther Brown, director of the Center for Culture and Learning at Delta State University in Cleveland, thirty-six miles south of Clarkdale, points to the intersection of two dirt roads just south of the famous Dockery Farms straddling the border between Bolivar and LeFlore counties.[3] Marked merely by two rusty, slanted stop signs, the only signs of life are a small, fenced-in horse pasture, a dilapidated stable, and an ancient, rusted school bus on cinderblocks reincarnated as a tool shed. If one tarries there long enough, perhaps the eerie silence will be interrupted by a slow-moving pick-up truck—whose tinny radio is tuned to a country and western station playing Toby Keith's latest single release. Even so, it is easy to imagine Robert Johnson striking a deal with the devil here, especially since one has to pass a tiny cemetery after turning onto the dirt road off of Highway 8. And yet, the suspicion lingers that the main reason for this intersection's elevation to mythical status over sundry virtually identical ones all across the Delta had something to do with its convenient proximity to Dockery Farms, a must-stop for any blues tourist anyway, and to Delta State, Professor Brown's employer, as well as its easy access from the highway.

So in the end, the mythical crossroads defies exact geographic designation, and it is therefore only fitting that, just as there are three crossroads, there are also three gravesites for Robert Johnson.[4] Blues researcher Steve Cheeseborough explains the matter thus: "A few years ago, a guy working with some filmmakers asked me where they could find the 'real' crossroads for their film. I told him about various spots. But he kept asking where the 'real' one was. Finally, I explained that if they wanted to shoot pictures of Santa Claus, I could take them to the mall. But if they insisted on shooting the 'real' Santa Claus, I'd have to tell them that Santa Claus is a mythical figure, not a real person. Well, that's how it is with the crossroads, too" (qtd. in Stolle 47). Nevertheless, at least for the blues aficionado, the myth of the crossroads remains every bit as powerful as the myth of Santa Claus.

The legends raking around Robert Johnson in particular and blues in general as well as the landscape of the Mississippi Delta itself cloak the whole art form and its history in a titillating aura of backwoods mystery— an aura avidly maintained by record labels, agents, promoters, chambers of commerce, even academic researchers and some musicians themselves. It therefore seems like a paradox that blues is actually a thoroughly *modernist* art form, and always has been. For insight into the blues as modernism, we need look no further than the aptly titled autobiography of W. C. Handy, the *Father of the Blues*. In the tenth chapter, "Blue Diamonds in the Rough: Polished and Mounted," Handy allows us to catch a glimpse of his compositional method: "The primitive tone or a correlated note of the blues was born in my brain when a boy. In the valley of the Tennessee River was McFarland's Bottoms, which our school overlooked. In the spring, when doors and windows were thrown open, the song of a Negro plowman half a mile away fell on my ears" (137). After having carefully transcribed the plowman's six-bar field holler, whose lyrics consisted solely of the singer's refusal to live in Cairo, Handy continues,

> All through the years this snatch of song had been ringing in my ears. Many times I wondered what was on the singer's mind. What was wrong with Cairo? Was Cairo too far south in Illinois to be "up North," or too far north to be considered "down South"? In any event, such bits of music or snatches of song generated the motif for my blues and with an imagination stimulated by such lines as "I wouldn't live in Cairo," I wrote my lyrics. If I had published at that time a composition called *The Cairo Blues*, and this simple four-bar theme had been developed into a four-page musical classic, every grown-up who had then heard that four-bar wail would now claim that Handy didn't write this number. And you would hear them say, "I heard it when I was knee-high to a grasshopper." Politely put, this would be a misstatement of fact; bluntly written, it would be a falsehood. That two-line snatch couldn't form a four-page composition any more than the two letters *i-n* could spell the word *information*. (137–38)[5]

Handy adduces more "snatches of song" he transformed into fully fledged blues compositions, "embellished by my harmonization and rhythm" (138). One need only recall the most famous blues of all time, Handy's "St. Louis

Blues," inspired, the composer tells us, by yet another "snatch" he first heard as a young homeless man from an inebriated woman wandering the levee of that midwestern city (118–21).[6] Its embellishments included the middle section in what Handy calls a tango rhythm, for which he drew on a more recent sojourn to Cuba. Mapping what Paul Gilroy almost a century later would influentially dub "the Black Atlantic," the classically trained Handy avers that "[a]ltogether, I aimed to use all that is characteristic of the Negro from Africa to Alabama" in "St. Louis Blues" (121). He later elaborated,

> Another frequent question is why I used a tango rhythm in the familiar minor strain, beginning with the words "St. Louis woman wid her diamon rings." The answer is that the tango was originally an African jungle dance called "Tangana" and may therefore legitimately be considered typical Negro music. It was brought into Spain by Moors and eventually reached the Argentine, where it was refined and freed from its primitive vulgarity. Simultaneously it reached Cuba by way of the Negro slaves and was given the name of "Habanera" because of its popularity in the city of Havana. This is the same rhythmic pattern that Bizet used in his "Carmen." So the "St. Louis Blues" may be said to complete a cycle which began in the jungle and finally reached the operatic stages and the swank night clubs of the world. ("Handy" 16)

Therefore, Handy's blues are a product of pastiche and collage and result from the collision of the snatches of folk songs, field hollers, and other vernacular musics on the one hand, with his classical training and inclinations on the other, and are thus thoroughly modernist. Their historical conscience lies in Handy's awareness that they belong to a cycle—the same cycle of black New World culture Frederick Douglass heard in the slave songs, the same cycle the ring shout ritual enacts, the same cycle whose arcs Jean Toomer used to preface the three sections of *Cane*. Handy also insists that his music is not borne out of mere harmonic and rhythmic experimentation for experimentation's sake, but that he sees his music, for all its eclecticism, standing firmly within a greater African American tradition. As he says it best in one of his lyrics, "May the world borrow gladness from sorrow, / Way down South where the blues began." That the "St. Louis Blues" also apparently borrowed from the now obscure "I Got the Blues," penned by Italian-American Antonio Maggio in 1908 and the first-ever sheet music to be published bearing the word "blues" in its title, and that Handy spent his formative years touring as musical director of the Irish Mahara brothers' Mahara's Minstrels, may posit an insurmountable problem for the critic intent on unearthing the 'authentic' sources of black blues, but it is right in tune with the aesthetic of Afro-modernism (Wald 15–16). Perhaps somewhat unexpectedly then, and certainly unintentionally, the blues' 'official' crossroads so designated by the Clarksdale Chamber of Commerce and flanked by the greasy venerability of Abe's Bar-B-Q on one side, the cookie-cutter capitalism of Church's Chicken on the other, is the one that comes closest to the spirit of the music with its idiosyncratic side-by-side of old and new, myth and commerce, tradition and fragmentation, history and progress, authenticity and ersatz.

Handy, as much as anyone else, codified not just the now quintessential AAB stanza form of the blues, but also recognized the so-called "blue notes" as the *sine qua non* of the genre. Handy's own description of these blue notes is, for all its latent essentialism and class prejudice, as good as any: again apropos his most famous composition, Handy relates that

> [t]he primitive Southern Negro as he sang was sure to bear down on the third and seventh tones of the scale, slurring between major and minor. Whether in the cotton fields of the Delta or on the levee up St. Louis way, it was always the same. Till then, however, I had never heard this slur used by a more sophisticated Negro, or by any white man. I had tried to convey this effect in *Memphis Blues* by introducing flat thirds and sevenths (now called "blue notes") into my song, although its prevailing key was the major; and I carried this device into my new melody as well. I also struck upon the idea of using the dominant seventh as the opening chord of the verse. This was a distinct departure, but as it turned out, it touched the spot. (*Father* 120)[7]

What is crucial in Handy's gloss is that this blue "slur" defies musical notation; all that Handy can do is approximate it in writing. What are commonly referred to as flatted thirds and sevenths—and later in bebop the notorious flatted fifth—are in fact notes that cannot be represented accurately on the staff. A blue note, explains Gunther Schuller, is "a microtonal variant" that produces an "harmonic ambiguity" vis-à-vis the European tempered scale (*Swing* 862; *Early* 46–47, 50–51). The catalyst for this harmonic ambiguity, the blue note in a way sounds the geographical location of Cairo, neither south nor north, in the plowman's song young William Christopher heard in Alabama. The blue note, it may be said, is the musical equivalent of Robert Johnson's crossroads: neither here nor there, defying the fixity of space and text, and yet a vital aspect of the story being told. The blue note is therefore the utterly modernist axis on which the blues turn, and which gives voice to Afro-modernism's historical conscience.[8]

The inherent harmonic ambiguity produced by the blue notes and reverberating in the blues scale is also echoed in the politics of race that surround the blues. On the one hand, blues is indubitably a distinctly African American art form; at the same time, its modernist hybridity has often been repressed in critical discourse, subordinated to a mythology of undiluted origins and authentic 'blackness.' Despite—or, perhaps, because of—the fact that blues has influenced each and every genre of popular American music, this myth is still alive and well in the twenty-first century. As for example sociologist David Grazian's important study of Chicago clubs shows, the country's most vibrant blues scene still conceives of the music as the ultimate receptacle of authentic blackness, a blackness connoting "an extreme sense of authenticity, or what we might call the cultural construction of 'soul' as a dominant racial stereotype" (36). In this realm where blackness is at a premium, nonblack musicians often find themselves marginalized. According to one performer interviewed by Grazian, "The truth is, if you're white you have to go out there and prove yourself even more. . . . I have to work twice as hard, play twice as good, because I'm *white*. In the world of blues, *I* am affirmative action" (qtd. in Grazian 139). Yet "[t]he blues," the legendary Memphis Slim stated categorically, "started from slavery," and Amiri Baraka seconded irrefutably that "blues could not exist if the African captives had not become American captives" (qtd. in Tracy 6; Baraka, *Blues* 17). And so it is that nonblack participation in and use of the blues is still raising provocative questions of cultural property and cultural propriety.

This problem is exacerbated by the recurrent exploitation of black music and black musicians by a music industry historically dominated by whites, amounting to what Baraka has accurately termed "the Great American Music Robbery" (Baraka, "Great" 328–30; Gennari 21–22, 47–49). It is a problem that has its roots in the minstrel show of the nineteenth century, as Eric Lott has shown: "These are the two narrative paradigms of minstrelsy's origins: one in which mixing takes place by an elision of expropriation, through absorption (in both senses); the other in which it takes place by a transfer of ownership through theft." The two paradigms "share an anxiety over the fact of cultural 'borrowing,'" and both "have as their purpose the resolution of some intractable social contradiction or problem that the issue of expropriation represents. That of the first is miscegenation; that of the second slavery itself" (57). In blues, a dynamic of "love and theft" became particularly regnant in the 1950s and 1960s, when the burgeoning folk movement and the so-called British Invasion prompted the 'rediscovery' of black blues musicians by white enthusiasts (Lott 4–7; O'Neal 346–53, 378–79). Eddie Boyd for instance, back in the 1950s a young Delta transplant witnessing firsthand the stirrings of the blues revival, still bristled years later at the way white producers and record labels sought to manage the music and the musicians: "You know, back in those days, man, those cats used to sit and talk about how they niggerized these blues singers, you understand?" (262). With the benefit of hindsight, a contrite Phil Spiro, radio disc jockey and blues fan, agrees with Boyd and muses:

> And what did we give them [the blues musicians being 'rediscovered']? For the ones who had recorded before, like Son [House] and Skip [James] and Booker ["Bukka" White], we kept comparing them to their younger selves, and they knew it. How could they help knowing, when perhaps three-quarters of the people that they met were asking them questions about what color shirt they wore on that muggy delta day in 1931 when . . . Nobody seemed to give a flying fuck that they were *still* living on the wrong side of this poverty line, and that the income from their music was not enough to significantly improve their lot over welfare in most cases. We also consciously or unconsciously tried to shape the music that they played on stage. . . . Our motivation was a strange combination of ego, scholasticism, and power. I wonder now what would have happened if we had just left them alone instead of telling them what songs to sing and what instruments to play on. The rediscoverers fought over the artists. . . . Worst of all, aside from a couple of people like Chris Strachwitz and Dick Waterman, the rediscoverers all too often didn't see the old guys as real, breathing, feeling, intelligent people. In general, we were collectors of people, who we tended to treat as if they were the rarest of records—only one copy known to exist. (qtd. in von Schmidt and Rooney 538)

The crossroads of power and property: in some ways, the cultural territory of the era echoed in disturbing ways antebellum America, the inherent modernism of blues notwithstanding. It was even more difficult for the newly 'discovered' musicians when the benchmark of authentic blackness was a handful of recordings by a man long dead—Robert Johnson. For young British rockers such as Keith Richards and Eric Clapton, Johnson was the ultimate blues musician, pure "soul" (Clapton 23; Richards 21–22).

The fabrication of authentic blackness and the accompanying myth of the crossroads are the products of a postromantic, antimodernist impulse.

The white romanticizing of black blues is not just problematic in terms of cultural appropriation: complicit in this process of romanticization is the once again deferred access of black musicians—and, thus, by extension, black *people*—to modernity. The popularized myth of the crossroads recasts the black blues musician in the European archetype of *l'artiste maudit*. It is a myth that requires the blues troubadour to still the artistic hunger by tarrying at the intersection outside of Cleveland until after midnight, but that would not want to grant him or her admission to, say, a Church's Chicken—even if it is the one in Clarksdale—should the long wait for a certain gentleman suddenly cause a pang of physical hunger.[9] Elijah Wald hints at the unsettling echoes of minstrelsy resounding at the intersection of the myth of Robert Johnson and the fabrication of authentic blackness:

> the modern blues audience hears Robert Johnson's music very differently from the way his peers heard it in 1935, and makes very different demands on those musicians who consider themselves his heirs. In a sense, the white audience turned blues into a sort of acting. At first, it demanded "real" blues singers, black men and women who had already established themselves as performers in their own communities. Since one of the measures of "realness" was that the music create the atmosphere of another world, that it carry the listener from Carnegie Hall or a Cambridge coffeehouse to a dilapidated porch in rural Mississippi or a barroom on the South Side of Chicago, this audience automatically gravitated toward the blues artist who made those connections most obviously. An audience of poor black Texans knew that T-Bone Walker was still one of them even though he was wearing a zoot suit and diamonds, dancing onstage and playing guitar behind his head. A white revivalist audience worried that someone that sharp and snappy was some kind of faker, adulterating the music's pure country roots. (254)

To be sure, Robert Johnson's crossroads are not entirely a fabrication of white myth-making. The crossroads in African American folk culture hark back to the West African deity Eshu-Elegbara, or Esu, guardian of the symbolic juncture of risk and opportunity, meaning and interpretation, of earthly life and the realm of the ancestors. But it is significant that in the Yoruba belief system, Esu is not a devilish, malevolent deity.[10] It is also worth pointing out that there is not even a veiled reference to the devil on Johnson's "Cross Road Blues." Instead, it is the Lord to whom Johnson appeals for spiritual salvation, late one afternoon, at a well-traversed intersection:

I went to the crossroads, fell down on my knees.
I went to the crossroads, fell down on my knees.
Asked the Lord above, "Have mercy: save poor Bob if you please."

Mmmm, standing at the crossroads, I tried to flag a ride.
Standing at the crossroads, I tried to flag a ride.
Didn't nobody seem to know me, everybody pass me by.

Mmmm, the sun going down, boy, dark gon' catch me here
Oooeee, oh dark gon' catch me here.
I ain't got no loving sweet woman that love and feel my care.[11]

And so, Robert Johnson—during his lifetime a performer with limited appeal and influence—posthumously became a mythical, larger-than-life figure only through the intervention of mostly white aficionados, whose tastes and expectations were shaped not by New World retentions of Yoruban beliefs, but by the Euro-American, postromantic view of the artist as a tortured genius consumed by his art and misunderstood by a callous, hostile world around him.

In this racially charged realm of sound, commerce, and power, the Allman Brothers Band occupies a particularly salient place. Emerging on the heels of what historian C. Vann Woodward has called the Second Reconstruction, the Allman Brothers Band was not only the flagship of southern rock but was also the genre's first, and for a long time the only, racially integrated combo (Woodward 107, 172–78).[12] The band was formed by Nashville-born guitarist Duane Allman, and its titular other half consisted of his younger brother Gregg on keyboards and vocals. Duane, a brilliant instrumentalist and charismatic personality, had made a name for himself as a session hand at the FAME Studios in Muscle Shoals, Alabama, just two or three miles south of Handy's birthplace. There, his talent as both musician and arranger shaped classic recordings by soul acts Aretha Franklin, King Curtis, and Wilson Pickett, and caught the ear of Otis Redding's former manager, Phil Walden. Walden urged him to put a new band together after Duane's then current group, Hour Glass, split with their record label. And so, in early 1969 the Allman Brothers Band— ABB for short—formed in Daytona Beach, Florida, and subsequently relocated to Macon, Georgia, where they became the cornerstone of Walden's newly founded independent label, Capricorn.

But even though they became so successful as to ride the crest of the '70s wave of stadium rock, the myth of Robert Johnson at the crossroads has loomed large over the Allman Brothers Band. Fans, managers, promoters, and assorted hangers-on have readily latched on to otherworldly theories in promoting the band's auratic mystique. They point to two earlier Duane Allman-led incubations of what would eventually become the ABB, which were called The Second Coming and Beelzebub, respectively. Then there was Macon's spooky Rose Hill Cemetery, where the band liked to congregate for nocturnal rehearsals and where cofounder Dickey Betts composed his classic "In Memory of Elizabeth Reed," inspired by the inscription on a nineteenth-century gravestone of a little girl. There was Gregg Allman's involvement with the criminal activities of the so-called Southern Mafia as well as his stormy and short-lived marriage to pop starlet Cher. There was the original members' copious consumption of virtually every hard drug known to humankind. All of these affairs alone, amplifying and indeed partly cowriting the classic rock-star narrative of spectacular rise, damning fall, and wondrous redemption, read to many like Flannery O'Connor's rock 'n' roll version of southern gothic, a tale of rhythm and bruise, and suggested that the band had hellhounds on their trails, too.

And then there were the crossroads. On October 29, 1971, Duane Allman lost his life after he swiped the back end of a flatbed truck (carrying a load of Georgia peaches, or so the rumors would later insist) and lost control of his modified Harley Davidson chopper. The accident occurred in Macon, at the intersection of Hillcrest and Bartlett. Duane had been the heart and soul of the band in many ways, a leader with an irresistible charisma. "He had this sort of glow about him," affirms keyboardist Chuck Leavell (Leavell and Craig 88). Roadie and close friend Joseph "Red Dog" Campbell muses, "He was, and no disrespect intended, like our Jesus Christ. We followed him and his word. You might say the rest of the band went along and preached with him. How lucky we were to have six great preachers in one church" (102). Despite this irreplaceable loss, the band decided to soldier on and hired Leavell to complement the frontline. But many simply couldn't get over the loss of Duane.

Bass player Berry Oakley took his leader's death the hardest. A year to the day before the accident, so the story goes, he had prayed over Duane, unconscious from a near-fatal heroin overdose, in a Nashville motel room, begging for just one more year of life for his idol. Now, Oakley began to listen obsessively to Robert Johnson's records, especially "Hellhound on My Trail," and was wont to hint darkly at otherworldly spirits seeking to do him harm. Riding his heavy Triumph motorcycle to a Macon jam session in the afternoon of November 11, 1972, the bassist collided with a bus; refusing medical attention on the scene, he died that night in the same hospital where Duane Allman had been pronounced dead little more than a year before. The second fatal accident to haunt the band occurred at the intersection of Napier and Inverness—a mere three blocks away from the crossroads where Duane had lost his life. The elder Allman's body still hadn't been buried and was lying in cold storage, so he and Oakley were laid to rest together, under matching tombstones, in the Civil War section of Macon's Rose Hill Cemetery. "Duane was the Preacher and Berry was the Deacon," says Campbell; "Like brother Duane told me the night before he departed this earthly dimension, 'This is a religion we are spreading. The music will always bring us back'" (28–29). Even so, tragedy continued to follow the ABB: Twiggs Lydon, the band's road manager for many years and a close friend of Duane's, would fall to his death in a skydiving accident just outside of a town in upstate New York named Duanesburg, spawning rumors of suicide and even foul play. Lamar Williams, Oakley's replacement and the second African American to join the band, would die exactly ten years after Duane from lung cancer that had been caused, the doctors speculated, by Williams's prolonged exposure to Agent Orange in Vietnam.[13]

In glaring contrast to the crossroads mythology surrounding the band, Robert Johnson is almost entirely absent from the ABB's discography. As if to dissociate themselves from the rampant myth-mongering of white blues fans, they have covered the Mississippian only very rarely in concert, suggesting a conscious choice not to indulge in the romanticizing hagiography that has made "Cross Road Blues" a cornerstone of the legend.[14] Unlike many who discovered the blues in the hippie era, Duane Allman and the rest of the band were interested less in milking myth than in making music. Although he didn't sing, only made the announcements from the stage, Duane was the brain behind and the undisputed leader of the sextet. He and brother Gregg, like so many other white southerners of their generation aspiring to be musicians, had grown up listening to and admiring black music. As the guitarist summarized the musical foundation of the band, "When we first started, Gregg and me were playing rhythm and blues. . . . We always had blues roots, and the only way we could break into the scene was to try to play black music in white clubs. The best thing that happened was that the British intervention on the scene made it possible to play what you wanted to play, and do what you wanted to do. . . . We didn't have to be restricted. Everyone began to dig the blues and everyone was getting into it" (qtd. in Freeman, *Midnight* 20). But from the very beginning, the Allman Brothers Band was interested in much more than simply streamlining and 'updating' the acoustic guitar of Robert Johnson's songs by plugging in, cranking up, and pounding away, as so many of the Allmans' contemporaries did after the invasion from across the sea had been launched and they first heard Cream, the Yardbirds, or John Mayall's Blues Breakers.[15]

The ABB's original, classic lineup already intimates that their music was designed to be something different from "love and theft": the two Allmans were complemented by Floridian guitarist Dickey Betts, whose country and western roots were accompanied by a deep admiration for the jazz manouche of Django Reinhardt as well as for the free jazz of Ornette Coleman; by Chicagoan Oakley, bass player and the only Yankee in the group, who had been subbing in various Florida beach bands when his future boss met him; and by the most unusual drum tandem of Butch Trucks and Johnny Lee Johnson. The classically trained Floridian Trucks, who also likes to double on tympani occasionally, came out of the folk music scene. By contrast, Alabaman Johnson, who shortened his name to "Jaimoe" early on, had always wanted to be a jazz drummer. When he was recruited by Duane, he had just toured with Otis Redding but found himself out of work when the singer had to leave him behind for the European tour because Jaimoe had no passport. The contrast between Trucks and Jaimoe could hardly be greater. Over three decades later, Warren Haynes, who would fill Duane Allman's spot in the band's umpteenth reincarnation, still wonders, "The thing that Butch and Jaimoe have together is the unspoken chemistry that you could never expect. . . . Those guys wouldn't even know each other were it not for music" (qtd. in Myers 58–59).

All members of the original group except Jaimoe were white—though Dickey Betts has some Native American background—and the addition of a black drummer to a white rock group was anything but ordinary. Butch Trucks remembers vividly his reaction when the elder Allman introduced him to his future percussion partner: "So he's sitting there: giant muscles, and tank top on, that bear tooth thing around his neck—and I'm going, 'damn, a militant n[igg]er, he's gonna kill me!'" (qtd. in "Southern"). For Jaimoe's part, his motivation for accepting what back in 1969 was a most unusual job proposition was rather pragmatic: "This friend of mine, he said, 'If you want to make money,' he said, 'go play with them white boys.' A little light bulb went off in my head—bing!—oh, make money, huh? So what the hell" (qtd. in "Southern"). Make money he did, eventually, but the reason he gives for staying is equally as telling as the economic disadvantage many black musicians experienced: "There was a lot of freedom in the stuff we were doing," Jaimoe affirms simply (qtd. in "Southern"). Trucks soon recognized the decisive influence Jaimoe was beginning to exert over the development of the band's unique sound: "Jaimoe turned us on to Miles Davis and [John] Coltrane and that's about all we listened to for a long time. . . . We didn't listen to any rock 'n' roll at all. We started getting a little more complex and experimenting with rhythms and melodies" (qtd. in Freeman, *Midnight* 63). Thus, progressive jazz combined with the blues' Afro-modernism to provide, in sound, a space of freedom that allowed the individual to express himself according to his own desires, yet still remain within a supportive collective.

It is this creative freedom Jaimoe cites for which cultural diversity was a decisive catalyst, which in turn grew out of the high premium on improvisation marking all the musics contributing to the ABB's stylistic mélange. The variety of the individual members' musical backgrounds, a modernist pastiche of sound, was mirrored by wide-ranging influences, where Miles and Trane met Robert Johnson and Rahsaan Roland Kirk (Freeman, *Midnight* 63–64; Myers 55; Perlah). And when Derek Trucks, Butch's nephew, eventually joined the band, he brought with him a pronounced interest in classical Indian and Middle Eastern musics, fusing them in what he calls "world-blues" (qtd. in Mattison 40; Hadley 33). Rather than romanticizing black music and black musicians—a path that, for example, Eric Clapton would follow devotedly, culminating in his 2002 album *Me and Mr. Johnson*—the ABB's approach was as thoroughly modernist as Handy's in that it sought to shore up in its music the fragments of its members' various influences and interests. Not surprisingly, given this modernist eclecticism, the ABB has always rejected the label 'southern rock.' As Gregg Allman likes to point out, "Southern rock is a term some guy came up with so they'd have a place to put our records in shops. Anyway, rock 'n' roll was born in the South, so southern rock is like saying rock rock. The Allman Brothers are a contemporary blues and jazz band. That's about what it is. That's what we called ourselves before the term southern rock came along" (qtd. in Perlah).[16] The adjectival clarification of the ABB playing *contemporary* music corroborates that the band is interested not in the faithful recreation of 'authentic' sounds, but rather in sounding out the possibilities offered by their two main sources, blues and jazz. Consequently, the ABB has always preferred the spontaneity and unpredictability of the stage to the constraints of the studio.

This sounding-out of possibilities arising from the spontaneity of performance has been a hallmark of the band irrespective of its various personnel reconfigurations. Neither their self-titled 1969 debut album nor the follow-up *Idlewild South* a year later made much of a splash, though they were well received by reviewers. The high point came with the sextet's third offering: the taping of the live shows of March 12 and 13, 1971, at New York's legendary Fillmore East almost single-handedly made Capricorn Records into the world's largest independent record label (Suarez 91). Portions of those four shows total were released originally as two double

LPs, *The Allman Brothers Band at Fillmore East* and *Eat a Peach,* the latter also containing new studio material. *At Fillmore East* constitutes the early culmination of the ABB's aesthetic, a benchmark of artistry recognized also by the Library of Congress: in 2004 it inducted the iconic album into the National Recording Registry ("National"). "This," avers their agent Phil Walden, "was really an expression of their region, their environment, of their culture" (qtd. in "Southern").

Accordingly, the album commences with the ABB's nod to their musical roots: the blues. The first track is Blind Willie McTell's "Statesboro Blues." Initially, Duane had come across the song when he attended a Taj Mahal concert, and it was lead guitarist Ed Davis's solo that prompted Duane to learn slide. But Duane soon sought out the original, too (Freeman, *Midnight* 31–32; Poe 56–57; Swenson 5). The mysterious Georgia native McTell recorded "Statesboro Blues" during his first session for Victor on October 17, 1928, in Atlanta, and it showcases his harplike, dexterous fingerpicking technique on his twelve-string acoustic guitar.[17] As is often the case in early country blues, the original version does not adhere completely to the classic twelve-bar formula codified by Handy and others: rather than a regular division into bars, the duration of a segment is determined by the musical phrase being played and/or the verse being sung. Significantly, McTell's filigreed guitar here employs Handy's blue notes only very sparingly, and almost exclusively their diminished seventh; there is but a smattering of flatted thirds across the performance. The ABB's version, on the other hand, is more than a mere appropriation or 'translation' of McTell into the electrified idiom. Although they continued to credit McTell as sole composer, the band's arrangement of "Statesboro Blues" is actually more a reinvention. Slowing down the original's sprightly tempo some to a hurtling groove, they not only rearrange the lyrics—largely using Taj Mahal's version—but completely recontextualize the music. The governing lick that opens the performance is actually the famous five-note riff from Muddy Waters's "Hoochie Coochie Man" that has become the ensign of electric Chicago blues.[18] Duane answers the band's riffing in classic call-and-response fashion on bottleneck; he even slides around a boppish flatted fifth or two later on. What is more, the authoritative guitar combines with the churning beat to intimate that, perhaps, the song's persona is now, several decades later, much more determined and willing to be "going to the country: baby, do you want to go? / But if you can't make it, baby, / Your sister Lucille say she wanna go." Bridging McTell's fleet-fingered acoustic country blues with Waters's meaty, electrified Chicago blues, the ABB's reinvention of "Statesboro Blues" is deeply attuned to what Amiri Baraka calls "the blues continuum": "as the developing strata of the city emphasized, the blues could extend in a kind of continuum from rhythm & blues all the way back to country blues. In the cities all these forms sat side by side in whatever new confusion urban life offered, and the radio made them all equally of the moment" (*Blues* 173, 169–73). The dual drums' hard-charging backbeat and especially Duane's searing slide guitar, the thoroughly modernist reshuffling of various stylistic frag-ments, make this continuum explicit.

After all, it's this same continuum that had famously given W. C. Handy's career a new direction in the sleepy Mississippi Delta town of Tutwiler sometime in the first decade of the twentieth century:

> [A]s I nodded in the railroad station while waiting for a train that had been delayed nine hours, life suddenly took me by the shoulder and awakened me with a start. A lean, loose-jointed Negro had commenced plunking a guitar beside me while I slept. His clothes were rags; his feet peeped out of his shoes. His face had on it some of the sadness of the ages. As he played, he pressed a knife on the strings of the guitar in a manner popularized by Hawaiian guitarists who used steel bars. The effect was unforgettable. His song, too, struck me instantly.
>
> Goin' where the Southern cross' the Dog.
>
> The singer repeated the line three times, accompanying himself on the guitar with the weirdest music I had ever heard. The tune stayed in my mind. (*Father* 74)[19]

To be sure, the memoirist—always the savvy marketer of the Handy brand—contributes his own share of lucrative mythmaking here. Handy knew that most of his audience was composed of white urbanites who, then as now, proliferated what Berndt Ostendorf refers to as "the danger-ous pyschopathological implications of pastoral purism. For many of them [white fans] blues are not genuine if the singer does not qualify in most of the following points: He should be illiterate, of indeterminate age, pref-erably ugly, recently dragged from his plough and mule into a makeshift studio, unwilling to make any money off his music and, most importantly, unwilling to leave the South" (81). But there is no reason to doubt that it was indeed the Delta where Handy first heard the "weirdest" sounds emanating from a slide guitar—even if that sound had partly come, as Handy intimates and some blues scholars argue (as does none other than Son House, by the way), courtesy of the many hugely popular Hawaiian traveling shows that were crisscrossing the country in the early 1900s (Spottswood 5; Wald 281–82).

Whatever the amount of romantic audience-pandering Handy injected into his description, the fact remains that the material conditions in the Mississippi Delta around 1900 most certainly forced many of its black inhabitants to wear ragged clothing and shoes with holes in them. And just as Frederick Douglass's frostbitten feet represented a historical conscience to which his pen gave voice, so does the anonymous musician at the Tutwiler train station (regardless of how 'creative' Handy's nonfiction here is) personify historical conscience, and the blue notes emanating from his guitar its voice. There is, then, a direct line reaching from early, rural Mississippi Delta blues to Duane Allman and his bandmates. Riffing on and expanding Baraka's blues continuum, "lean, loose-jointed," pale Duane Allman and his cohorts may exemplify what can be called the southern groove continuum. Coming of age in the apartheid South, they, except for Jaimoe, were not directly privy to the experiential history of Americans of African descent. But their music and their understanding of its roots, an understanding expressing itself in a modernist aesthetic born of the blues continuum, suggested that petrified mappings of raciological taxonomy need not apply automatically when it comes to southern *sound*-scapes.

It is therefore perhaps no coincidence that "Statesboro Blues" would become the Allman Brothers Band's traditional concert opener. Slotted first on the *Fillmore* album, it is followed by Elmore James's "Done Somebody Wrong," the T. Bone Walker classic "Stormy Monday," and Willie Cobbs's "You Don't Love Me." Hence, the album's first four tracks continue to limn the southern groove continuum as spawned by the blues. They traverse the genre's entire spectrum, from McTell's country blues to Cobbs's rocking, electrified Chicago blues reincarnated as a funkefied boogie. The instrumental "Hot 'Lanta," the album's first ABB original, begins to push the classic blues formula. It in turn is followed by another instrumental, Dickey Betts's "In Memory of Elizabeth Reed." Extending the blues sensibility considerably, it marks a stylistic shift: paralleling Carlos Santana's emergence, "In Memory" is a Latin-flavored tune characterized by Jelly Roll Morton's famous "Spanish tinge" (qtd. in Youngren 23). "In Memory" combines a complex, multilayered rhythmic groove with extended improvisations over a two-chord vamp. The album concludes with a tour de force of the Gregg Allman original "Whipping Post," the song most indelibly associated with the ABB.

"Whipping Post" had been conceived shortly after Gregg's return from the West Coast in late March of 1969. For the time being, the singer had moved into the upstairs room of Berry Oakley's apartment house but was awakened one night by the cries of the Oakleys' new baby. Without lights or electrical outlets in the tiny room, without pen or paper, Gregg proceeded to write the song with a box of stick matches on an ironing board cover—to the great dismay of Linda Oakley.[20] On the ABB's debut album, "Whipping Post" clocked in at an easily digestible 5:18. On stage, it would undergo more and more alterations, though it retained the original's structural modules, until it extended to over twenty-three minutes at the second show of the Fillmore concerts on March 13. By that time, it had also been wedded to another tune, "Mountain Jam," that the band had been performing at first separately. "Mountain Jam," never recorded in the studio, was based on "There Is a Mountain" by Scottish folkie Donovan, but the ABB defamiliarized the ditty so dramatically that Donovan granted the band co-composer credits when it was released commercially. Stripped of Donovan's psychedelic hippie lyrics—"The caterpillar sheds his skin / To find the butterfly within"—the ABB's version rumbled on for over half an hour. Since it wouldn't fit on what was already a double LP (and a live double album at the time was considered to be career suicide in the industry), "Mountain Jam" was released only on the follow-up, *Eat a Peach*. But as originally performed, the two tunes resulted in almost an hour of uninterrupted music.

Two features of the extended medley are significant. First, there are Gregg Allman's lyrics. Though not strictly a blues in terms of form, "Whipping Post" utilizes the standard blues narrative of love betrayed: "I been run down, / And I been lied to. / And I don't know why / I let that mean woman make me out a fool." Having absconded with Gregg's persona's cash and totaled his newly acquired car, she is now "with one of my good-time buddies / Drinking in some cross-town bar." In the chorus, Gregg moans, "Sometimes I feel— / Oh baby, sometimes I feel / Like I been tied to the whipping post. // Good Lord, I feel like I'm dying." The song thus traverses the same ritual ground as Wright's "Long Black Song," limning the intersection of love (or sex), violence, and ownership, and constructing the song's persona as what Adam Gussow calls a "blues subject": "the blues subject [is] a site on which a peculiarly southern dialectic of torture and sexuality is played out" (139). The chorus's analogy expressing the agony of Allman's persona references a symbol of chattel slavery in the American South.[21] But Allman's identity as a *white* southerner is only heightened by the oft-repeated assertion that "nobody sings the blues like Gregg does—at least not with blond hair" (qtd. in Myers 58). Moreover, following an archetypal narrative construction, Allman's identity as a white *male* southerner is marked by a journey into the figurative blackness of American history from which the protagonist obviously would like to emerge again via what Ralph Ellison calls "a ritual of exorcism" (*Shadow* 103).[22] The identity thus injected into the blues subject's dialectic precludes the application of Angela Davis's contention of love as a metaphor for freedom in blues (9–10). This, after all, is a music invented by a people for whom any kind of love had been a very precarious proposition indeed for at least two centuries after arriving in the New World. As Toni Morrison's Paul D muses, "to go to a place where you could love anything you chose—not to need permission for desire—well now, *that* was freedom" (*Beloved* 162). As circumscribed as the (artistic) freedom of the ABB may have been initially due to their regional provenance—Walden remembers that Atlantic, Capricorn's distributor, urged him to drop the band after the sluggish sales of their debut album "because nothing was ever gonna emerge from the South" and, moreover, "that there was no way I could have any luck with a white musician"—it wasn't nearly as compromised as the freedom, artistic and socioeconomic, of Paul D's descendants, the African American blues artists 'rediscovered' by Phil Spiro and others (qtd. in "Southern"; qtd. in Leavell and Craig 66).

What is more, only the trivialization of the experiential consequences of slavery, experiences from which Allman's ancestors were absolved solely by virtue of their skin color, allows the equation of the persona's broken heart and the slave's corporal punishment. This problematic kind of appropriation can be diagnosed as a manifestation of the so-called "black through white syndrome," and, consequently, the lyrics of "Whipping Post" enact the reconfigured rites of the minstrel show (Black 229–31; Hewitt 33–54). However, the chorus's simile is an expression of empathy, not of derision as in the minstrel show of the nineteenth century, nor, obviously, is it a romanticization of slavery as in the plantation tradition. Nevertheless, the declaration of emotional solidarity presupposes a trivialization of the physical terror exerted in the peculiar institution and its aftermath. In the evolution of the music, asserts Gussow, "[t]orture and dismemberment are pressing concerns of blues performers and blues song for reasons that trace directly back to the popular racial spectacle lynching suddenly became in the early 1890s, a kind of spectacle that had no real precedent in black memory," and a kind of spectacle in which white southerners were the perpetrators, not the victims as in the sonic spectacle of "Whipping Post" (29). That the state of Georgia saw more lynchings of African Americans in the four decades or so after the end of Reconstruction than any other state makes the trivialization even more problematic (Gussow 167; Lincoln, *Negro* 81).

The rhetorical blackface Gregg Allman dons is reinforced when the guitars of Betts and Allman, playing in unison, build toward the climax of the song. They take a four-note pattern up the A dorian scale in a rousing crescendo, culminating with two As as quarter notes, a pause, and one half note a full octave higher, thus mimicking the lash of the whip and the scream of the victim.[23] This is particularly unsettling to hear in a 2003 performance by the revamped lineup in Raleigh, North Carolina. The twin guitars of Warren Haynes and Derek Trucks, augmented by Gregg's organ and Oteil Burbridge's six-string bass, build to the familiar crescendo. But then the guitars' figurative cries of pain are accompanied by simultaneous cries of cognizant joy from the audience. And there is no reason to assume that this particular audience was significantly different in demographic makeup from what is the norm at ABB concerts, that is, almost exclusively white and predominantly male. In this regard, then, "Whipping Post," having become a favorite audience sing-along, constitutes the contemporary version of the minstrel show. There, as Eric Lott explains, the performers' "racial ventriloquism" met with an audience that "indulged in displaced blackface versions of themselves, 'went black'":

> In terms of ego-ideology, the male spectator was alternately his "black" self and black people's "manly" white superior, when, of course, "blackness" did not simply underscore a resistant sense of white "manliness" . . . It was in terms of his alter-ideology that he became a planter. The spectator may have intermittently identified with black characters [or, in this case, the whipping post so inextricably linked with slavery]—he had to if the minstrel show was to have its impact—but he always knew what he was *not:* a slave, whether of wages or of the plantation; *he* was no feminized (proletarian) subaltern. Here was a convenient fiction born in part of male panic, a gendered fantasy of renewed mastery over inferiors whose blandishments the mechanic enjoyed and whose pleasures he commanded. (197)

It is precisely this psychological dynamic that "Whipping Post" still conjures up in concert, early in the third millennium.[24] The chorus and climax of "Whipping Post" constitute a form of neominstrelsy, rhetorical and sonic, that trivializes the historical conscience represented by the pen measuring the gashes in Douglass's feet, or by the notes played by Handy's Tutwiler muse.

But where the minstrel show of the nineteenth century was designed to assuage all kinds of fissures tearing at the psychosocial fabric of the country's political economy—Ostendorf calls nineteenth-century minstrelsy a "symbolic substitute for material and economic bondage, a new contractual symbolism designed to take over from the whip and the lash" (70)—the ABB's "Whipping Post" cannot be dismissed entirely as updated minstrelsy because its music in fact *celebrates* fissures, deliberately creates them in the spontaneous flow of improvised performance. In other words, the discursive minstrelsy of the song's lyrics, Gregg Allman's racial ventriloquism, is counterweighted by the recognition of W. C. Handy's modus operandi, tapping the sheer limitless potential of the blues as an inherently *modernist* aesthetic. It is again worth pointing out here that Handy, too, got his start crisscrossing the South as a purveyor of minstrelsy, touring as the musical director of the highly regarded Mahara's Minstrels. As Lott also emphasizes, the minstrel show, "the first formal public acknowledgment by whites of black culture, was based on small but significant crimes against settled ideas of racial demarcation, which indeed appear to be inevitable when white Americans enter the haunted realm of racial fantasy" (4).[25] The "significant crimes," the subversion of socially sanctioned taxonomies of race and sound, occur in the *sonic* modernism of "Whipping Post," furnishing a paradoxical juxtaposition to the rhetorical minstrelsy of the lyrics.

First of all, (instrumental) music is a much more abstract system than language. Its much more complex referential capabilities issue from "the instability with which music, because of its unique emotional qualities and sensory recall mechanisms, threatens all discourse, especially writing," as Bruce Martin points out (21). Musicologist John Blackling has argued that in improvised musics in particular, sound is as meaningful as language in that it, too, constitutes (indeed, creates) systems of interdependent signs whose constantly changing processes must be understood in context (85–89). The one moment of sonic minstrelsy in "Whipping Post," the twin guitars' anguished cry of pain, is after all conditioned by the lyrics' *text*, and is not spontaneous either. Furthermore, this kind of metaphorical displacement of violence from lyrics to music grows out of the black blues tradition, too, perhaps most famously voiced in John Lee Hooker's "Boom Boom" (Gussow 228–32). As if to magnify the "significant crimes" and deemphasize the racial ventriloquism of discursive minstrelsy, the 2003 rendition of "Whipping Post" features tenor saxophonist Branford Marsalis as guest soloist. The Durham resident and Crescent City native reaches deeply into his Sonny Rollins bag of motivic improvisation for his solo and strategically deploys Trane-ish sheets of sound and altissimo screams as well, hence underscoring the ABB's jazz influences. Moreover, Marsalis has always been an artist attuned to the political implications of music—one of his earlier albums, recorded by the quintet he co-led with brother Wynton, was entitled *Black Codes (From the Underground)*—and has also consistently refused to be pigeonholed as a performer.[26] Finally, the edition of the ABB playing at the Alltel Pavilion that night fielded the most multicultural roster by far: joining the three remaining charter members Trucks, Jaimoe, and Gregg Allman, plus newcomers Haynes and Derek Trucks, were bass player Oteil Burbridge, who claims a part-Egyptian heritage, and jazz-fusion percussionist Marc Quinones, who is of Latin American descent.

Second, the ABB once again foregoes stylistic mimicry in favor of a dynamic, fluid performance, tapping deeply into the southern groove continuum's inherent modernism by improvisationally fragmenting the song into segments with different time signatures as well as weaving in musical "snatches" from a wide variety of source material. Like storytelling, music, especially when improvised, entails embellishing the passage of time, and the solos in "Whipping Post" tell a different story from the lyrics. On the 1971 *Fillmore* album, the song begins with Berry Oakley's menacing bass introduction in a most unusual time signature, namely, 11/8, followed by the counterpoint of the dual guitars. With the rest of the band joining in, the song switches to 6/8 for the head—or a swift waltz time, not coincidentally a favorite time signature with John Coltrane's classic quartet—and then Gregg Allman tears into his persona's blues.[27] Shifting gears to 2/4 for the chorus, a brief interlude again in 11/8 follows before Duane launches into his solo. Behind him, his brother's organ and Betts's guitar are comping a four-chord vamp of A minor seventh, B half-diminished, C major, and B half-diminished, but the solo section is already edging into the territory of modal improvisation, especially with Oakley's bass moving nimbly up and down the A dorian *scale*, not the chords.[28] Just as there is no set chorus length in modal jazz—which eschews the 32-bar AABA form of the standard or the 12- or 16-bar form of the blues—so do the solos here unfold not according to the underlying harmonic structure, but follow their own dramaturgy. In other words, the soloist, Duane in this case, is done with his solo when its own development of tension and release dictates. Bookending the first guitar solo is Gregg's restatement of the head in 6/8, the chorus in 2/4, and a brief interlude in 11/8 before it's Betts's turn. Betts, who seems much surer here of his phrasing and his rhythm than on the previous night, shifts to a 2/4 beat halfway through, egged on by Trucks, whereas the rest of the band maintains the steady 6/8 groove, resulting in a polyrhythmic layering. Toward the end of his solo, he pulls the band first briefly into 4/4, then into a rubato section before suspending the beat altogether. It is here that Betts weaves in a lick borrowed from Ornette Coleman's free jazz classic "Lonely Woman" before returning to 6/8 again. Another free rubato section precedes a 2/4 bridge, which in turn morphs into 6/8 again.

Then comes the menacing crescendo toward the song's climax, the disturbing call and response of the whip's lash and the victim's cry. Into the brief moment of silence that follows arrives Gregg's voice, unaccompanied for the first few words of the chorus before the whole band joins. Another free rubato segment propels Betts into resuming his solo, only this time he uses the A ionian scale. Again, it is he—possibly taking a page out of the playbook of beboppers such as Charlie Parker or Dexter Gordon—who weaves in another musical quote. What at first may sound like the lullaby "Frère Jacques" is actually a reference to one of Betts's heroes, Django Reinhardt, and his recording of "Danse Norvégienne," which in turn is derived from an Edvard Grieg composition based on Norwegian folk sources.[29] For the ensuing rubato that flirts with 4/4 time, Duane takes over from Betts, only in a minor scale again, and engages Trucks's tympani in a game of call and response that glides into a massive crescendo on B minor. Gregg restates the chorus in free time, the call and response now between the two Allmans and the two drummers. The song ends in a grandiose finale, out of which peel Trucks's tympani, which blend seamlessly into the next tune, "Mountain Jam."

The two guitarists first hint at the theme, taken in 4/4 time, in call-and-response fashion, tossing each other melodic phrases and fragments. After the theme, it is again Duane who takes the first solo. Now almost the entire performance is modal, with the musicians improvising over the E ionian scale.[30] His brother follows with a rare organ solo of his own, in which he utilizes the blues scale almost exclusively, ending it with a sly quote from Led Zeppelin's "Dazed and Confused," only one among many such interpolations throughout.[31] Dickey Betts, in his solo, displays another affinity with the bebop of the 1940s: an improvised phrase he would later develop into a fully fledged composition of his own, namely, the chart-topper "Jessica" (the ABB's sole single to take the top spot). This, of course, is the same procedure that Charlie Parker and others were wont to follow (Dyer 186). The call-and-response interlude with Duane that ensues shifts to chordal improvisation over E major and D major and ends with Duane's signature bird calls, high up on the neck of his Les Paul.

Then follows another trademark of the ABB sound, a lengthy drum solo by Trucks and Jaimoe. There have been other bands featuring two drummers: 38 Special, for instance, or most famously The Grateful Dead, and many of the classic Motown hits were recorded with two drummers as well, but none let their sound be defined and explored the possibilities offered by double drum sets as thoroughly: Trucks and Jaimoe truly are the ABB's engine room. Duane had originally gotten the idea at a James Brown concert: Brown—the Godfather of Soul or, as Ishmael Reed referred to him, "the Godfather of Everything" (Reed 30)—had been featuring two drummers in concert for a while, where matching the different yet complementary sensibilities of John "Jabo" Starks and Clyde Stubble-field supercharged the funk beat (Brown and Tucker 178; Freeman, *Midnight* 37; Guralnick 221–22; *Standing*). The juxtaposition of the different approaches of Starks and Stubblefield in Brown's band was accentuated even more by Jaimoe and Trucks in the ABB. Trucks, the former folkie, was usually responsible for anchoring the beat, while Jaimoe, the diehard jazzer, played over, under, and around his partner, but their truly telepathic interplay rendered this role assignment only a general trend. As Camp-bell, their drum technician, put it so memorably, "In those days, Butch and Jaimoe looked like two Cobras playing together and off of each other when they played the drums" (63). Here, on "Mountain Jam," Trucks leads off, all the while accompanied by Jaimoe, whose big ears accentuate Trucks's solo. When Jaimoe takes over, he dissects and deconstructs the beat—launching even into a few bars of hard rock—and especially his bass drum betrays the Gene Krupa influence, with a generous dose of Max Roach (Myers 58). Trucks then takes it back into the pocket, setting the stage for Berry Oakley's bass solo.

Oakley's function in the band also transcended the restrictive support-ing role usually accorded to bassists. In the ABB, his instrument became less of a rhythmic anchor and more of a third voice in the frontline, a prominence he achieved in part because of his characteristic sound marked by an aggressive attack courtesy of a thumb plectrum. Harking back to the mélange of different time signatures comprising "Whipping Post," Oakley's solo guides the drummers from 4/4 to 6/8 and merges with the twin guitars (quoting Jimi Hendrix's "Third Stone from the Sun") in 4/4 again. The full band joins in a 2/4 shuffle beat, launching Duane into a slide guitar solo. Several different shifts, from shuffle to 6/8 and to 2/4 and from modal to chordal, end in Duane leading the band into "Will the Circle Be Unbroken" in a stately 4/4. The rubato ending leads back to the theme of the song, with Duane and Betts again engaging in call and response. Another rubato section featuring Betts leads to the finale and the two chords that are the bedrock of the blues, the dominant and the subdominant seventh.

Therefore, "Whipping Post" alone meanders in and out of five differ-ent time signatures. Significantly, these recurrent shifts are mostly not prearranged, but grow organically out of collective improvisation.[32] As jazzer George Lewis points out, "In performances of improvised music, the possibility of internalizing alternative value systems is implicit from the start. The focus of musical discourse suddenly shifts from the individual, autonomous creator to the collective—the individual as a part of *global humanity*," and concludes that "improvised music, seen in historical terms,

[is] a transcultural practice" (110, 113; emphasis added). "Without Improvisation," seconds Joshua Redman, "Tradition and Innovation are reduced to imaginary and impotent adversaries, bickering fruitlessly over territory to which neither can lay rightful claim" (liner notes). In combination with "Mountain Jam," then, the ABB shows how the southern groove continuum extends not only from Christian hymns to electric Chicago blues, but from Handy's Mississippi River and Macon's Ocmulgee River— muddy waters indeed—to the Parisian Seine, Scotland's lochs, Hawaii's beaches, and the fjords of Norway. And so, the ABB's music, at its best, exemplifies in its modernism what Baraka in *Blues People* calls "the *lateral* (exchanging) form of synthesis, whereby difference is used to enrich and broaden, and the value of any form lies in its eventual use" (191). And it is the possibility of this kind of lateral transference that is sustained in the Afro-modernism of blues and jazz, the ABB's twin inspirations. The lateral synthesis achieved in the band's music therefore challenges received systems of taxonomy—musical, racial, regional, or other systems. Given this international, multiracial matrix, the Allman Brothers Band offers music—soundscapes—as a figurative ritual ground most conducive to decolonizing visually inscribed, petrified mappings of raciological categorization and thus swinging open, however fleetingly, doors to spaces that allow for the possibility of combining seemingly divergent and opposite forms of human experience and expression. For producer Tom Dowd, whose *palmarès* after all included such other classics as Coltrane's *A Love Supreme*, the ABB's *At Fillmore East* was simply "the greatest fusion album I've ever heard" (qtd. in Swenson 12).

To be sure, the ABB were not the first to hear in the ritual grounds of southern soundscapes a more democratic, egalitarian alternative—or, perhaps, utopia—highlighting the cultural transference of the blues aesthetic, of the southern groove continuum, across lines of color and genre where the South's historical burdens and the social practices arising from them are at least temporarily suspended. Blues shouter Eddie Boyd, usually very outspoken about the racism he encountered as a traveling performer, relays just such a temporary suspension, occasioned by transracial sounds of music, of the racial exigencies of southern society. Of one memorable gig at the Night and Day Club, a white-owned establishment on the outskirts of Clarksdale, Mississippi, the Delta capital of the blues, he recounts:

> So, they had a little dressing room out back of the club, and this white man, he put a strand of hay-baling wire across there and hung a whole string of potato sacks up there and put on one side "Niggers" and (on the

other side) "White Folks" (laughs). Those white boys [fellow musicians who also performed at the Club] took a knife and cut that sack down from end to end and piled it up in front of that nightclub and poured kerosene on it and set it afire. That was the hillbilly boys. That's why I have never been able to be no racist, because I learned better than that early. 'Cause there's a lot of people doesn't understand that how good some people is, and how real. 'Cause these cats didn't have to do that, man. They were Mississippians and that was in Mississippi. They really had a funny way of talking, 'cause they were uneducated cats, man, they played those fiddles and banjos. But they could play, man, and sing those hillbilly songs. He said, "What the hell this son of a bitch talkin' about? Putting a damn sheet up here between us and y'all. It ain't hardly step-pin' room in here. We play on the same stage. He [the owner] doesn't know music is natural international, don't give a damn what color he is." I say, "Hello, brother, welcome to the club." (237)

Boyd here limns a different crossroads of cultural exchange than does the Robert Johnson myth. In his account, the premises of the Night and Day Club have superimposed upon them the figurative club of musicianship, a "club" that is "natural international" and that transcends race.[33] In this club echoes the "Long Black Song" of Sarah's (utopian) vision, resounding with the harmonies of "men, black men and white men, land and houses, green cornfields and grey skies, gladness and dreams" that "were all part of that which made life good. Yes, somehow they were linked, like the spokes in a spinning wagon wheel" (154). For Ralph Ellison also knew, long before the Allmans did, that "[t]he master artisans of the South were slaves, and white Americans have been walking Negro walks, talking Negro-flavored talk (and printing it when spoken by Southern belles), dancing Negro dances and singing Negro melodies far too long to talk of a 'mainstream' of American culture to which they're alien" (*Shadow* 286). And conversely, the Father of the Blues himself initially made a living gig-ging in the Delta with music that was (or seems) decidedly unbluesy: "In the old days we had to play for dances the following: Mazurka, Polonaize, Berlin, Schottish, Quadrilles, lancers, yorkes, minuettes, etc. and Jim Turner and our bunch made up such dances impromptu that have never been set to music, which if done would compare very favorably with com-positions by leading composers of that style," catalogues W. C. Handy (Letter to Margaret Tubb).

Thus, music *can* transcend race. It did, for example, also in the famous Muscle Shoals Studios in 1960s Alabama, or at Stax in Memphis, where mostly white session musicians—Duane Allman among them—helped the

Queen of Soul, Aretha Franklin, and others record classic *black* music. It is difficult to argue with Les Black's contention that what was created in Muscle Shoals, deep in the heart of apartheid America, was a music that "blurred the lines of racial segregation through coloring sound. This was black music practiced and innovated by both blacks and whites" staking out "utopian soundscapes" that "provided the means to communicate across the line of color and produce a music that was culturally composite and also embodied an identifiable black cultural legacy" (251). But this sonic utopia was confined almost entirely to the oasis of the recording studio and did not exist outside of history, either. As veteran songsmith and vocalist Dan Penn muses, "In a strange kinda way we were in the background and it was the black folks who were up front. Suddenly, after Dr. King's death, it was over" (qtd. in Black 248). Seconds David Hood, bassist of the legendary Muscle Shoals Rhythm Section, "I learned so much about music from Otis Redding and all the other artists I worked with. They taught me how to play. But it was different after the assassination. That was the turning point" (qtd. in Kemp 6). And Stax pioneer Rufus Thomas confirms, "The death of Martin—the whole complexion of everything changed. It had to" (qtd. in *Respect*).

After the slaying of Martin Luther King, the rise of the ABB displayed perhaps the most visible continuance of interracial collaboration that had been so successful in the Stax and Muscle Shoals studios—certainly as far as the South was concerned (Guralnick 353–56). The ABB's multiracial personnel was unusual enough to be noticed early on by other southern rockers: Richard Young, who would go on to co-lead the Kentucky Head-hunters with his twin brother Fred, maintains that "[t]he thing about the Allman Brothers is that the word *brother* meant something. They had a black dude in that band, and you knew that they all had to wash in the same water spigot. Well, that was a big deal back then. It meant something. It stood for something" (qtd. in Kemp 219). The ABB's modernism grew out of an understanding of the historical divisions within southern ritual grounds and a confrontation with them. The musical inclusiveness of the southern groove continuum in performance was matched by a heightened social and political awareness of the band—Betts's engagement for Native American causes, or the band's support of Jimmy Carter's presidential campaign, for instance. There was also, in the early days, the ABB's unusual booking policy: when touring in the South, the band insisted on racially integrated seating. For example, the contract Capricorn's office negotiated with Albany Junior College (today Darton College) near the Georgia-Alabama state line in late 1970—more than a year before the release of *At Fillmore East* would propel the band to superstardom—contained a "RIDER TO BE ATTACHED AND MADE PART OF AFM CONTRACT NO. <u>524</u> DATED <u>December 10, 1970</u> BETWEEN <u>ALLMAN BROTHERS BAND</u> (HEREINAFTER REFERRED TO AS EMPLOYEE), AND <u>ALBANY JR COLLEGE</u> (HEREINAFTER REFERRED TO AS EMPLOYER.)," whose seventh paragraph read:

> 7. Employer agrees that admission to the engagement shall be open to all regardless of race, color or creed and that there shall be no segregated seating facilities based on race, color or creed. Artist shall be free to engage the services of supporting musicians of their choice without regard to race, color or creed. Non-compliance by the employer with the provisions of this paragraph shall give artist the right to cancel forthwith this agreement and in such event, any compensation paid or retained by artist and they shall be free of any obligations to employer for losses incurred and without prejudice to employees [*sic*] right to retain the full contract price. (American Federation)

This rider was part of all contracts the ABB made at that time, and the nature of the rider's other stipulations—all relating to general organizational technicalities such as catering, stage setup, power supply, and the like—as well as the convoluted syntax and mechanical error of paragraph 7 suggest the direct involvement of at least Duane Allman, the countersigner on all contracts (ABB 1971). It is also the only paragraph detailing consequences in the event of the employer's noncompliance.[34]

At the same time, however, the high likelihood of the ABB performing the discursive neominstrelsy of "Whipping Post" in the gym of Albany Junior College, just as they would more than three decades later in Raleigh, paradoxically accompanies the band's social activism and celebration of the southern groove continuum. The band's early home base, Macon, Georgia, exemplified yet another crossroads of the continuum. For Newton "Newt" Collier, Macon native and veteran of the bands of Otis Redding as well as Sam and Dave, his hometown was the last of "the three Ms in music" after Memphis and Muscle Shoals. Collier remembers a thriving music scene of about two dozen clubs and adds, "Otis Redding was the catalyst for everything."[35] Although "musicians [had] started to integrate themselves in different bands," the clubs themselves remained thoroughly segregated, and the only white musician who could play in the city's black clubs was Redding's best friend, Wayne Cochran, often billed as "the white James Brown" (Freeman, *Otis!* 71–73). Even the socially progressive ABB, insists Collier, remained "basically outsiders" throughout their sojourn in Macon. At least part of the reason for the band's now legendary free concerts in Atlanta's Piedmont Park was the fact that they didn't have any playing opportunities in Macon's black clubs: even Duane admitted that "the *only* way we could break into the scene was to try to play black music in white clubs" (qtd. in Freeman, *Midnight* 20; emphasis added). The band arrived in Macon at the nadir of the town's race relations: King's murder—here as elsewhere—had led to violent racial unrest, which was accompanied by the growing controversies over the desegregation of Baconsfield Park and Bibb County Schools as well as by the slaying of a black man by a white police officer (Manis 236–68). Ironically though, the success of the ABB worsened relations between Macon's black and white musicians. Collier is still bitter about Walden's Capricorn label shifting its focus exclusively to white rock and in effect forcing many of Macon's black musicians to relocate (Brent 47–55; Freeman, *Otis!* 113–45; Malone and Stricklin 111–16).

What both the story and the music of the ABB inadvertently amplify is the *tension* that marks southern ritual grounds as well as the southern groove continuum. "Whipping Post" is, then, a long black song, too, in a way, in that it foregrounds this tension: for all its democratic inclusiveness, ultimately music cannot transcend history, and "Whipping Post" fails to imagine a new *rhetorical* posture toward existence. Music, like narrative, entails the embellishing of time passing by. But just as the passage of time never occurs in a vacuum, so do storytelling and music-making, especially improvisation, never occur outside of the specific context in which they are performed. The historical whipping posts resound on the song's deeper (Ellisonian) frequencies as a telling inarticulacy that 'unmasks' the minstrelsy of "Whipping Post." Harking back to Oliver Nelson, then, the abstract truth is that music *can* transcend race. The *concrete* truth, however, is that music can never really transcend *history*. Not southern music, and not southern history, at any rate.

So—is the ABB's music 'black' music? Does, in other words, the field of tension that constitutes Afro-modernism overlap with the southern groove continuum? Given the direct connection between W. C. Handy's compositional techniques and the ABB's improvised performances, it would appear so. Which, in turn, raises one final, and very old, question: can white folks sing the blues? If blues is understood as a repository for an essentialized, 'authentic blackness'—a "blood ritual" as Baraka heard it—then the answer is clearly no (*Blues* 149). But if the blues aesthetic is understood as a product of an Afro-modernist sensibility, a sensibility that questions and challenges the socially and historically received binary pairs of the larger American culture—black and white, or blues and rock, for example—then, perhaps, what is 'authentic' in 'authentic' blackness is that the blackness of blackness in fact thrives on hybridity, that it har-nesses the possibilities of cultural production as well as simultaneously affirming the African American tradition. Perhaps, then, the southern groove continuum at its best manages to negotiate this field of tension successfully—perhaps, then, the southern groove continuum at its best is Afro-modernism straining to hear its historical conscience, sometimes succeeding ("Statesboro Blues"), and sometimes failing (the chorus and climax of "Whipping Post"). Trombonist George Lewis, for one, a long-standing member of the free jazz collective AACM (Association for the Advancement of Creative Musicians), insists that "African-American music, like any music, can be performed by a person of any 'race' without losing its character as historically Afrological," just as, say, a Schubert lied sung by Marian Anderson does not lose its character as what Lewis would call historically Eurological (93).[36] And so the blues, to Steven Tracy's ears, are "twelve sweet measures of humanity large enough to fit us all, but tight like that just the same" (7).

Thus, the crossroads of Robert Johnson are not just a locale where danger and opportunity, this world and the next, life and death, Euro-pean romanticism and Yoruban gods meet. In the third millennium, the meetings between white and black continue at that same crossroads still, engaging in rituals at once reactionary and visionary, trying to forge a bet-ter future but unable to transcend completely the exigencies of the past. And this, then, is perhaps the real abstract truth of the blues.

CHAPTER 5

Life and Death in the Dirty South

The Urban Ritual Grounds of Tayari Jones

The Allman Brothers Band is certainly the granddaddy of what the recording industry christened "new southern rock" around the turn of the millennium. The newest of the New Souths also seemed to demand a new southern rock music—yet most of the young white rock bands embraced neither the label nor the particular New South in which they had grown up, the South of the Sunbelt. It was a seemingly different South altogether that sounded the clarion call of musical resurgence in the last decade of the previous century. By 2004 the erstwhile dominant rap establishments on the East and West Coast respectively had been superseded by the

Dirty South, as almost half of the hip-hop music played on commercial radio that year originated south of the Mason-Dixon Line (Sanneh; Murray E1). The prediction that "The South's gonna do it again" had come to pass—just not in quite the way the Charlie Daniels Band's flag-waver imagined back in 1975. The Dirty South quickly became such an iconic ritual ground that its influence reached even into that other resurgent genre, new southern rock. Among its banner-bearers are the Alabama-bred Drive-By Truckers, who began as a rough-and-tumble country-rock band and then morphed into a latter-day Lynyrd Skynyrd for a time (the Truckers still retain Skynyrd's trademark triple-guitar attack) before finding a distinct voice of their own. Curiously at first glance, their path toward aesthetic independence culminated in the 2004 album they titled *The Dirty South*. Partly recorded in Muscle Shoals' FAME studios just south of W. C. Handy's birthplace, the record continues the Truckers' irreverent updating of the staples of southern mythology: requisite references to moonshine, televangelists, Elvis, church, NASCAR, outlaws—and, of course, the devil—are accompanied by a motley panoply in which NASA joins John Henry, Sam Phillips, Buford Pusser, a celluloid John Wayne, and Carl Perkins's Cadillac.

Although one reviewer clucked that the Truckers' new disc had "a clever title but remarkably little crunk," the album is also a nod to that part of the region that has produced what the band considers the most important new music (qtd. in M. Miller, "Dirty"). Leader Patterson Hood—son of David Hood, bassist of the legendary Muscle Shoals Rhythm Section that had backed Aretha Franklin, Wilson Pickett, and many other soul stars—has stated repeatedly that southern hip-hop had been absolutely vital in the band's development. *The Dirty South* was conceived during a phase when the Truckers, according to Hood junior, listened to nothing but "old-timey country and rap records" (qtd. in Lesemann; Hood, Interview). Most of the stories the songs tell are set in the late 1970s and early '80s—just before, Hood gripes in the liner notes, "they strip-mined and strip-malled us into bland suburbia and conformist complacency. . . . Hell, even our small towns have sprawl. In some cases, the sprawl predates the town. Many of the hard times being sung about in these songs have been replaced by even harder times. Sam's Club has got baloney in them big ol' sticks and we got free samples out the ass but our small towns and court house squares are being boarded up and torn down" (liner notes). Though the lyrics of hard luck and bad times emphasize that not all was good back then, there is nevertheless a certain nostalgia that suffuses the predominantly semirural, small-town settings of the songs. In this respect, *The Dirty South* is in line with a long tradition in white southern culture, where 'southernness,' however ambivalent and ambiguous a collective identity, is perpetually under siege.[1]

This, then, is what simultaneously echoes and differentiates the Truckers' South from the Dirty South of African American popular culture. The latter ritual ground is almost always thoroughly urban and rarely displays a sense of nostalgia for the olden days. By contrast, in contemporary black literary criticism the southern city is a setting that is not explored all that often, a tendency that finds its pendant in critical paradigms valorizing the vernacular and the folk, celebrating a "romance of the residual" (Dubey 158–70; duCille 80). The novels of Tayari Jones, however, provide ample opportunity to investigate southern cityscapes. Her urban ritual grounds of 'the ATL,' the undisputed capital of the Dirty South and what is often said to be the least 'southern' of all southern cities, undermine not only the sense of community and indeed humanity of their inhabitants, but also (vernacular) language and storytelling itself, and yet they still occupy a symbolical crossroads of history and modernity, race and class, life and death, love and loss. Jones's 2002 debut, Leaving Atlanta, set in the same era as the Drive-By Truckers' version of the Dirty South, explores the effects of the infamous Atlanta Child Murders on the lives of three fifth-graders, Tasha, Rodney, and Octavia, and their community.

James Baldwin had called it "the Terror" (27): the investigation of the Fulton County Task Force into the abduction and gruesome killing of twenty-nine children, mostly boys, that had begun in the summer of 1979 eventually led to the arrest of Wayne Williams, considered by some to be the first documented black serial killer. In January of 1982, Williams was convicted on two murder charges and brought to Hancock State Prison—a close-security facility located in, of all places, Jean Toomer's Sparta—where he continues to serve two life sentences today. But Leaving Atlanta focuses not on the grisly crimes, the ongoing controversies over both the police investigation and the trial, or the many conspiracy theories surrounding the killing spree.[2] Nor does it aspire to be a philosophical treatise on the geopolitics of race like Baldwin's take on the murders, The Evidence of Things Not Seen, or to supplement Toni Cade Bambara's 'docu-novel,' Those Bones Are Not My Child. Instead, Leaving Atlanta centers on the children themselves, but in doing so, it also probes an epistemological crisis that pits word against world, language against experience, sign against referent.

Leaving Atlanta, like Toomer's Cane, is divided into three sections, the first of which is titled "Magic Words." Set in the fall of 1979, when the string of killings was just beginning to register on the media's radar screens, the opening paragraph's southern-gothic setting already foreshadows the protagonist's fall from innocence into experience: "Hard, ugly, summer-vacation-spoiling rain fell for three straight months in 1979. Atlanta downpours destroyed hopscotch markers carefully chalked onto asphalt and stole the bounce from yellow tennis balls forgotten in back-yards" (3). The "growling thunder and purple zigzag lightning" was God talking, the children are told, as they "listened to the water smack against the window panes and figured that God's message must not have been meant for them to understand" (3).[3] The mystery of God's language as well as the section's title also point to Jones's ironic treatment of one salient theme in the African American literary tradition, the trope of lit-eracy. Upon her return to school, the protagonist, eleven-year-old LaTasha "Tasha" Baxter, is confronted with a world that does not seem to make sense anymore: she has diligently perfected her rope-jumping technique over the summer only to discover on the first day of classes that her peers dismiss it now as "baby stuff"; she finds herself ostracized at lunch hour by the complex politics of ever-shifting fifth-grade alliances; and, worst of all, her father, who has been having an affair, has moved out of their work-ing-class household (5). Tasha's first day back at Oglethorpe Elementary School is characterized by mystery and uncertainty, and for all of it the catalyst is the meaning of the word *separated*. Attempting to defend the state of affairs between her parents, Tasha clarifies to her nemesis Monica that "'[t]hey're not *separated*. They're *living apart* right now. It's different.' She paused for a minute, trying to explain what was different about her household and Monica's, or that of any of the other kids who didn't have a father anymore. She still had her daddy. He called her on the telephone almost every night and picked her up from ballet lessons on Tuesdays. *Separated* was different, harsher. Almost as bad as divorce. And not once had her parents used that word" (7). "Separated," her little sister DeShaun adduces later, "was kids who only had a mother to come and hear them say a poem on Black History Day. Or the ones who had stepfathers that they called by their first names" (11–12).

Piece by piece, Tasha's world begins to fall apart. Even though her father moves back in with her mother after the killings start, Tasha's tribulations continue as she struggles to make sense of the confusing world around her. Time and time again, it is the fallibility of words that is ulti-mately the source for all the uncertainty and fear that engulfs the eleven-year-old: "If it hadn't been for Monica saying *separated* that day, none of this would be happening," she even muses (52).[4] But Tasha also discovers that while language and words lack any mimetic, referential power in rendering the world around her more comprehensible, they can have a premonitory authority that is in fact destructive and deadly. In a schoolyard scuffle with Jashante, a thirteen-year-old classmate on whom Tasha actually develops her very first crush, she yells, "'I hope you die. I hope the man snatches you and . . . ' she searched in her mind for the word she had heard on the news. 'I hope you get asphyxiated and when they find you you are going to be . . . ' What was the other word? 'Decomposed'" (45). Later, when her father drives her home from the local skating rink where they happened upon Jashante and his friends, he observes that the boy will "be lucky to see the other side of eighteen" (68). Before long, the evening news reports that Jashante has gone missing, and Tasha blames herself for having cursed him, tearfully promising her mother "to be more careful with my words" (74). The axis of representation has spun completely out of control.

But it is not only the eleven-year-old Tasha whose navigation of the southern ritual grounds is disrupted. The grown-ups, too, struggle to construct a narrative with a representational axis to the puzzling cityscape they inhabit. Tasha's initiation into the realities of the southern ritual ground, modern, urban, and yet still fraught with the historical legacies of the South, comes when she stealthily overhears a conversation between her parents after dinner. Earlier that day, her father had joined a volunteer search party that ventured into a white suburb: "Out there where we went, is like where I grew up. It's a trip. Twenty-five miles outside of Atlanta and *bam*, back in Alabama" (78). As the father—angry, frustrated, confused, and terrified—begins to relate the events of the day in stops and starts, his wife attempts to soothe him, indicating that this was a story he did not really have to share. Hovering in the upstairs hallway, however, their eavesdropping daughter hopes to hear news, any news, of Jashante, who is still missing: "'Mama, let him say it,' Tasha whispered. Only words can undo words. Kids say that to take something back you have to say it backward. Like a filmstrip run the wrong way. *Die you hope I. Eighteen of side other*" (79). Instead, her father continues to seek out, desperately so, a connection between language and life as he pleads with his wife, "That's what I'm talking about. How can I say that I can't stand to talk about it? And how can you say that you can't stand to *hear* it when other people are *living* it?" (79). But once again, his story of the search explains very little, if anything at all. It certainly does not explain how and what Tasha is living—nor does it really explain what the community at large is living as the southern ritual ground traversed by the volunteers only widens the gap between sign and referent, defying any meaningful narrative deployed to unravel its mysteries: the father goes on to relate that he found only a dead dog in a garbage bag, but that another search party had happened upon skeletal remains in a lake, not too far from the Baxters' house in fact.

Not only is the father confused by the geography of the immediate terrain of his own neighborhood—he had not been aware of the existence of a lake so close by—the bones are not Jashante's either, but those of a little girl (80).

It is ultimately the father's story that Tasha overhears that completes her fall from innocence into experience, her initiation into the exigencies of the urban ritual ground she inhabits, a ground so treacherous that its very own rituals resist delineation in language and words. As she sneaks back to the bedroom she shares with DeShaun, her frightened little sister reminds her of a promise she had impatiently made weeks earlier:

> "Remember you said that there was a magic word to keep you safe."
> "Oh, that magic word," Tasha said, as if there were only one. Words could be magic, but not in the abracadabra way that DeShaun believed. The magic that came from lips could be as cruel as children and as erratic as a rubber ball ricocheting off concrete.
> "Shaun," Tasha said, "there's no such thing as a magic word."
> "Not at all?"
> "Not like you mean."
> "Oh," DeShaun said, with almost tangible disappointment.
> "Well," Tasha told her, "there is power. But—" She stopped, wanting to comfort her sister with more than flawed, uncontrollable words.
> "But what?" DeShaun pressed.
> "It's not a word; it's a charm." (81–82)

Tasha's epiphany reveals language as not necessarily powerless or ineffective, but certainly as mysterious, obfuscating, evasive, allusive, incomprehensible—as magic. In a gesture of helpless resignation, the charm Tasha passes on to her little sister is one of the green, tree-shaped air fresheners Jashante had been peddling on the side, the one he had given her at the skating rink shortly before his disappearance. Whatever powers language may possess, they cannot be harnessed to make sense of the world—neither Tasha's nor DeShaun's. And in whatever shapes they bend their words, they won't fit their souls, let alone protect them. Frederick Douglass's mighty pen has been replaced by a tiny air freshener. As a recurrent motif in the novel, the tree-shaped air freshener also harks back to Jean Toomer's *Cane* and its various narrator-observers' futile attempts to "[p]ush back the fringe of pines upon new horizons" (18). Consequently, the novel's first section releases the two sisters into a barren, urban wasteland, a postapocalyptic landscape whose symbolism freezes them in a perpetual suspension between nostalgic memory and ominous reality: "In autumn, oak trees drop acorns on Atlanta lawns and cover them with a quilt of decaying leaves. LaTasha Renee Baxter held her little sister's hand after school as they walked across their lawn, forcing the acorns under their feet into the red earth. The air stank of leaves burning in barrels, but Tasha recalled the clean outdoor smell of pine" (82).[5]

The nostalgia to which Tasha clings at the end of "Magic Words" is developed to a tragic extreme in the middle section, "The Direction Opposite of Home." Its protagonist is Rodney—portly, bespectacled, and highly intelligent, but "locked inside his own head," he is an outcast not only at school but also in his own home (44). He comes from a black upper-middle-class home, yet his authoritarian father is abusive, his maladroit mother bumbling. In contrast to the conventional third-person narrator of "Magic Words," the distinguishing feature of "The Direction Opposite of Home" is its narrative point of view: the disembodied narrative voice addresses the protagonist directly in the second-person singular. What is more, this narrative voice has total and complete access to Rodney's mind; it could access other minds just as easily and exhaustively, but it chooses not to.[6] The shift from the previous section's narration in past tense to the present tense here suggests that this disembodied, all-knowing narrative voice not only shadows Rodney step by step, but actually choreographs his every action and thought. The axis of representation is turned around: the narrative voice does not so much record mimetically Rodney's actions and thoughts as dictate them. The effect is that in this section, the narrative voice itself becomes stalkerlike: its relentless immediacy completely envelops Rodney and smothers (asphyxiates) whatever vestiges of agency and self-determination he may have been able to tap.[7] In her docu-novel of the Atlanta Child Murders, Toni Cade Bambara also uses a second-person narrative voice: *Those Bones Are Not My Child* is framed by two brief expository chapters summarizing the circumstances that led to the arrest of Wayne Williams and its aftermath. However, the narrative voice of the prologue and epilogue is a sympathetic companion to the nameless black mother, Bambara's alter ego, engaged in writing a book about the murders (C. A. Taylor 262, 271). Jones's experimentation with point of view in *Leaving Atlanta* is much more reminiscent of Toni Morrison's *Jazz* or Ann Petry's *The Street*—or William Faulkner's *The Sound and the Fury* and *As I Lay Dying*—than of Bambara's otherwise conventional narrative (Bleikasten 72–75, 201–8; Grandt 201–2).

In "The Direction Opposite of Home," the narrative voice's power—cool, even sarcastic at times, and deadly in its laserlike precision—contrasts dramatically with Rodney's own inability to express himself. "Since your words are almost invariably misinterpreted, you avoid speech in general and abstain entirely from rhetorical questions," instructs the narrative voice (87). Unlike his classmate Tasha, Rodney is already aware of the abyss between sign and referent, between the horrifying potentials residing in the urban ritual grounds and the language deployed to describe and contain them. Following Jashante's disappearance and the discovery of more bodies, the Atlanta Police Department sends a (white) officer to Oglethorpe Elementary to apprise the children of preventive measures and warn them of the possibility that the perpetrator may be posing as a member of law enforcement. But Rodney and the rest of the fifth-graders, terrified as they are, remain unresponsive, suspicious: "No one speaks. What all of you already know is too terrible to trust to unreliable words. . . . You know now, as undeniably as if you had read it in the World Book Encyclopedia, that Officer Brown has nothing useful to share. As a matter of fact, you are more fearful than ever to know that this man is all that stands between your generation and an early death" (94–95). Once again, the horrifying ritual that has the city in its grip resists verbal description.

It is not just the public drama of the killings that widens the chasm between word and world, but also the private, individual drama of Rodney. A tenuous friendship between him and the other social outcast, Octavia, is beginning to blossom, but, like Tasha, clinging to the belief that "[t]he antidote for words must be a spoken one," Rodney is misunderstood even in the simple act of uttering her name (101). Later, Rodney's father arrives at school to discipline him in front of his class for shoplifting candy, but the first word of his forced confession—a simple "I stole"—beaten out of him by his father's belt, is misinterpreted as "a cry of pain or admission of defeat," and during the second word, "Father speaks louder than you and the word is lost" (138). Even his confidential second confession, to his friend Octavia, is misunderstood: "'You told?' she says. 'Told what to who?' 'Never mind.' You reach into your pockets and give her . . . two cherry lollipops" (139). The innocent gesture here echoes that of his classmate Tasha in the earlier section, a pathetic gesture devoid of language.

Where Tasha's nostalgic yearning is for a time and a world that includes a living Jashante, Rodney's is much more escapist. Tasha's fall from innocence to experience occurs with her realization of the inefficacy of language in her world; Rodney's occurred with his birth into, considering the narrative voice, the world of language: "That night, you lie in bed trying to remember the time before you were born. Father said once, 'Boy, we talking about things that happened before you were even *thought* about.' This is the time that you want to recapture. You are curious about the state of not being, because this is certainly where people go when they leave their bodies in the woods for the police to find" (113). His suicidal nostalgia is intensified by the humiliating punishment he endures at the hands of his father, and at the end of that school day, Rodney does not embark on his usual route: "Nothing you know is in the direction you're heading. Home is the other way. You keep moving. . . . At Martin Luther King Drive you dart across four lanes of traffic against the blinking warning of the cross signal. Car horns scream, but the drivers accelerate when you find yourself alive and disappointed on the north side of the road. . . . Home is the other way" (139–40). When a blue sedan pulls up beside him with a driver claiming to be a police officer investigating a bank robbery nearby, Rodney not only notices a green air freshener shaped like a tree dangling from the rearview mirror, but immediately recognizes the badge the driver produces as a crude fake. Nevertheless, Rodney climbs into the car and is whisked away to certain death.

Symbolically, the terrain Rodney navigates here at the end of the novel's middle section is steeped in multiple layers of tragic irony. First of all, it is the disembodied narrative voice itself that literally sends Rodney to his death. In Frederick Douglass's archetypal southern ritual ground, the discovery of the power of literacy illuminated "the pathway from slavery to freedom"; here, language is just as powerful, but it is deployed—or, rather, deploys itself—to kill, not to liberate (38).[8] Moreover, Rodney's flight across Martin Luther King Drive harks back to the perilous journey of the runaway slave; only now, the only freedom to be found north of "the direction opposite of home," even in the newest of the New Souths, is the liberty that comes with death. Significantly, Rodney's last act after he has crossed the busy road named after the hero of the Civil Rights movement is one of passive resistance. Ironically, tragically, King's strategy to integrate the South Rodney turns on its head here: his act of climbing into the serial killer's car is an act of passive resistance against his violent, domineering father, his outsider status at almost all-black Oglethorpe Elementary, his seemingly hopeless life. Cruelly, the danger to Rodney and his peers—the still unfulfilled promises of the Emancipation Proclamation and the Civil Rights movement—emanates from within the black community itself (although the driver of the blue sedan, fittingly, is not identified as Wayne Williams). But perhaps the cruelest irony of them all is that the narrative voice may very well protect the community in sending Rodney to his certain death, for Rodney's mind and background actually point to some alarming possibilities: his obsession with death; his abusive father and distant mother; his outsider status at home, where his parents dote on his younger sister but, at best, ignore him; his outsider status at school, where he suffers constant teasing and bullying; his indifference to moral precepts (he realizes very well that shoplifting is 'wrong,' but never expresses any sincere guilt or remorse at all)—all of this amounts to a textbook background profile of a psychopathic serial killer. So at the end, perhaps with pitiless but final foresight, the narrative voice has Rodney "snatched" by the bigger, badder, grownup version of himself. Either way, Rodney's fate echoes Atlanta's original name—Terminus.[9]

The other outcast of Oglethorpe Elementary, Octavia Fuller, is the protagonist of the novel's last section, "Sweet Pea." Living in the projects with her single working mother, Octavia is heckled by her schoolmates as "the Watusi" for her jet-black skin (40).[10] Unlike Rodney or Tasha, precocious Octavia tells her own story in her own words. Even so, her section, too, highlights the unreliability of language from the very beginning: "My mother tells lies. She tells them all the time. For all kinds of reasons. Some of them make sense and other times it's like she lies just to hear herself talk. It gets tricky because she can mix a lie and the truth together so it ends up like Kool-Aid, and you can't really separate what's water, what's mix, and what's sugar" (143). More than any of the other characters, she is acutely aware of the chasm not just between sign and referent, but between signifier and signified, too. When her concerned mother attempts to defuse her daughter's fears with the usual euphemisms, Octavia retorts, "'Why everybody always say you lost somebody? Rodney not lost. They make it sound like you mislaid your lunch box or something.' Now I was the one irritated. People need to say the words they mean. Rodney not *lost*, he *dead*" (251).[11] The dissociation of word from world Octavia also notices in the shifting, multiple perceptions that attempt to circumscribe the rapidly changing ritual grounds of the newest of the New Souths: "Chicago is the windy city, but what is Atlanta? I asked Miss Grier [Octavia's teacher] one time and she say, 'Atlanta is the city too busy to hate.' Mama say it's the 'Chocolate City.' Kay-Kay [Octavia's cousin in Macon] probably think everybody up here smile all the time and eat Hershey Kisses wearing velvet dresses" (184).

In this respect, Jones's novel echoes Bambara's Atlanta, which is also marked by the paradoxical juxtaposition of the Second Reconstruction with the actual terror and confusion engendered by the killings: the newly polished image of the city is that of "*Gone With the Wind* Atlanta. New International City Atlanta. Black Mecca of the South. Second Reconstruction City. Hope of a bulk of Fortune 500 companies. Scheduled host of the World's Fair in the year 2000. Proposed site of the World University. Slated to make the Top Ten of the world's great financial centers" (18). In reality, Atlanta has become "a magnet for every bounty hunter, kook, amateur sleuth, soothsayer, do-gooder, right-wing provocateur, left-wing adventurer, porno filmmaker, crack-shot supercop, crackpot analysts, paramilitary thug, hustler, and free-lance fool" (5). And for James Baldwin, "Atlanta became, for a season, a kind of grotesque Disneyland" (11). All three of these narratives—Jones's, Bambara's, and Baldwin's—navigate the same crossroads of time intersecting in Atlanta, a city that, according to Eric Anderson, remains characterized by "natural and built urban environments that have, since the late 1970s, borne the conflicting burdens of memory and forgetting, of terror and banality, of old and new and never-changing and ever-changing Souths" (206).

It is precisely this burden that Octavia feels weighing heavily on her shoulders. Although of all the characters, she is best able to contend with the tragedies surrounding her, her mother, with a heavy heart, decides to send her away to live with her estranged father, who teaches at a South Carolina college. On the day of Octavia's departure, mother and daughter attend the funeral of Octavia's friend, Rodney Green. Her story ends as she and her mother wait for the taxicab outside of the church:

> She speaks and the lies curl from between her lips like smoke, getting into the fabric of my clothes and twining through my hair. "I love you," she says.
>
> Today is an ugly day. The clouds, dark and cold, hang close to the ground, like they might start raining gray ice and broken glass.
>
> I turn my face away from Mama and look toward Fair Street. I don't see the yellow taxi. For Mrs. Grier, all it took was a car trip and a eyelet pillowcase to make her forget her home. But not me.
>
> I'll be missing my mama for the rest of my life. (255)[12]

Ironically, and sadly, this is one of the very few instances in the novel where words *do* fit the world, where the accuracy of language is not undermined or diminished, where a character succeeds in shaping words to fit her soul. Octavia's mother truly *does* love her, and Octavia's loss of the camaraderie she has shared with her *is* real and permanent. The tone of the emotionally charged ending is in stark contrast with the concluding author's note, where Jones summarizes, in three short paragraphs and a language that is deliberately cool and detached, the Atlanta Child Murders and the Wayne Williams case. The note emphasizes a salient theme in "Sweet Pea," namely the complex relationship between the 'truth' and a 'lie' and how that relationship evinces itself in language. The author's note attempts to put forth, in a matter-of-fact, impartial language, a summary of the 'truth,' which Jones ends with the aloof *non sequitur* "I have made slight alterations to the chronology as it suits the purposes of the novel" (257). Everything preceding the author's note is a work of fiction and hence, by definition, a 'lie.' Tasha, Octavia, and especially Rodney exist only as verbal constructs, as text. However, these fictive constructs tell us much more about what it means to be human in a most terrifying southern ritual ground, and thus are much more 'truthful,' than the author's note—or, for that matter, the voluminous FBI case file, or any other nonfiction account. "Fiction," says Eudora Welty, "is a lie. Never in its inside thoughts. Always in its outside dress" (119). This, then, is also the reason why the author herself makes brief cameo appearances in each section: in "Magic Words," Tasha significantly mentions that she likes to sit next to little Tayari Jones, her classmate, in the cafeteria, "because she was really good at imitating people's voices"; in "The Direction Opposite of Home," Rodney spots Tayari sniffing glue during art class; and in "Sweet Pea," Octavia is relieved to hear her classmates direct their gossipy attention to Tayari's mother, president of the PTA, who "always came to the school wearing weird square shoes with laces up the front" (54, 165–66). Thus, in a novel that is very much about the epistemological crisis occasioned by the dissociation of word from world, the appearance of the one 'real' person, Tayari Jones, is not just the author's confrontation with herself, but also the author's confrontation with her craft—which, after all, is in some ways all about being "really good at imitating people's voices." It suggests that the chasm between sign and referent *can* be bridged after all, if 'only' imaginatively.

To put it differently, *Leaving Atlanta* corroborates what Ralph Ellison has called "the novel's capacity for telling the truth while actually telling a 'lie,' which is the Afro-American folk term for an improvised story" (Introduction xxii).[13] Jones's novel is therefore less a postmodernist text, despite its self-reflexivity, but engages a modernism with an historical conscience, and its postmodernist touches are extensions of an Afro-modernist aesthetic. The narrative technique of "The Direction Opposite of Home" constitutes perhaps the most recognizably postmodernist element, where Rodney Green's story comes into existence only in the interplay between the protagonist as the signified and the narrative voice as the signifier. The section exemplifies a postmodernism in which, as John Duvall puts it, "the self is always unavoidably elsewhere, only emerging in the act of inscription" (68). At the same time, Rodney's section, like the entire book, is suffused with a discourse of corporeality—recall, for example, the fifth-grader's obsession with dying or decomposing human bodies, his wish to escape his own physical existence, or the humiliating beating his father metes out at school. Rodney-as-text hence 'embodies' Christian Moraru's assertion that postmodernist texts can "pervade their material horizon because they are material, because their 'bodies matter,' too" (*Postmodern* 32).

Thus, even though Rodney does not, cannot, know how he fits into the larger text of history, the fact that his body isn't 'real' does not diminish the corporeality of those who actually lived through this particular time in history—on the contrary. For Jones herself, the Atlanta Child Murders are a "memory that we never spoke aloud but carried with us in our bones" ("Toxic" E1). Writing an op-ed piece for her hometown paper, the *Journal-Constitution*, on the reopening of the case in 2005, she lamented that "[t]he world has forgotten these murders because the victims were black and mostly poor. And I believe that on many levels this simple explanation is sadly accurate. But it cannot explain away the silence in my own community, the hush in southwest Atlanta, the home of many of the murdered children, the area of the city where many of those whose lives were directly touched still reside. The question still eats at me" (E1). Thus, bearing witness was not enough: "For us," she concluded, the memory

> is like a bone poorly set—painful, crooked, and gimpy. The events of 1979–81 so ravaged our community that we have been unable to speak of them in the years since. The arrest and conviction of Williams for the murders of two adults, and the subsequent closing of the children's cases, was neither balm nor tincture. Rather, it was just a plaster cast, ensuring that the fractured bones of our community would never properly mend.
>
> Re-examining this case will cause great pain to Atlanta, the city of my birth, the place where my family still lives. I don't anticipate that this will be easy. Tempers will flare, as will old rivalries and grudges. But as we know, the only way to repair a bone badly set is to break it again, and then set it right. (E1)

Thus, Jones's shaping words to fit her memory is done not only to reawaken historical consciousness, but, much like Frederick Douglass placing his pen in the gashes on his feet (or later standing before Niccolò Paganini's violin), to tap a historical *conscience*—an act that surpasses mere witnessing and remembering.

In the world of *Leaving Atlanta*, the southern ritual grounds' historical legacies manifest themselves also in the characters of the fathers. Tasha's father, as I have already pointed out, is reminded that the new, post–Civil Rights urban South he inhabits has not left behind southern history after all, even though the younger generation may not be aware of it, when he volunteers to join the search party. Rodney's father, an unapologetic advocate and practitioner of corporal punishment, lectures his son over breakfast about the benefits of the Washingtonian pull-yourself-up-by-your-own-bootstraps philosophy his own father had passed on to him, and when his wife attempts to defend Rodney's failing grades by arguing that he may not be challenged enough at school, Claude retorts sneeringly, "Challenged? . . . This boy's problem is he never had to pick cotton. When you pick cotton you don't sit out there and see if you can be *challenged* by the cotton. You don't bring your bag in empty at the end of the day and tell that white man that the cotton didn't *challenge* you. You just pick the goddamn cotton!" (128). In a sense, then, Claude Green is therefore perhaps as much a victim of southern history as he is a perpetrator of abuse.[14]

The father figure, however, is noticeably absent in the novel's last section. Ray, as Octavia refers to her father, appears only as a voice on the telephone. But "Sweet Pea" does not need a father figure because Octavia, precocious as she is, has already been exposed to and is beginning to understand, if only dimly, the exigencies of southern history, both personal and communal, in her contemporary ritual grounds. First of all, Octavia is learning how to face her personal history by telling her story in the past tense. Second, her mother's stories of growing up in racially segregated Macon—the original Allman Brothers Band's home base—have prepared her, in contrast to Tasha and Rodney, to recognize the continuities, subtle as they may be, between the pre- and the post-Civil-Rights-era South, her communal history. Accordingly, the open-ended "Sweet Pea" delineates a southern ritual ground that contains possibilities as well, beset with profound ambiguities though they are. As Ellison maintains, "fiction is but a game of 'as if,'" yet "therein lies its true function" (Introduction xx). While the quasi-postapocalyptic urban landscape of the final goodbye-scene echoes the gothic foreboding of the initial setting of "Magic Words," Octavia, at the end, is facing "Fair Street," suggestive of a future that holds at least the possibility of renewal and redemption—quite unlike the fate of her unfortunate friend, Rodney. On the other hand, Octavia, like her literary ancestor Huck Finn, none too thrilled at the prospect of being "sivilized," is about to be sent to South Carolina—after all, the first state to secede from the Union. There is, for her, no more territory "to light out for" in the Sunbelt South (Twain 49, 367). Even so, her father, who is a professor at a college in Orangeburg, is presumably teaching at South Carolina State or at Claflin University, two historically black institutions, where Octavia will therefore be at least somewhat sheltered from the more egregious, lingering manifestations of unreconstructed racism. There *is* a future for her beyond the terrain haunted by the Atlanta child murderer, even as that future comes at the cost of being separated from her mother. Accordingly, Octavia's narration shifts from the past tense to the present tense in the novel's very last scene, and then shifts to future tense in Octavia's touching last words, "I'll be missing my mama for the rest of my life" (255).

For the time being, though, Octavia feels unjustly disempowered. It is this sense of entrapment delineating the fate of each of the three major characters, albeit to various degrees, that informs this urban ritual ground of the post-Civil Rights era. Nelson George, riffing on Stephen Henderson's "'Soul-Field' of the black experience," has called its African American denizens the "post-soul generation," and indeed, the urbanized southern ritual grounds traversed in *Leaving Atlanta* bear a striking resemblance to what has become but the latest reincarnation of the New South, the Dirty South (Henderson 49; George 3–11; Neal 3). In its original cartography by the Atlanta-based hip-hop group Goodie Mob on their 1995 debut album *Soul Food*, which primarily maps the East Point suburb and its vicinity, the Dirty South is a territory fraught with injustice, betrayal, and confusion. Although *Soul Food* is not fueled by the disconnect between sign and referent as is *Leaving Atlanta*—after all, hip-hop is a musical genre in which rhetorical prowess and virtuosity are at a premium—the album's ritual grounds similarly engender a pervasive sense of disorientation. On the claustrophobic track "Thought Process," guest vocalist André 3000 (one half of the Atlanta rap duo OutKast) notes that

> Now as an outkast I was born,
> Wasn't warned of the harm
> That would come to meet me like Met Life,
> But yet life done sent me through a lot of ups and downs like it ain't
> > nothin'—
> Like elevators, but I ain't the one that's pushing the buttons.
> I got off at the thirteenth floor when they told me that it wasn't one;
> They said it skipped from twelve to fourteen.

The sense of disorientation acquires special poignancy here considering that the elevator analogy harks back to the rhetoric of racial uplift—and is set in the same southern city that, by 1908, had implemented racially segregated elevators (Woodward, *Origins* 355). The starkness of this ritual ground is reinforced, here as elsewhere throughout the album, by the minimalist beats and arrangements of the production squad Organized Noize. It is therefore no coincidence that in this urban landscape of disorientation and confusion where "[w]e trapped off in this maze with walls made of layers," the infamous "child snatcher" also has a cameo appearance: "Huh, the only thing we feared was Williams, Wayne," André volunteers. The child murders had exposed a side of Atlanta, "the Black Mecca of the South" and "the city too busy to hate," that had remained invisible to many during its dizzying economic rise: in 1980 about one-third of the city's population subsisted below the national poverty level, and almost all of the victims came from the underclass of the working poor (Headley 14, 26). Fifteen years later, Goodie Mob reminded those atwitter with the excitement of hosting the world for the 1996 Olympic Games that this 'other' Atlanta was still very much around.

Like the characters in *Leaving Atlanta,* Goodie Mob and their collaborators inhabit a territory where they appear to be trapped, tragically so, in an inescapable present. *Soul Food*'s splintered, fragmented, confusing southern landscape is also suffused with a pervasive sense of entrapment: on the satirical "Live at the O.M.N.I.," for example, Goodie Mob transform the name of the Atlanta landmark from an entertainment and sports venue into an acronym for "One million niggers inside." It is a Dirty South that *seems* to have left history behind. This, then, also reflects the significant shift in African American cultural production that Mark Anthony Neal has diagnosed:

> The post-soul generation becomes the first generation of African Americans who would perceive the significant presence of African-American iconography within mass consumer culture/mass media as a state of normalcy. It is within this context that mass culture fills the void of both community and history for the post-soul generation, while producing a generation of consumers for which the iconography of blackness is consumed in lieu of personal relations, real experience, and historical knowledge. (121)

However, "Dirty South," the track that codified this, the newest of the New Souths, also implies that the current, bleak present of crime, drugs, corruption, poverty, and despair is indeed in part the legacy of southern history: "See, life's a bitch, then you figure out / Why you really got dropped in the Dirty South. / See, in the third grade, this is what you told: / You was bought—you was sold." Just as Tasha's father complains bitterly, "I won't hush. That's the problem. We been hushed up too long. These children don't know nothing about lynching. They don't know about white folks burning niggers alive" (76–77). Goodie Mob, in the booming 1990s, attack not just a sociopolitical power structure that continues to thrive—if by other, more complex means—on the continued subjugation of Americans of African descent, but also a complicit educational system that trivializes the history of blacks in the New World and ignores their suffering. The result is not just a sense of betrayal but also a pervasive uncertainty: if Goodie Mob's Dirty South does not so much defy the very language deployed to map its geography, their rhymes still capitulate often before the underlying reasons that inform the rituals of death and deprivation taking place within its boundaries: "I struggle and fight to stay alive / Hoping that one day I'd earn the chance to die. / Pallbearer to this one, pallbearer to that one— / Can't seem to get a grip 'cause the palms sweatin'" ("I Didn't Ask to Come").[15] The origin for this pervasive uncertainty, Toni Morrison would now counsel, lies in the absence of "[t]he advising, benevolent, protective, wise Black ancestor" who "is imagined as surviving in the village but not in the city," and certainly there is no such ancestral spirit in either Jones's Atlanta nor in Goodie Mob's Dirty South ("City" 39). Even so, *Leaving Atlanta* and *Soul Food* do not represent so much a break with the (literary) past as a transference of the rural Black Belt's vernacular semiotics into the city: yes, the ancestral spirit is present indeed in Jean Toomer's *Cane*—in the person of Father John, for instance—but Toomer's various observer-narrators consistently fail to capture its essence in words. The absence of any ancestral spirits in the Dirty South of Tayari Jones and Goodie Mob is counterbalanced by a *conscience* that recognizes the legacies of history in a landscape that places "one million niggers inside" a postmodern temple of mass spectacle—a landscape that continues to put Americans of African descent 'in their place.'

To be sure, since Goodie Mob's initial staking out of Atlanta as the capital of the Dirty South, this territory and its rituals have undergone many alterations and transformations. Southern hip-hop, previously dismissed somewhat derisively as "south coast" or "third coast" rap, found in the flexibility of its ritual grounds a launching pad that catapulted the Dirty South from the rap underground into the cultural mainstream (Krims 145–46; M. Miller, "Rap" 181). But even in some of its commercially successful variations, often utterly devoid of historical consciousness, let alone conscience, its urban landscapes sometimes defy, if not language itself, then any reasonable explanations for why "you really got dropped / In the Dirty South." This is the case in fellow Atlanta rapper Ludacris's "Growing Pains" from his 2001 hit album *Word of Mouf*. The Dirty South of Ludacris and his Disturbing Da Peace posse is "dirty" in a different way from the ritual grounds navigated by Goodie Mob. Ludacris's Atlanta is characterized by stability and certainty: its braggadocios, gregarious macho-hedonism leaves little room, if any, for social satire or political commentary, certainly not for contemplative uncertainty. Even so, "Growing Pains," though uncharacteristic of the rest of the album, is, like *Leaving Atlanta*, suffused with a pervasive sense of nostalgia tempered by violent death. In its specificity, Jones's novel might at face value be mistaken for merely a contemporary update of the local color school of writing, but it actually negotiates a tension between a nostalgic look back at childhood on the one hand and violent death on the other very similar to that of "Growing Pains" (a nostalgia not unlike the one both cultivated and satirized on the Drive-By Truckers' *The Dirty South*):

> Played with Transformers, G.I. Joes and Thundercats—
> We was loving that
> Before they started jacking Jags,
> 'Fore notes from Red Oaks had folks scared to come through
> College Park after dark—
> Crown Victorias, police unmarked cars,
> Be aware: Wayne Williams was out there.
> But we didn't care kids was getting stabbed and ditched out there:
> Too busy playing double-dare.

The specter of Wayne Williams, evoking here a very different facet of southern history, disrupts the nostalgic look back, if only briefly, and is in stark, ironic contrast to the 'old school' sample—the signature guitar riff is lifted from William Bell's Stax hit "I Forgot to Be Your Lover"—and to the voices of children at play that frame the track. "Growing Pains" thus corroborates Jeff Abernathy's point that "[t]he American Eden—ever a racially charged atmosphere—is always ready for the fall," in the South in particular (156).

It is the loss of innocence that is also at the center of Jones's second novel, *The Untelling*, set in the West End neighborhood of pre-Olympics Atlanta.[16] Like its predecessor, this novel too revisits and revises the central tropes of the African American literary tradition such as invisibility, naming, and literacy. But now it is no longer so much the southern landscape itself that is the site of confusion and disorientation, but the southern body, especially the female body.[17] The catalysts for the individual, quieter dramas of *The Untelling* are found in the body of Aria Jackson, the narrator, who experiences a false pregnancy and is later diagnosed with extremely rare premature menopause at the age of twenty-five. "A sensible person," muses Aria upon leaving the doctor's office,

> would have taken a home pregnancy test first. I hadn't because I was convinced I knew my body. Now I couldn't even take the expression seriously. What did it mean, to know your body? This was a phrase that I'd picked up from women's magazines and television talk shows. I'd been living in this body twenty-five years and it was a stranger to me. I had gone through the Change and hadn't even seen the signs. Dr. Blackwelder had said that it was easy enough to miss, that my body had been responding to the years of birth control pills I'd swallowed, taking

its cues from the synthetic hormones. But still, a person who knew her body should have known that something was seriously wrong. I felt like an idiot, like the wives who are always the last to know. (162)

Aria's alienation from her own body, her rare physical condition, and her strong desire to bear a child are exacerbated by the fact that seemingly everyone she knows has children of their own already, even if they hadn't wanted any: seventeen-year-old Keisha, Aria's foil, is pregnant with her second child, which she also wants to give up for adoption; Aria's boyfriend, Dwayne—a locksmith, no less—has a son living in Alabama; her baby sister was born despite her mother's tied tubes and is hence referred to as the Jacksons' "miracle child" (2); her older sister Hermione bears witness to the family legacy after having married her prematurely deceased father's best friend and given her firstborn her father's name; and her best friend and roommate, Rochelle (who is herself adopted), had an abortion in college.

It is Rochelle who sports the most visible corporeal idiosyncrasy: she is the same age as Aria, but her hair color has aged prematurely and is "as white and sparkly as the snow" (209). Her trademark is an expensive pen "stabbed . . . into her hair like a chignon stick" (36). Back in college, she and Aria became friends when she confided that she was pregnant and Aria agreed to lend her money for an abortion. What convinced Aria that Rochelle had not lied to her, did not have a drug problem, but really did need help, was when Rochelle "leaned forward, showing me the groove where she'd split her hair apart with the pen. The part, marked with blue ink, was flanked by Rochelle's new growth; her real hair was kinky in texture and the soft gray color of old roads" (57–58). Aria lent her what little money she had because, she concluded, Rochelle "had told me her truth and shown me her hair" (59). Thus, the pen in Rochelle's hair fulfills the same symbolic function as the pen in the gashes of Frederick Douglass's feet, tracing the same old road: the instrument of literacy as a measurement of the wounds of the past and their import in the present. Like Douglass's, Rochelle's parentage is uncertain, and like the nineteenth-century autobiographer, she too is concerned with literacy as a form of social activism: Rochelle works at the Literacy Action Resource Center (LARC for short), which trains juvenile delinquents, all of whom are black and female. That Rochelle has neither the time nor the inclination to write the invitations for her upcoming wedding and outsources the job to Keisha, the pregnant seventeen-year-old charge of LARC who is functionally illiterate but extremely talented at calligraphy, is just another one of the many ironies marking *The Untelling*'s southern ritual grounds.

But, even more so than in *Leaving Atlanta*, these are personal dramas, nowhere near as epic as Douglass's battle of civilization against barbarity. For the characters, though, their significance is little smaller. They may not have developed a historical conscience of their own, or may be only dimly aware of it, but *The Untelling* certainly is, and the novel casts it also in one of the most southern of southern symbols, the magnolia tree: it is such a tree, a century old and surrounded by dogwoods, that years ago claimed the lives of Aria's father and baby sister in a car accident—on their way to the annual spring recital at the Phillis Wheatley YWCA, so named after another former slave who availed herself of the power of literacy. The final two paragraphs of Aria's story end the novel with a Faulknerian (or Ellisonian) indeterminacy, one that is again linked to the continuing reassessment of historical conscience in the form of the magnolia tree overgrown with dogwoods:

> There is balm in the telling, and in the hearing too. These words, these truths, will ride on the air like ragged scrap of song. With every lamp burning I will speak while Dwayne touches my hands and listens. I will ask him what he knows about the dogwoods, crooked and ashamed, their stained petals an annual remembrance. Although Hermione is right about a great many things, she was wrong about the nature of things gone by. This is what I have come to know: Our past is never passed and there is no such thing as moving on. But there is this telling and there is such a thing as passing through. (324)[18]

The sudden stateliness of the diction, its self-consciousness that recalls Jean Toomer's hapless narrator-observers bent on catching the "spirit" of the place, casts doubt on the integrity of the epiphany, especially since Aria is someone who is given to acting out roles well disseminated throughout mass culture—from sitcoms such as *Good Times* to Anita Baker songs or movies such as *Lady Sings the Blues*—and most especially in her desire for marriage and motherhood. But Aria has begun to transform herself, from a mere witness of family history to an advocate of its meanings, through acknowledging the historical conscience symbolized by the dogwoods. The Toomeresque songs carrying "truths" she imagines wafting through the Atlanta air, the shaping of words to fit her soul, will probably take on manifestations different from the songs of the Drive-By Truckers. But they arise out of the same puzzling, paradoxical Dirty South.

The semiotics of the Dirty South as arranged by Goodie Mob, the South of Tayari Jones's post-soul generation, suggest that there are new borders to be negotiated within southern culture in general and southern literature in particular. And so, for Jones, "Atlanta is the perfect setting for dramatizing the modern American predicament. . . . In my view, this is where the rubber hits the road in America" ("(Un-)Telling" 71–72). At the same time, Jones's relationship to her native region remains as ambivalent and complex as that of her literary forebears. She recalls that her first big lecture tour took her

> out on the Southern Circuit. That would be Jackson, Oxford, Memphis, Blythesville, Arkansas—you get the idea. And I found myself interacting with self-avowed 'southern' writers and the people who love them. While many of the people were quite kind and even interested, it was clear that my brand of southernness . . . one that is black and urban and middle class, was clearly out of place in these settings. I still hold on to my 'southern' badge however, because the South is my home. But I feel sort of uneasy. (72)

It is that same uneasiness which Jones lends her protagonist in *The Untelling*. There, Aria remarks about someone who would not feel displaced anywhere within the territory of the old Confederacy, "His accent was sugary, southern white. Whenever I heard someone speak that way, the words so lazy they seemed to be lying down, it made me feel like only white people were really southerners. That the rest of us were just squatters" (65–66).

Jones's Afro-modernism therefore recalls what Hugh Kenner apprehended back in 1975, and what seems still relevant in the new millennium: "the homemade world of American Modernism terminates not in climactic masterworks but in an 'age of transition'—we live in it—where the very question gets raised, what the written word may be good for" (*Homemade* xvi). Accordingly, the image of Du Bois's blackboard recurs in Jones's Sunbelt South as well. In *Leaving Atlanta*, for example, Octavia seeks counsel from her former second-grade teacher and mentor, Ms. Grier, as she is worried about being sent away to live with her biological father in South Carolina. Ms. Grier tries to console her by sharing a story from her own childhood, about the premature death of her parents and her growing up in the home of relatives. As she is recounting these reminiscences, Octavia is cleaning the blackboard in the classroom—or trying to: "I had the whole board wiped down but soon as it dried, traces of the chalk letters started showing through again. I dunked my rag in the water and started over" (234). Octavia, ironically the most articulate of the children in the novel, confesses to having "word problems" and even has her spelling book stolen at school (140). Yet, her story is the most "telling," one whose articulacy on an emotional level surpasses even the laserlike precision of the narrative voice stalking her friend Rodney. Words, stories, may be infested with incurable inarticulacy—but, as Nathaniel Mackey's phrase underlines, it is a *telling* inarticulacy: language remains the primary means by which we attempt to make sense of the world around us and by which we seek to explain our humanity to it, and to ourselves.

In *The Untelling*, Du Bois's blackboard has been slightly transformed. After Aria follows her friend Rochelle to a teaching position at LARC, she is shocked at the Center's dilapidated, ramshackle infrastructure. The blackboard has been demoted to a dry-erase board, but there is an overhead projector:

> I dimmed the light and clicked on the overhead projector. In the dark, with the door closed and the shades down, I was aware of the room's narrow dimensions. It was silly, really, to think that an old house could be converted into a school. . . . Idealistic and silly. This room was not a classroom. Where was the chalkboard and the pull-down map of the world? This was a bedroom and a small one at that. We were eleven people crammed into metal desk chairs, which were then all crammed into a guest bedroom. What did we really think we were accomplishing here? To teach students this far behind you needed computers, current hip textbooks. Hell, you needed a real teacher. Not just me and Rochelle, people hired for our "energy."
>
> I heard myself asking for a volunteer to read a passage beamed onto the white bedsheet used as a projection screen. (164)

Aria's sense of claustrophobia, deprivation, and futility not only echoes Goodie Mob's but also reinforces the dramatic division into two distinct territories, for LARC is indeed a world away from, say, Atlanta's Emory University, or even Aria and Rochelle's alma mater, Spelman. And so, Aria the college graduate, still behind the veil, reenacts the role of Du Bois the former Fisk University student. Revisiting this particular tract of his southern ritual grounds in his autobiography, Du Bois conspicuously leaves out the pale blackboard; instead, he adds the following sentences tailing the description of the treacherous floorboards: "All the appointments of my school were primitive: a windowless log cabin; hastily manufactured benches; no blackboards; almost no books, long, long distances to walk. On the other hand, I heard the sorrow songs sung with primitive beauty and grandeur. I saw the hard, ugly drudgery of country life and the writhing of landless, ignorant peasants. I saw the race problem at nearly its lowest terms" (117). Whether post-Reconstruction, rural Watertown, Tennessee, or pre-Olympics, metropolitan Atlanta—"the meaning of progress," it seems, can often be measured in inches.

It is quite exciting to hold the center of the national stage,
with the spectators not knowing whether to laugh or to weep.

—Zora Neale Hurston, "How It Feels to Be Colored Me"

CONCLUSION

"The Biggest Colored Show on Earth"

Afro-Modernism, Hip-Hop, and Postmodern Blackness

"I have never, in all my journeys, felt more of an interloper, a
stranger, than I felt in Atlanta," confessed James Baldwin in his
treatise on the child murders, *The Evidence of Things Not Seen* (55).
Visiting the "new" Atlanta only a few years after the ghastly string
of killings, professional tourist V. S. Naipaul continued to be befud-
dled by the city as well (25–27, 57). His diagnosis of Atlanta's race
relations deduced that "there were two world views here almost,
two ways of feeling and seeing that could not be reconciled" (58).
At the end of his "turn in the South" he mused in Toomeresque
tones, "But in this flat land of small fields and small ruins there
were also certain emotions that were too deep for words" (296).

Both Baldwin and Naipaul discovered the same paradox W. E. B. Du Bois had accentuated almost a century earlier, when he referred to Atlanta as the "Gateway to the Land of the Sun" and as the capital of "the Land of the Color-line," exemplifying how the South in general was a very "odd world" indeed (*Souls* 48, 128, 43). In a sense, they all had been on the hunt for answers to the famous questions posed in another unmistakably southern tale: "*Tell about the South. What's it like there. What do they do there. Why do they live there. Why do they live at all*" (Faulkner, *Absalom* 142). William Faulkner's Shreve, the Canadian medical student, discovered when he posed these questions to Quentin, the quintessential white southerner, in their frigid New England dorm room, that there is a South that keeps eluding words. And, paradoxically, for this exact reason it is all the more vital to "tell about the South" again and again, to reimagine it anew.

In some ways then, Goodie Mob's Dirty South echoes Baldwin's sense of alienation even as it attempts to provide an answer to Shreve's queries. Listening to the Dirty South's topography as the soundtrack to Tayari Jones's fiction also limns a trajectory of Afro-modernism that segues into postmodernism. As musicologist Adam Krims notes: "It seems, at times, that rap music would have to have been invented by postmodern theory, had it not been there, poised to exact its tribute" (8). Extending Craig Werner's paradigm of the three key themes of modernism, hip-hop makes readily audible (and visible) the three key themes of postmodernism: disjunction, textuality and parody, and simulacra. Generally, where modernism's concerns tend to revolve around the dissociation of sign from referent, postmodernism tends to explore the interplay between signifier and signified. Hip-hop's electronic sampling of beats and melodic fragments indulges in an aesthetic of disjunction; textuality (in its widest sense) and parody are evident in rap's relentless self-referentiality and aggressive competitiveness; and there is the proliferation of simulacra, the performative demarcation of a geographic terrain—the "'hood" as *genius loci*—whose borders are often patrolled by highly stylized personae. Hip-hop scholar Russell Potter is among those who have pointed out how the cultures of the African diaspora anticipated, by centuries actually, in many ways not just modernism, but postmodernism as well: "Living, talking, making music, and writing in the subjectivity of resistance that was built—*had* to be built—against the economic and philosophical bulwarks of slavery and colonialism, black cultures conceived *postmodernism* long before its 'time' as construed by writers who had to wait to take their cue from Derrida, Foucault, or Lyotard" (6).

In situating hip-hop squarely within a historical continuum, Potter at the same time also alludes to how contemporary African American cultural production often impugns the white noise of "*il n'y a pas de hors-texte*" that would demote both human experience and history to the status of, in Paul de Man's words, "a purely linguistic complication" (Derrida 158; de Man, "Resistance" 92; Lehman 93–104). Interestingly enough, Jacques Derrida's (in)famous proclamation that there was no outside-the-text, one of the more controversial flashpoints of the critical project of deconstruction that accompanies postmodernism, occurs in the section in *Of Grammatology* in which Derrida reads the autobiography of Jean-Jacques Rousseau, *Confessions*.[1] In the same paragraph, Derrida writes that

> in what one calls the real life of these existences "of flesh and bone," beyond and behind what one believes can be circumscribed as Rousseau's text, there has never been anything but writing; there have never been anything but supplements, substitutive significations which could only come forth in a chain of differential references, the "real" supervening, and being added only while taking on meaning from a trace and from an invocation of the supplement, etc. And thus to infinity, for we have read, *in the text*, that the absolute present, Nature, that which words like "real mother" name, have always already escaped, have never existed; that what opens meaning and language is writing as the disappearance of natural presence. (159)

Even if we should therefore have read, in Frederick Douglass's text, that the gashes in the autobiographer's feet "only come forth in a chain of differential references," the point is that *somebody's* frostbite scars surely did exist, but were never recorded by history-as-text. Moreover, "what opens meaning and language," for Douglass as much as for Goodie Mob, is 'writing' as an act that makes 'apparent' the shortcomings of (mis)representation of whatever the surrounding culture deems a "natural presence" at any given time, (mis)representations that can and do have an impact on "the real life of these [black] existences of 'flesh and bone.'"

Thus, Madhu Dubey notes that "[s]ome idea of the real that eschews both organicism and technological fetishism, innocent mimesis and textual inflation, seems urgently needed in the postmodern era," not least because in our own time, "[t]he question of referentiality stubbornly persists as a vexed problem in African-American fiction as well as literary criticism" (11, 49). Afro-modernism's historical conscience effects an ongoing interrogation of the act of representation; in African American postmodernism, this interrogation seems far from obsolete, but is in fact intensified. Taking his cue from bell hooks, Timothy Spaulding explains that post-modernist blackness "reflects the political ideology of black nationalism, the 'authority of experience' and identity politics of black feminism, and the deconstructive project of postmodernism. From these discourses, African American writers develop a concept of 'narrative authority' that reinvests the contemporary writer with political agency by radicalizing the act of storytelling" (17). This tenacity of "some idea of the real" in African American postmodernism stems, according to Toni Morrison, also from the fact that

> [i]t's not simply that human life originated in Africa in anthropological terms, but that modern life begins with slavery. . . . From a woman's point of view, in terms of confronting the problems of where the world is now, black women had to deal with 'post-modern' problems in the nineteenth century and earlier. These things had to be addressed by black people a long time ago. Certain kinds of dissolution, the loss of and the need to reconstruct certain kinds of stability. (qtd. in Gilroy, "Living" 178)

These, then, are also "'post-modern' problems" that the Afro-modernism of *The Untelling* addresses, a narrative that is very much 'about' the telling and the untelling, the telling inarticulacies, of the black female body. Andreas Huyssen illuminates the stakes when he points out that postmodernist practice born from poststructuralist theory, "where it simply denies the subject altogether, jettison[s] the chance of challenging *the ideology of the subject* (as male, white, and middle-class) by developing alternative and different notions of subjectivity" and adds that dismissing questions of authority and authorship altogether "merely duplicates on the level of aesthetics and theory what capitalism as a system of exchange relations produces tendentially in everyday life: the denial of subjectivity in the very process of its construction. Poststructuralism thus attacks the appearance of capitalist culture—individualism writ large—but misses its essence; like modernism, it is always also in sync with rather than opposed to the real processes of modernization" (213).[2]

Paradoxically, the perhaps most unabashedly capitalistic and most thoroughly postmodernist lot within the contemporary "tribal geography" is also the most fiercely territorial and individualistic one: hip-hop. Its performance rites, highly evocative of the Turner-Stepto conception of *communitas*, often demarcate symbolic ritual grounds that are not only celebrated enthusiastically but also carefully policed and vigorously defended (Benston 39; Smith 43–45, 107–9). The glorification of a mythical "'hood" is often accompanied by the ritual incantation to "keep it real." That these ritualistic claims to a "tribal" terrain actually result in the continuous fabrication of often contesting authenticities does not diminish the perceived 'realness' of the ritual ground in question, because in hip-hop identity is inextricably linked to geography (Krims 123–51; Ogbar 6–8, 23–24). At the same time, socially conscious hip-hop often harks back to Afro-modernism's historical conscience. In a process Derrick Alridge terms "imaging," the more socially aware hip-hoppers seek to graft historical references onto present-day concerns: imaging addresses "temporal limitations through techniques that morph time and provide a wider lens for seeing the organic, metaphorical, symbolic, and concrete connections" between hip-hop and the Civil Rights movement and the black liberation struggle in the New World (228–29). Says Goodie Mob's Khudjo, "We all living in the same struggle. It's just different times" (qtd. in Alridge 233).

Little Brother is another such trio, composed of rappers Phonte and Big Pooh and producer 9th Wonder. Based in Durham, North Carolina, they too hail from hip-hop's most lucrative territory, the Dirty South, although their aesthetic owes much more to Goodie Mob than to, say, Ludacris. Little Brother's sophomore outing, released in the fall of 2005, is a concept album whose title is program: *The Minstrel Show*. Recorded and mixed in Durham's "Chopp Shopp Studios," the record resonates with thoroughly postmodernist techniques (booklet 12). The governing principle is parody, that of a TV sitcom called "The Minstrel Show." Accordingly, the concept album begins with a jingle: "You are watching UBN, U Black Niggers Network, Channel 94, Raleigh-Durham, Chapel Hill," which is followed by guest vocalist Yazarah sweetly intoning the sitcom's theme song: "We'd like to welcome you to everything there is to know: / This is our life, this is our music, it's our minstrel show."

Postmodernist techniques not only are evident in the music, but extend to the packaging of the CD, announced repeatedly as "The biggest colored show on earth." On the cover, the trio strikes the classic minstrel pose: three disembodied heads, the only color contrast consisting of the gleaming white of eyes and teeth against dark brown skin. The front-cover logo as well as the entire booklet is a parody of *TV Guide* magazine, reconstituted here as *LB Weekly*. The announcement of a cover story on page 34 about "THE MINSTREL SHOW: THE NEW HIT SITCOM. SUNDAYS ON UBN" is counteracted by the fact that there is no page 34 in the booklet. Even the parental-advisory warning sticker—not a sticker in this case, but printed in the lower left-hand corner—reinforces the postmodernist play as it calls attention to the artifice of the album's guiding concept.

The inside of the booklet continues the parody: *LB Weekly* lists the songs like *TV Guide* lists shows, including air times and even star ratings. For example, "Hiding Place," airing at "1 P.M.," ranks guest rapper Elzhi with only one and a half stars out of three, whereas Big Pooh gets all three. The program announces that the broadcast of "Cheatin'" has been "cancelled" and "replaced with Percy Miracles, Live in Rome '78" (5). Of course, the CD does include the track: and much like the shifting identities of minstrels, Phonte Coleman, a.k.a MC Phonte, morphs into Percy Miracles here, in a hilarious sendup of R. Kelly's bedroom crooning. *LB Weekly* also includes an ad for "the second season finale of 'Lovin' It,'" another UBN sitcom, set to begin "This Monday night 8 P.M."—but in fact "Lovin' It" is track the tenth, slated to air on "Sunday, September 11, 2005" at "6:30 P.M." (5, 7). Other postmodernist simulacra inside the booklet include an ad for a new line of clothing called "5th & Fashion" and even a crossword puzzle (2, 12).

But at the same time, Little Brother's postmodernism is suffused with bell hooks's "authority of experience" (29).[3] In *LB Weekly*'s "Story of the Week"—the seriocomic liner notes—Derek Jennings insists that Little Brother "talk about real shit while everybody else talk shit about keeping it real. Our forebears hustled and struggled so that we would no longer have to scratch when we ain't itch, or smile when we ain't happy. But in 2005, even though you don't have to rock blackface to be in entertainment, it 'shole heps." On the track "Watch Me," for example, postmodern parody joins satire born from a social and historical conscience when Phonte raps,

> I'm Phonte, international stage ripper; done
> Made friends and made figures
> While you stuck on the front porch mad, like you fixin' to shave
>
> > Mister.
> That's reality, so color me purple.
> My name in history, nigga, that's all I work for.
> Better keep it moving like the laws of inertia
> Before these Carolina boys come to hurt 'cha:
> Better tell them about it!

On the one hand, Phonte's parody here mockingly displaces the bygone folk culture of the black South celebrated in Alice Walker's *The Color Purple* and in the pastoralism of Steven Spielberg's movie version by boasting about his ability to navigate the global economy. On the same track, Big Pooh begins his verse by stating simply that he "can't afford to not record"—and how successful the trio has been in its manipulation of the postmodern conditions of consumer-capitalism is brought 'home' in the booklet's acknowledgments, which list two people of Little Brother's extended posse whose sole task is apparently "international currency conversion" (12). Booker T. Washington would be proud—and Shug Avery perhaps surprised.

On the other hand, Phonte's postmodern parody is also an act of "imaging," and as such it invests its very target with an authority that speaks to the continued validity of a collective historical consciousness and conscience. "Watch Me," and the album as a whole, resounds with the "memorious discourse" of postmodernism: this is a discourse that, according to Christian Moraru, does not constitute "an irresponsible art of forgetfulness," but rather seizes on the postmodernist mode of representation "as a case of prodigious, 'compulsive' cultural recollection" (*Memorious* 37, 21). What Little Brother's parody recalls is not just the racist distortions of white minstrelsy but also the often more complex and differentiated performances of minstrelized blackness enacted by African Americans themselves. Little Brother's "biggest colored show on earth" harks back to the slogan "The greatest colored show on earth" that the famed Rabbit Foot Minstrels used to advertise their performances (Abbot and Seroff 289). Like W. C. Handy's Mahara's Minstrels, the Rabbit Foot Minstrels were an all-black outfit that at one point included blues shouter Ma Rainey, the "Mother of the Blues," who, according to legend, kidnapped a teenaged Bessie Smith in Chattanooga, Tennessee, and taught her to sing the blues as a member of the troupe (Lieb 4–19). The blues' Mother and Father both, as well as Bessie Smith, the "Empress of the Blues," and many other early blues artists such as Ida Cox or Perry Bradford, toured with minstrel troupes, indicating how crucial a part the black minstrel show played, and continues to play, in the lineage of contemporary American popular musics (Lhamon 110, 145–46; Stewart-Baxter 11–12, 36–47). In their own time, the very existence alone of outfits such as Mahara's or the Rabbit Foot Minstrels enabled their African American cast to project themselves "across the South as a glorious, enviable spectacle . . . when white racist reaction was concerned with restricting black freedom of movement through public space," as Adam Gussow observes (88). The introduction to "Watch Me"—"And right now, you in tuned to the biggest colored show on earth: The Minstrel Show, nigga"—is yet another reminder that the entire album is a historicized 'text' that explores the 'script' of the black body as a site of ongoing contests of representation and hence of power, an historicized text just like Walker's novel, or Ma Rainey's performances, or the pen in the gashes of Frederick Douglass's feet.

For his part, the Father of the Blues defended Mahara's Minstrels vigorously: "It goes without saying that minstrels were a disreputable lot in the eyes of a large section of upper-crust Negroes," Handy wrote,

> but it was also true that all the best talent of that generation came down the same drain. The composers, the singers, the musicians, the speakers, the stage performers—the minstrel show got them all. . . . Encyclopedists and historians of the American stage have slighted the old Negro minstrels while making much of the burnt cork artists who imitated them. But Negroes were the originators of this form of entertainment, and companies of them continued to perform as long as the vogue lasted. Mahara's outfit, like the Georgia Minstrels, the McCabe and Young Minstrels, and the Hicks and Sawyer Colored Minstrels, was the genuine article, a real Negro minstrel show. (*Father* 33–34)

The modernist concern over authenticity in Handy's slightly revisionist and oxymoronic gloss ("a *real* Negro minstrel show") is revisited in Little Brother's postmodernism: both insist that there *is* something "genuine" and "real" behind the minstrel's mask: Afro-modernism's historical conscience, hooks's "authority of experience." The kind of postmodern rewriting Little Brother are engaged in here amplifies their text as, in Moraru's words, "a modality of setting up—and straight—the cultural accounts of society, its memory, and its struggles" (*Postmodern* 173). And if, as Houston Baker contends, it is "the mastery of the minstrel mask by blacks that constitutes a primary move in Afro-American discursive modernism," then Little Brother indicate that black postmodernisms constitute an extension of the tradition, not a break from it (*Modernism* 17).[4]

This contiguity is evident, too, in the ways in which *The Minstrel Show* rewrites Paul Laurence Dunbar's famous masqueraders, who also "sing, but oh the clay is vile / Beneath our feet, and long the mile" (lines 12–13). But not only are Little Brother far from resigning themselves to a loss of narrative authority and control that corrupts the songs of Dunbar's tragic minstrels; "these Carolina boys" who have "come to hurt 'cha" also see very little "vile" in the clay of their ritual ground (Baker, *Modernism* 39–40; Spaulding 19). However, they still acknowledge that, like Dunbar's singers, they too perform in an *international* cultural marketplace that prefers to celebrate a "mask that grins and lies" but remains largely indifferent to the humanity of those behind the mask (Dunbar 1). The parody of *The Minstrel Show* thus oscillates between the postmodernist recognition that all identity is constructed and the modernist quest for an authentic self. Little Brother's brash reclamation of narrative authority at once subverts the tragic resignation of Dunbar's minstrels and affirms the authority of that which engendered both "We Wear the Mask" and their album's own postmodernist updating of minstrelsy, namely an historical conscience born from the variegated experience of what it means to be black in the New World. And so, even in the thoroughly postmodern, highly digitalized contexts of consumer-capitalism and the global economy, Mark Anthony Neal concludes that "[o]nce again, we're back to ownership: ownership of possibilities, language, and experiences; if not of blackness itself"—even and especially in the contemporary, urban South (188).

Thus, in their insistence that representation is power, Little Brother—who take their name in deference to the pioneers of hip-hop—position themselves squarely within the African American tradition, a tradition ranging from the poetry of Phillis Wheatley and the autobiographies of Frederick Douglass to the subversive minstrelsy of Bert Williams to the fiction of Toni Morrison. The legacies of this tradition and its historical conscience remain. As Phonte sums it up, "To me, THE MINSTREL SHOW is ultimately about responsibility. . . . As rappers, we have to take responsibility for what we say, and for the images we portray to our people. If not, we're doing essentially what minstrel shows did: perpetuating negative images and reinforcing these negative stereotypes" (qtd. in "Little"). It is a sentiment echoed by many, including historian Jeffrey Ogbar, who sees in more commercially oriented rappers such as Lil Jon, the King of Crunk, "the quintessential postmodern super coon" (31).[5] The African American postmodernism of Little Brother (if perhaps not that of the King of Crunk) exemplifies that, as Ralph Ellison put it, "Negro American consciousness is not a product (as so often seems true of so many American groups) of a will to historical forgetfulness. It is a product of our memory, sustained and constantly reinforced by events, by our watchful waiting, and by our hopeful suspension of final judgment as to the meaning of our grievances"—even into the third millennium (*Shadow* 171). For a people whose history and humanity have been consistently denied or distorted by a national 'master' narrative, the performance of an authentic *human* voice remains absolutely crucial.

In these performances, the ritual grounds of the American South resurface time and time again as a site of prime importance in the ongoing process of reinventing culture and identity. The ramifications of this collective process, as we have seen, extend far above and beyond the Mason-Dixon Line. Perhaps this is so because, as Goodie Mob could tell both Shreve and Derrida, succinctly and with postmodernist irreverence, "Shit just don't sleep / In the Dirty South."

Introduction

1. Basie's trumpeter Buck Clayton confirms: "People often wondered how we got some of these titles. . . . We were all sitting round the studio after a playback when [producer] John Hammond asked 'What are we calling that one?' 'Well, let me see . . . ,' Count said and straightaway we all said that should be the title" (qtd. in Sheridan 98). Reissues that include this and later recordings of "Gone With 'What' Wind?" variously list only Basie or occasionally also Goodman as co-composer.

2. See Stepto (5); Baker (*Blues* 3–4); Gates (*Figures* 236–50; *Signifying* 78–79, 181); and Morrison ("City" 42). Gates seems to move closer to Mackey's "telling inarticulacy" when he adds that Signifyin(g) "depends on the success of the signifier at invoking an absent meaning ambiguously 'present' in a carefully wrought statement" (*Signifying* 86). However, Gates's critical practice qualifies this statement substantially. Despite his claim of

being a poststructuralist, his readings are actually more akin to structuralism: if a text performs certain empirically verifiable linguistic and rhetorical rituals, then it is a constitutive text of the African American literary tradition (52). This is why, in his critical paradigm, Zora Neale Hurston is "true somehow to the unwritten text of a common blackness," but, say, Jessie Redmon Fauset isn't (183). In other words, what constitutes according to Gates the blackness of a black text may ulti- mately be 'unwritable,' but it can indeed be circumscribed by the critical practice of Signifyin(g). Likewise, Stepto's critical practice does indeed, if only implicitly, point to a reconfiguration of the southern ritual ground as situated in time and *mind* rather than time and *place*: "what is national about Afro-America is that it is without dominion" (77). Even so, at the base of his vertical paradigm of narratives of ascent and immersion respectively, one always finds the South.

3. The writers whose work Stepto analyzes in his study are all southerners by birth, except W. E. B. Du Bois—and Ralph Ellison, who nevertheless considered his years in Alabama formative: "In time I was to leave the South, although it has never left me, and the interests which I discovered there became my life" (*Shadow* 169).

4. In fact, black literature often exhibits an *anti*pastoral strain, ranging from Frederick Douglass's plantation garden in Maryland, to the terrifying lynching scene James Weldon Johnson's ex-coloured man witnesses in the Georgia countryside, to Toni Morrison's not-so "Sweet Home" Kentucky plantation (R. Butler 71–72).

5. All translations of Benjamin are my own, as are subsequently those of Erich Auerbach.

6. The fiction of William Faulkner at times approximates something of an Afro- modernism, as Craig Werner has argued (27–62). Still, history in Faulkner is almost always seen as overwhelming, as for Quentin Compson, or as irretrievably reced- ing, as for Sam Fathers—never as nourishing. It is also interesting to note that there seems to be an inverse correlation between modernist experimentation and salient southernisms: *The Sound and the Fury*, for example, is perhaps the novel that most consequently exploits the modernist alienation of word from world, but what Faulkner himself called the "immitigable chasm between all life and all print" is noticeably smaller in, say, *The Reivers* (qtd. in Bleikasten vii).

7. Kenner's hypothesis in a nutshell:

> Discussing a poetic, we circle toward a definition of a university system as understood by Americans: a system in which other people are learn- ing things you are not, and you look daily at blackboard traces left by professors whose subjects you are never likely to study, nor need you. The break that defined modernist poetics was preceded by a tacit break with the educational theories of the Renaissance, when they claimed to understand just what combination of learnings would constitute an educated man. ("Poets" 120)

This notion of the interface between higher education and literary modernism recalls the division of labor inherent in capitalist economic systems. And the Ameri- can system of capitalism—the *ur*-form of capitalism, so to speak—was of course designed in such a way as to force as many blacks as possible into peonage.

8. This symbolism was obviously important to Du Bois. In the chapter of his autobiography titled "I Go South," much is taken verbatim from *The Souls of Black Folk*'s "The Meaning of Progress," including the description of the classroom where

he taught for two consecutive summers. However, the pale blackboard is conspicuously missing.

9. Werner describes call and response thus: "Grounded in West African conceptions of the interrelationship of individual and community," the ritual of call and response

> begins with the call of a leader who expresses his/her voice through the vehicle of traditional song, story, or image. This call, which provides a communal context for exploration of the "individual" emotion, itself responds to a shared history that suffuses later stages of the process. If the community, as it exists in the ever-changing present, recognizes and shares the experience evoked by the call, it responds with another phrase, again usually traditional, which may either affirm or present a different perspective on the initial call. Whether it affirms or critiques the initial call, however, the response enables the leader to go on exploring the implications of the material. Rich in political implications, this cultural form enables both individual and community to define themselves, to validate their experiences in opposition to dominant social forces. (xviii)

Chapter 1

1. For more detailed accounts of the reaction to the issuance of the proclamation, see Foner (1–3, 23–27); Franklin (118–27); McFeely (215–16); McPherson (557–59); and Quarles (199–202).

2. To be sure, *Life and Times* is not a flawless work of art. Critics have variously pointed at a tone that is exceedingly self-congratulatory at times; at Douglass's rather embarrassing fawning admiration for whites in position of power, especially his former masters; and at a narrative structure that is somewhat rambling and not nearly as taut as that of his other autobiographies. However, one must ask, at least as far as the first two points of criticism are concerned, if these critics do not project their disappointment in Douglass the human being onto *Life and Times* as a work of art. And regarding the last point of contention, the less tightly structured narrative development of the last autobiography is, at least to some extent, precisely the result of Douglass's changed aesthetic of autobiography, which no longer grants primacy to the quest for literacy.

3. Critics who subscribe to a deconstructionist dismantling of mimesis sometimes privilege the text to the extent that it virtually eclipses context altogether: perhaps unwittingly echoing Paul de Man's contention that death was nothing other than "a displaced name for a linguistic predicament," Ann Kibbey and Michele Stepto, for example, read the famous scene describing Frederick's fight with Covey as a transfer of "the signifiers of slavery" back to the slaveholder and as a stand "against the fractured referentiality of the antilanguage of the 'white man'" (de Man, "Autobiography" 930; Kibbey and Stepto 184). Perhaps this is the kind of critical practice that causes Deborah McDowell to complain that often "the explanation of Douglass's strength depends overmuch on a focus on style emptied of its contents" ("In" 53). The opposite approach to reading Douglass's autobiographies, privileging context to

the detriment of text, retains a significant investment in the powers of mimesis, so that the text becomes an archeological dig that yields traces of an 'authentic' black folk culture. This approach argues that "Douglass's *Narrative* contains an unwritten text of folklore that the reader, and probably Douglass himself, may not be conscious of" (Rothenberg 48; Raybourn 29–38). Again, this school almost exclusively focuses on the 1845 *Narrative* because it is closest in time to Douglass's upbringing as a slave and thus implicitly yields the least 'diluted' account of an 'authentic blackness' in America. (And the first problem of this approach is presented by the intimation that only the culture of the black slave is truly authentic; that there existed a quite different culture among free blacks, for instance in New Orleans, is conveniently forgotten.)

4. Though Maryland was not part of the Confederacy, it was culturally and economically still very much part of the Old South. A slaveholding state, Maryland remained in the Union thanks largely to Lincoln's quick quelling of secessionist sympathizers, the stationing of troops, and the imposition of martial law (McPherson 284–90). After the war, the border state remained more southern than northern, with its commercial center, Baltimore, exemplifying the position of the whole state, according to historian C. Vann Woodward: "A mixture of the Old and the New Order, Baltimore was at one and the same time the last refuge of the Confederate spirit in exile and a lying-in hospital for the birth of the New Order" (*Origins* 162). Douglass himself always referred to Maryland as a part of the South.

5. What Douglass describes here is a rhetorical strategy common to African American speech habits that linguists have termed *signification* or *signifying*—other (mostly regional) variations of signifying include sounding, jiving, the dozens, shucking, *et cetera*—on which, in turn, Gates's literary theory of Signifyin(g) is based (Baugh 25–28; Labov 306–53; Smitherman 118–34).

6. This tension is exemplary of the genre in general. Paul John Eakin notes that "autobiography is nothing if not a referential art," but that it is also propelled by "the presence of an antimimetic impulse at the heart of what is ostensibly a mimetic aesthetic" (*Touching* 31). Eakin confirms Douglass's aesthetic again when he observes that "the autobiographical act is revealed as a mode of self-invention that is always practiced first in living and only eventually—sometimes—formalized in writing" (*Fictions* 8–9). Eakin goes on to acknowledge that culture plays a decisive part in this mode of self-invention because "the self is already constructed in interaction with the others of its culture before it begins self-consciously in maturity (and specifically in autobiography—where it exists) to think in terms of models of identity. . . . [C]ulture has exerted a decisive part, through the instrumentality of models of identity, in the process of identity formation, whether literary or psychological" (*Touching* 102). James Olney has made the case for African American autobiographical writing as a paradigm of autobiography in general, for "autobiography renders in a peculiarly direct and faithful way the experience and vision of a people, which is the same experience and the same vision lying behind and informing all the literature of that people" ("Autobiography" 13, 15–16). This has made the genre particularly attractive to African Americans, whom the mainstream had (or has) sought to exclude from writing the history of America. And if "the aestheticization of culture is a product of modernity" as Gregory Jusdanis affirms, then "[l]iterature in a sense is the nation's diary, telling the story of its past, present, and future. Literary culture has been indispensable to ethnic communities wishing to cement their

integrity as nations and to demonstrate (belatedly) their modern credentials" (82, 47).

7. The hard-core deconstructionist might now object that, short of touching Douglass's scarred feet, the Lacanian signifying chain remains unbroken (Derrida 157–64; Spivak lxii–lxvii). However, how 'true' the autobiographer's textual representations of his cracked feet actually are does not really affect the pertinence of historical conscience: the scars may have healed in the half century that lies between their first and their last representation in text, or Douglass may have exaggerated, perhaps prevaricated even (although there is no evidence to that effect). But, again, the point is that even if Frederick Douglass's feet weren't scarred from frostbite—*somebody's* feet surely were.

Chapter 2

1. I am adapting here Walter Benjamin's closing argument in his essay on Charles Baudelaire: "He indicated the price for which the sensation of modernity is to be had: the destruction of aura in the experience of shock" ("Über" 229). Benjamin sees in *Les fleurs du mal* a protomodernism related to, but much more radical and uncompromising than, the protomodernism of *Life and Times of Frederick Douglass*.

2. William Rankin has already commented on this subject matter in his essay "Ineffability in the Fiction of Jean Toomer and Katherine Mansfield." However, his brief analysis is mainly a comparative character study and remains largely on the surface of the texts examined. While there is indeed in *Cane* a "despair before the impossibility of precisely capturing emotions, feelings, and states of mind," the question of *why* these fail to be transmitted Rankin does not address, except for the somewhat perfunctory conclusion that "[t]he major literary weapon for expressing the inexpressible is metaphor" (160, 167).

3. George Hutchinson maintains that the story's title character is actually biracial: African American and Jewish (*Harlem* 407). However, he fails to take into account that it is really the first-person narrator—like Toomer, a genteel, educated observer from the North—who superimposes Judaeo-Christian attributes onto Fern. Confronted with the mystery that is Fern, the narrator seeks reference points that might be more familiar (more 'writable') to himself and his audience. Hutchinson's overreading of Fern's ethnicity is based on Hargis Westerfield's analysis, which links the *imagery* surrounding Fern, not the title character herself, to the myth of the Jewish Mother of God (269–71). Charles Scruggs and Lee VanDemarr point out that giving Fern Jewish characteristics is in fact Toomer's nod to *Our America*, written by his close friend and mentor Waldo Frank (149–50). Scruggs and VanDemarr correctly note that "[t]he real basis for [the narrator's] attraction to [Fern] lies in her authenticity, which derives from the context of this place," the ritual grounds of Georgia's Black Belt; "part of the pathos of the narrator's various scenarios that place her elsewhere is that it reflects his own uprootedness, not hers" (150).

4. Henderson's concept of saturation and Soul-Field clearly influenced C. Eric Lincoln's discussion of "soul," which is also very reminiscent of Benjaminian aura:

> Whatever else it is, soul is the essence of the black experience—the distillate of that whole body of events and occurrences, primary and

derivative, which went into the shaping of reality as black people live it and understand it. . . . Soul is a kind of *élan vital* developed through the experience of living and performing constantly on the margins of human society, under conditions of physical and psychological stress beyond the boundaries of ordinary human endurance. It is a quality and an art developed in the matrix of the African-American experience. (*Race* 243–44)

Aura differs from soul, saturation, and Soul-Field in that Benjamin was very much aware of the tautology Benston locates at the core of Henderson's critical enterprise and that, by extension, also besets Lincoln's concept of soul. Where Henderson maintains that saturation is linked to poetic structure and therefore at least in part empirically verifiable, Benjamin insists that aura defies reproducibility, linguistic or otherwise (with the tentative exception of very early photography, which nevertheless already augurs the aura's impending and irreversible destruction). It must be mentioned here that Benjamin's essay "The Work of Art in the Age of Technological Reproducibility," more so than "A Short History of Photography" that introduces the term, is as much political polemic as it is cultural criticism. In "The Work of Art," Benjamin actually advocates modern art's (Marxist) emancipation from notions of the auratic and from the aura's "parasitic existence in ritual," instead grounding itself in a different practice, namely politics ("Kunstwerk" 144–45). While his famous term "aura" is often interchangeable with "authenticity" (as in this passage from "The Work of Art") or "tradition," Benjamin never spelled out a definitive concept of the auratic (Rochlitz 138). Benjamin could tout enthusiastically the dawning of a new epoch of radical art here, while elsewhere—as for example in the essay "The Narrator: Observations on the Work of Nikolai Lesskov," written only a few months after completing the first draft of "The Work of Art"—he harked back with wistful nostalgia to an earlier time when tradition, culture, history, and indeed human experience, were not yet under relentless assault from the fragmenting forces of modernity (Lindner 202–5; Rochlitz 9, 218–19). Concludes John McCole, "Benjamin's work celebrates and mourns, by turns, the liquidation of tradition" (8).

5. Robert Jones argues that the narrator does reach an epiphany about Avey even before their meeting in the park, concluding that the modern world "induces her spiritual sterility" (*Jean* 42). However, Jones fails to recognize that the narrator of "Avey" is an unreliable one as he constantly tries to impose his 'reading' of, as he says, "what *I* meant to *her*" on his companion (Toomer, *Cane* 46; emphasis added). Similarly, when he receives a short letter from her, he "decided" that her handwriting was "slovenly" (46). Thus, if he does reach an epiphany regarding Avey at all, it is an insight deeply shaped by the conception of his own self in relation to her.

6. Similarly, Paul, who "can't talk love" to Bona, tries to explain the inexplicable to the black doorman of the club that they have just left together (76). His long explanation, precisely because it tries to explicate that which cannot be explained, is suffused with metaphors, but after he shakes hands with the doorman, he finds that Bona has disappeared. In "Theater," the anticlimax of John's daydream about the sensuous dance of Dorris occurs when "John reaches for a manuscript of his, and reads" (55). Thus Dorris, whose dance on stage has spurred John's daydream, finds her dance "a dead thing in the shadow which is his dream" (56). In all of these instances, language precludes men from tapping the spiritual essence of women. Laura Doyle observes astutely that Toomer's text

carries on a long tradition wherein movement into the educated class means distance from and containment of other bodies by way of texts. . . . *Cane* exposes this body-displacing tradition of texts while also retaining the assumption that women live the essential embodiment alienated by this tradition. In that sense *Cane* joins the body-displacing tradition by keeping its own distance, as male text, from female embodiment. . . . By attributing embodiment to women and authorship to men, *Cane* thus reinscribes the function of the embodied woman as material instrument of men's culture. It affirms the racial-patriarchal aesthetic myth, which we saw operating in Romanticism, of female content and male form, with form as the governing metaphysical mechanism. *Cane* eschews metaphysical hierarchies without, however, withdrawing from the gendered oppositions that inflect those hierarchies. (94)

7. Significantly, the only instance in which Lewis and Kabnis connect is a moment devoid of speech:

His [Lewis's] eyes turn to Kabnis. In the instant of their shifting, a vision of the life they are to meet. Kabnis, a promise of a soil-soaked beauty; uprooted, thinning out. Suspended a few feet above the soil whose touch would resurrect him. Arm's length removed from him whose will to help . . . There is a swift intuitive interchange of consciousness. Kabnis has a sudden need to rush into the arms of this man. His eyes call, "Brother." (98)

As between the narrator and title character in "Fern," a momentary spiritual connection is established here not through language, but through the eyes. However, Kabnis gives in to "a savage, cynical twistabout within him" that "mocks his impulse and strengthens him to repulse Lewis." Kabnis's "thinning out," parallel to the thinning out of the beauty and power Toomer himself once believed he had managed to arrest in *Cane*, continues unhindered (98).

8. In addition to the modernist gesture of combining different literary forms, this, then, is also the reason why "Kabnis" was written as a closet play. "The value of a performative . . . employment of 'race,'" writes J. Martin Favor, "is precisely the ability of the performer to be at once 'inside' and 'outside' racial discourse, both 'really' black and not 'black' at all" (151). We never see the church choir perform "My Lord, What a Mourning" because in *Cane*'s symbolic territory they are "'really' black," while the lead character in "Kabnis" is, of all of Toomer's characters in Sempter, the one most painfully confronted with his alienation, being neither "'really' black" nor "not 'black' at all."

Chapter 3

1. The graphophone was developed by Charles Sumner Tainter along with Alexander Graham Bell and his cousin Chichester Bell in the last quarter of the nineteenth century as an improvement on and alternative to Edison's phonograph. The graphophone was initially conceived as a dictation device, its distinguishing feature a wax-covered cylinder that was more accurate and sensitive than the tin foil

favored by Edison. However, the Columbia Phonograph Company, founded in 1889, was the only company successful in marketing the graphophone, largely because it sold cylinders of music—the John Philip Sousa marches were a particular boon for the corporation. Also in part because of company mergers and various lawsuits and countersuits concerning copyright infringements, the graphophone was already outdated technology by the turn of the century. Though Tainter's innovations laid the foundation for the success of Columbia and had a long-lasting impact on the further evolution of recording technology, the graphophone's unwieldy six-inch wax cylinder could not compete with Edison's and never succeeded in the marketplace. By the 1910s the terms *graphophone* and *phonograph* were used interchangeably, also because releases in Edison's Diamond Disc Series were distributed as both increasingly popular discs and, until 1929, cylinders, if only in sharply declining numbers (Millard 64–69; Morton, *Sound* 16–42, *Off* 17, 76–79). Given the "sharp, scratching noise" Sarah hears as the salesman cranks up the device, this is a phonograph playing a disc, not an Amberal cylinder—as is, incidentally, the "graphophone" Cash Bundren aims to purchase from V. K. Suratt in William Faulkner's *As I Lay Dying* (Wright, "Long" 132; Faulkner, *As* 258, 261; Frow 47).

2. The manuscript of "Long Black Song" contained a fifth section that was dropped in the final version published in *Uncle Tom's Children*. In this final section, Tom arrives on the scene with Sarah's brothers, all three of them recently discharged from the military and still wearing their uniforms. The veterans die fighting at Silas's burning house, with Sarah, as in the published version, about to flee across the hills (Sollors 118).

3. Significantly, Silas threatens Sarah with the whip first. The black-on-black violence exerted by the master's preferred tool of regulatory violence prefigures here Zora Neale Hurston's contention of the black woman as "de mule uh de world" (*Their* 14). Silas's character also recalls the whip-wielding Sykes in Hurston's short story "Sweat" (949). Later, when Sarah sees the two white men wrestling with Silas "on the ground, rolling in dust, grappling for the whip" the latter had intended to use on his wife, the earth-mother figure, the whip again symbolizes the power to define and police the South (149). Werner Sollors has pointed out the similarities of "Long Black Song" to another of Hurston's stories: "The Gilded Six-Bits" also dramatizes the encounter of the 'natural' time of black folk with the clocked time of capitalist modernity leading to the protagonist's adultery (123–28).

4. Echoing the final scene between Fern and the narrator, an embrace in which it is not clear what happens, so is Wright's wording of this disturbing passage ambiguous, and many critics read it as a rape scene (J. A. Joyce 380; M. Walker 117–18, 184–85). Furthermore, Sarah is linked to the same objective correlative as Fern— again with obvious sexual overtones—namely a nail: as Sarah recedes from the advances of the white salesman into the house, "[h]er numbed fingers grabbed at a rusty nail in the post at the porch" (137). In "Fern," the narrator says of the object of his desire, "If you walked up the Dixie Pike most any time of day, you'd be most like to see her resting listless-like on the railing of her porch, back propped against a post, head tilted a little forward because there was a nail in the porch just where her head came which for some reason or other she never took the trouble to pull out" (17).

5. Sarah's sexual arousal occasioned by the sounds of "When the Roll Is Called Up Yonder" is very reminiscent of an episode in Wright's own childhood. At the age

of twelve, young Richard became infatuated with an elder's wife in his grandmother's church. As he would later write in *Black Boy*,

> I felt no qualms about my first lust for the flesh being born on holy ground; the contrast between budding carnal desires and the aching loneliness of the hymns never evoked any sense of guilt in me. It was possible that the sweetly sonorous hymns stimulated me sexually, and it might have been that my fleshy fantasies, in turn, having as their foundation my already inflated sensibility, made me love the masochistic prayers. (131–32)

Around that same time, Richard promised his grandmother he would make a serious effort at praying. Locking himself in his room for prayer, an unexpected by-product of this ritual were his first literary efforts:

> My attempts at praying became a nuisance, spoiling my days; and I regretted the promise I had given Granny. But I stumbled on a way to pass the time in my room, a way that made the hours fly with the speed of the wind. I took the Bible, pencil, paper, and a rhyming dictionary and tried to write verses for hymns. I justified this by telling myself that, if I wrote a really good hymn, Granny might forgive me. But I failed even in that; the Holy Ghost was simply nowhere near me. . . . (140)

6. As far as I have been able to determine, the 1915 version of "When the Roll Is Called Up Yonder" was the first to be available on disc. The hymn would later be covered by artists as diverse as Johnny Cash and Hampton Hawes, the Five Blind Boys of Alabama and Johnny Paycheck. That 1919 is the year in which the story is set is made clear by Silas's news that Tom had returned from the war. The demobilization and repatriation through the early part of 1919 of black troops from the European theater sounded the prelude to the devastating race riots of the infamous "Red Summer" of 1919 (D. Lewis 3–24).

7. Though the Edison Mixed Quartet's vocal arrangement has the lead baritone and tenor trade lines on the chorus section with the contralto and soprano, this does not constitute call and response. Call and response, as a musical strategy, entails the interaction between leader and collective (or congregation) (Fulton, "Singing").

8. Interestingly enough, when HBO decided to turn the Richard Wright story into a half-hour made-for-TV short for its "America's Dream" series, starring Danny Glover as Silas and Tina Lifford as his wife, the song that leads to catastrophe is "Body and Soul" (O'Connor). I thank Warren J. Carson for bringing this movie to my attention.

9. In "Long Black Song," Wright also appears to apply his own version of ironic typology. The biblical names of the three black characters ironically refracture scripture: in Genesis, Sarah is the wife of Abraham, remaining childless until the age of 90. Silas accompanies Paul on his journeys and is also credited with being the bearer of the First Epistle of Peter. And the Book of Ruth tells a story of fidelity, loyalty, and, eventually, idyllic bliss—not at all how "Long Black Song" presents baby Ruth's mother (DeCosta-Willis 546–48; McCarthy 735–37; Sollors 142).

10. This, of course, is a recurring contention in the slave narratives, that the peculiar institution is as injurious to the master as it is to the human chattel.

11. The role of religious music for Wright remained the same outside of the southern ritual grounds, too. In "The Man Who Lived Underground," originally begun in

1941, the protagonist witnesses a church service immediately after he has fled from the police into New York City's sewer system (Rowley 254–55, 262–63). Hearing the black congregation sing "*Jesus, take me to your home above / And fold me in the bosom of thy love*" in their subbasement church makes him feel "that he was gazing upon something abysmally obscene, yet he could not bring himself to leave" (*Eight* 24). Later, right before he is apprehended by police, he hears the same churchgoers sing, "*The lamb, the Lamb, the Lamb / Tell me again your story / The Lamb, the Lamb, the Lamb / Flood my soul with your glory*" (67). Written almost two decades later, the radio play "Man, God Ain't Like That," also published in *Eight Men*, is set in Africa and Paris (Rowley 490–91). Babu inspires his 'master,' the American painter John Franklin, by singing the hymns he has learned from Methodist missionaries, among them

> At the cross, at the cross,
> Where I first saw the light,
> And the burden of my heart rolled away,
> It was there by faith I received my sight,
> And now I am happy all the day . . . (*Eight* 161)

In Paris, Babu comes to believe that Franklin is God and brutally murders him when the painter insists on sending him back to Africa. Eluding trial despite a confession to French police, Babu returns to his native land, where he becomes the leader of a religious cult preaching the imminent return of Jesus in the shape of John Franklin.

12. These writings were often the result of economic necessity, not artistic interest. Wright's attitude toward the blues seems as ambivalent as his assessment of black (southern) folk culture in general. In *Black Boy*, his persona is disturbed by "how lacking in genuine passion we were, how void of great hope, how timid our joy, how bare our traditions, how hollow our memories, how lacking we were in those intangible sentiments that bind man to man, and how shallow was even our despair" (43). In direct opposition to the inner life of Sarah in "Long Black Song," the jeremiad continues:

> (Whenever I thought of the essential bleakness of black life in America, I knew that Negroes had never been allowed to catch the full spirit of Western civilization, that they lived somehow in it but not of it. And when I brooded upon the cultural barrenness of black life, I wondered if clean, positive tenderness, love, honor, loyalty, and the capacity to remember were native with man. I asked myself if these human qualities were not fostered, won, struggled, and suffered for, preserved in ritual form from one generation to another.) (43)

Certainly, the blues is just such a "ritual form," but Wright recognized this only in his foreword to Oliver's book and, fleetingly, in *Twelve Million Black Voices*. Deploring the "cultural barrenness" of black life served the persona of the alienated, questing hero he sought to project in his autobiography (Sollors 146–47). Elsewhere, his assessment of black vernacular culture could be much more differentiated. The following passage from *Twelve Million Black Voices*, a book much less quoted than his persona's invective in *Black Boy*, is particularly insightful also because it concerns the very medium of Richard Wright's craft:

> We [the African slaves] stole words from the grudging lips of the Lords of the Land, who did not want us to know too many of them or their meaning. And we charged this meager horde of stolen sounds with all the emotions and longings we had; we proceeded to build our language in inflections of voice, through tonal variety, by hurried speech, in honeyed drawls, by rolling our eyes, by flourishing our hands, by assigning to common, simple words new meanings, meanings which enabled us to speak of revolt in the actual presence of the Lords of the Land without their being aware! Our secret language extended our understanding of what slavery meant and gave us the freedom to speak to our brothers in captivity; we polished our new words, caressed them, gave them new shape and color, a new order and tempo, until, though they were the words of the Lords of the Land, they became *our* words, *our* language. (40)

13. See, for instance, Hurd (42–56) or McCarthy (736–37). In my view the story's shortcomings arise out of Wright's inability to combine in the central figure of Sarah two different functions: on the one hand, Sarah is to be read, in the first part of the tale especially, as southern earth mother embodying the territory over whose ownership black and white are fighting and dying. Accordingly, she is a creature of impulses, so much so that she later even falls asleep when her husband is about to be lynched. A certain dehumanization of Sarah is the prize Wright pays for pressing her character into an archetype: she is in a way like a doll that reacts only when squeezed, and the recurrent references to Sarah's "black teats" position her more as mammal than as woman (126, 128). At the same time, Sarah is also the moral conscience of the tale, offering a morally superior alternative, utopian though it may be, to her husband's Washingtonian ideology. But Sarah's vision does seem out of character considering how Wright introduces her in the earlier sections of the text.

Chapter 4

1. For more on Johnson and the legend of the crossroads, see Marcus (21–40); Palmer (111–17, 124–28); Pearson and McCulloch (18–64, 87–102); Schroeder (27–52, 99–100); and Stolle (40+).

2. Personal conversation with Frank L. "Rat" Ratliff (30 May 2005) and Roger Stolle (31 May 2005).

3. Dockery Farms is to the blues what New Orleans is to jazz. Charley Patton, who lived and worked there in the early 1920s, is considered to be the single most important figure in shaping what is now called the Delta blues. Patton partnered often with Willie Brown, and it was Brown who mentored Robert Johnson and is credited for his role in the latter's "Cross Road Blues" (Evans 41–49).

4. The most likely burial site, unmarked until recently, is in the cemetery at Little Zion M. B. Church just outside of nearby Greenwood. A second gravestone is in Morgan City's Mount Zion M. B. Church, which is the 'official' burial site of Johnson, at least according to his death certificate. The third is in Quito, on the grounds of the Payne Chapel M. B. Church, about halfway between Morgan City and Itta Bena on Highway 7, a hamlet so tiny one does need recourse to supernatural powers to find it, because the official highway map of Mississippi does not even list it.

Johnson did indeed find his untimely end in Quito, at the Three Forks Store, which reportedly was in the yellow one-story building, long since abandoned, after the highway bridge and flanking the dirt road that leads to the Payne Chapel. A fourth possible location of Johnson's crossroads is rumored to be outside of Robinsonville, just southwest of Memphis, but no one is able to say for certain where this one is. Last, and more mundane perhaps, given the perennial push-and-pull between commercial crossover appeal and artistic integrity that has been marking the history of black music in the New World, the most concrete crossroads may be the New York City studio whence Black Entertainment Television, BET, airs its hugely successful *106 & Park* top-ten video countdown every weekday.

5. It is commonly assumed that Arna Bontemps, who "edited" the memoir, was responsible for the more poetic touches in the text (Nichols 12; K. Jones 102). However, my research indicates the opposite: the two manuscripts housed in the archives of the W. C. Handy Birthplace, Museum, and Library in Florence, Alabama, reveal that the famous opening paragraph was Handy's own, with only slight amendments by Bontemps. In a telling letter, Handy complains that he was less than happy with his editor:

> I thank you for the correction, Taylor [Texas, a stop on one of Handy's concert tours] which I remembered, but being blind, my editor took so many liberties with my manuscript, that I wouldn't let him see the last seven chapters, because I was dealing then, with something he knew nothing about. In fact, if you will read the opening paragraph, "Where the Tennessee River," and so forth, he got that out and said, "I came into the world singing the blues." He wanted the book to be more about the blues, and cut out much of my background, which I put in, and that's maybe how Tyler crepted in. (Letter to Hank Patterson)

Though Handy's memory is rather selective here—the published version does begin with the idyllic image of Florence overlooking the Tennessee River, although an earlier manuscript displays Bontemps's radical corrections, some handwritten, in that very opening paragraph—it still reveals the diverging priorities of memoirist and editor (Handy, *Father of the Blues as Edited by Arna Bontemps* 1; K. Jones 96). "Maybe my editorship of Handy's book will gain consideration for me in the field of folk music," Bontemps had hoped initially ("Letter" 7 Feb. 1941 74). However, he confessed to his friend Langston Hughes that "[t]he Handy book is a headache. He jumps on my neck when I jazz it up; Trounstine [Handy's lawyer] screams when I fail to. I'm afraid it'll come to no good end" ("Letter" 14 Nov. 1939 42). "The Handy book should go to press soon," he later wrote, "vastly diluted since I last saw it, no doubt. I take no credit or blame for its final shape" ("Letter" 26 Jan. 1940 54). And indeed, when *Father of the Blues* did come out, Handy had not acknowledged Bontemps at all, causing the latter to sniff in turn that "Handy mashed it up a lot in the interest of dignity, etc." ("Letter" 2 July 1941 84).

The first typescript is entitled *Fight It Out* and looks to be entirely Handy's own, bearing only Handy's name on the inside title page (Handy, *Father* xiii). In this manuscript, the passage about the plowman's song and Handy's compositional modus operandi reads as follows—I have used proofreader's marks to indicate the handwritten corrections and changes:

The primitive tone or correlated note of "ⱯSt. LouisⱯ ᴧtheᴧ Blues" was born in my brain when a boy. In the valley of the Tennessee River Ywas whatY was Yknown asY McFarland's bottoms, which our school over-looked. In the Spring, when doors and windows were thrown open, Yone dayY the song of a Negro plowman half a mile away fell on my ears. This is what he sang:

"Aye-oh-you, Aye-oh-O
I wouldn't live in Cairo-O!"

All thru the years this snatch of song had been ringing in my ears. Many times I wondered what was in the singer's mind. What was wrong with Cairo? Was Cairo too far South in Illinois to be "up North"; or too far North to be considered "down South"?

In any event, such bits of music or snatches of song generated the motif for my Blues and with an imagination stimulated by such lines as, "I wouldn't live in Cairo," I wrote my lyrics.

At that time if I had published a composition called "The Cairo Blues," and this simple four-bar theme had been developed into a four-page musical classic, every grown-up now, who heard that four-bar wail then, would claim that Handy didn't write this number and you would hear them say, "I heard it when I was knee-high to a grasshopper." Politely put this would be a mis-statement of fact; bluntly written, it would be a Ybig lie mixed with small truthY ʌfalsehoodʌ. That two-line snatch couldn't form a four page composition any more than two letters, "i-n," could spell the word information. (XII.1)

In the other manuscript, titled *Father of the Blues as Edited by Arna Bontemps*—an unnumbered page inside the manuscript, between pages 25 and 26, identifies this version as "Re-written and arranged by Arna Bontemps"—the same passage appears as follows:

When I was a boy, I once stood in an open doorway listening to a plow-man's voice floating across the spring-green fields. Presently I made out words and a snatch of melody.

Aye-oh-you, aye-oh-O,
I wouldn't live in Cairo-O!

Through many years that fragment lingered in my mind. Often I tried to imagine what could have been in the singer's mind. What was wrong with old Cairo? Was it too far South to be "up North," or too far North to be "down South"? In any case, there was the music, brief, plaintive and inconclusive.

Now suppose I had taken this slight, four-bar theme and built upon it a composition of four pages in length and called the piece The Cairo Blues. What would my fine-feathered friends say? Exactly what some of them have said about other blues compositions of mine. "Aw, I heard that there song when I was knee-high to a grasshopper." And while they would be telling truth, in a remote sense, they would be making a very childish observation. For that two-line snatch could no more form a full-length composition than the letters i-n could spell information. (183)

The letters and other materials in the Handy archive further confirm Handy's compositional method and general modernist sensibility as a composer and arranger. Unfortunately, a thorough and comprehensive assessment of the holdings of Florence's Handy Museum is beyond the scope of my present study, but this is important work that I feel ought to be undertaken most urgently.

6. It appears that Handy's "St. Louis Blues" was mined for a most famous "snatch" itself: The bridge of Handy's composition betrays a striking resemblance to George Gershwin's "Summertime."

7. In *Father of the Blues as Edited by Arna Bontemps*, the passage reads:

> The primitive Southern Negro exaggerated the minor third and seventh tones of the scale. I had noticeΛdΛ this tendency. With them it was universal. Whether in the cotton fields of the delta or on the levee up St. Louis way, it was always the same. Till then, however, I had never heard it used by a more sophisticated Negro or by any white man. I introduceΛdΛ these two notes into my song that nightΛ.Λ Yand I think I can say they proved effective. Y Widely employed now, they are known as "blue notes." Another first was chalked up when I struck upon the idea of using the seventh in the opening measure of the verse instead of by resolution. This was a distinct departure in composition, but it touched the spot like two fingers of rye. (116)

There is no equivalent passage in *Fight It Out*, only the pithy explanation, "See the blue notes?—The Blues then were a composite of the snatches, phrases, and idioms illustrated herein" (XII.5).

8. Some blues scholars, however, have also asserted that the blue note is in some ways akin to a countermodernist affirmation of the individual self: for Rod Gruver, for instance, "organic man, man the irrepressible, wins a major victory in the blue note itself; for the blue note is a symbol of man's refusal to give up his unpredictable orneryness, his inalienable right to be himself and nobody else's" (223). This affirmation of the self, though, is won through the fragmentation of the western tonal scale and is therefore yet another manifestation of Afro-modernism's intrinsic difference from high modernism. It is, once again, Ellison who distills the ramifications of the more strictly musicological aspects: "The blues is an art of ambiguity; an assertion of the irrepressibly human over all circumstance, whether created by others or by one's own human failings" (*Shadow* 277).

9. Most obviously, the Faust legend comes to mind. To pick just one example of the legend's translation from the Old World to the New, the Igor Stravinsky–Charles Ferdinand Ramuz collaboration of 1918, *L'histoire du soldat*, finds its irreverent southern rock counterpart in the Charlie Daniels Band's "The Devil Went Down to Georgia."

10. For more on Esu's role at the crossroads, see A. Davis (472); Floyd (24–26, 72–76); Gates (*Figures* 48–49; *Signifying* 5–42); and Rudinow (134).

11. The lyrics are from the second take of "Cross Road Blues."

12. Though the Allman Brothers Band is considered to be the "first" southern rock band, period, most if not all of the genre's criteria actually fit Elvis Presley's Sun recordings as well as Ike Turner's "Rocket 88," the song that birthed rock 'n' roll (Palmer, *Deep* 222, *Rock* 201). Given my aim of remapping southern (figurative)

territory as well as the Allman Brothers Band's own rejection of the label, it is more accurate to place the band in a stylistic continuum.

13. The events surrounding the deaths of Allman, Oakley, Lydon, and Williams are recounted in detail in Scott Freeman's band biography, *Midnight Riders,* and Randy Poe's biography of Duane Allman, as well as in the memoirs of Joseph Campbell, Chuck Leavell, and Willie Perkins.

14. The only Robert Johnson song the band ever recorded in the studio is 1991's "Come On in My Kitchen." Though recorded 'unplugged,' the retro-arrangement does not attempt to recreate the original. What does begin as a slow, twangy, archetypal blues eventually becomes an upbeat, jaunty little piece, complete with gospel choir and New Orleans–style second-line rhythms. The only other reference in the ABB catalogue to the myth of Robert Johnson's crossroads—other than a very early version of "Cross Road Blues" by the Allman Joys—occurs in *Eat a Peach's* "Melissa," among the first songs the band recorded after Duane's fatal accident (though it had been written some years earlier). "Melissa" concerns the compulsive wanderings of a "gypsy" who "flies from coast to coast":

> Crossroads,
> Will you ever let him go? Lord, Lord—
> Will you hide the dead man's ghost,
> Or will he lie beneath the clay,
> Or will his spirit roll away?

The ABB's eschewing of the Johnson song catalogue prefigures the more recent revisionism of some white blues artists. For example, genre-bending slide guitar virtuoso Hank Shizzoe, a veritable encyclopedia of American blues, refuses to play "Cross Road Blues" because of his aversion to the commodification and distortion of the myth of the crossroads (personal communication, 17 Nov. 2005).

15. Not quite coincidentally, it was Duane Allman who breathed new life into the famous *Layla* sessions. British guitarero Eric Clapton and the studio musicians he had hired (recording under the pseudonym "Derek and the Dominos") had gotten bogged down in creative aimlessness, so Clapton decided to bring in Allman to restore focus to the proceedings. Though not credited anywhere on the resulting album other than as guitarist, Allman contributed significantly, most notably the famous seven-note introductory riff on "Layla" (Brent 74–75; Freeman, *Midnight* 78–84).

16. They also resist the 'jam band' label that became so fashionably hip in the 1990s. It's left once again to Gregg Allman to set the record straight: "We jam, but we're not a jam band . . . [I]mprovising happens spontaneously. Jamming is not something you set out to do" (qtd. in Perlah). And Allman is correct indeed in that it was the record company MCA that created the brand label "southern rock" in 1974 specifically for that other stalwart combo of the genre, Lynyrd Skynyrd. Though nowhere near as musically adventurous as the ABB, Skynyrd, too, resisted cooptation to a certain degree, as evidenced in their tongue-in-cheek hit song "Workin' for MCA." And lead singer Ronnie Van Zant agreed with his colleague: "Southern Rock's a dead label, a hype thing for the magazines to blow out of proportion" (qtd. in O'Brien and McKaie 4) At the same time, they also displayed much less awareness of the historical exigencies of their own southern ritual grounds when, albeit

at the behest of MCA, they toured in support of their 1974 *Second Helping* album using the Stars and Bars as stage backdrop. Their smash hit "Sweet Home Alabama," to this day the unofficial anthem of the South, evinces this self-contradiction that stays unresolved, in turn condemning and praising the state's segregationist governor George C. Wallace. The Confederate battle flag has remained a staple of Lynyrd Skynyrd shows ever since (O'Brien and McKaie 16–17; Odom and Dorman 98–110). The ABB's influence on the band had already been explicit on their debut album, where the anthem "Free Bird" was a tribute to the recently departed Duane Allman.

17. McTell is a fascinating figure in his own right. He was born in Thomson, Georgia, probably in 1901, and his wanderings took him all over the South, North, and the Midwest. Containing copious ballads and spirituals as well as blues, McTell's discography is one typical of the traveling musician who had to cater to the diverse tastes of diverse audiences and is much more varied than Robert Johnson's. This is perhaps the reason why John Lomax, who 're-discovered' McTell playing in the driveway of an Atlanta rib shack, never issued the 1940 recordings he did with the singer. Like much of his life, McTell's death is shrouded in legend, too: succumbing to an apparent brain hemorrhage in 1959, he was reportedly seen, Elvis-like, at Curley Weaver's 1962 funeral, or playing at an Atlanta storefront church in 1972 (Bastin 213–14; D. Kent, liner notes).

18. The band recorded the Willie Dixon-penned classic, Oakley's only lead vocal, for their *Idlewild South* album. Characteristically, as they would later do with "Statesboro Blues," they were not satisfied with simply covering the song: the original riff they grafted onto "Statesboro Blues," but reversed it for "Hoochie Coochie Man." In the original hit version for Muddy Waters—as well as in "Statesboro"—the riff is ascending; in the Allmans' version of the Dixon song, it is *descending*. Likewise, the Taj Mahal version of "Statesboro Blues" that initially captured Duane is significantly different from the rearrangement that found its way to the top of the ABB bandbook: for one, Mahal's rendition lacks the riff from "Hoochie-Coochie Man" and deploys a much more pronounced shuffle beat, mostly a result of Mahal's use of only one drummer.

19. In *Fight It Out*, the passage appears as follows:

> One day, at Tutwiler, while waiting for a train that had been delayed nine hours, I enjoyed a sleep to be awakened by a guitar played by a colored man, and in a manner new to me. He was using a knife pressed on the strings in a way since made popular by Hawaiian musicians, who make use of a steel bar. The chords he struck would waken any one. Question: how many years—or centuries—had a knife antedated the steel bar? Knife or steel bar, in any event, produced unforgetable [sic] tones. The man was singing:
>
> "Goin' Where the Southern Cross the Dog."
>
> He would repeat the line three times, accompanying it on his guitar with the wierdest [sic] melody I have ever heard. The tone stayed in my mind. (VI.3)
>
> *Father of the Blues as Edited by Arna Bontemps* describes the event thus:

Then one night at Tutwiler as I nodded in the railroad station while waiting for a train that had been delayed nine hours, life suddenly took me by
the shoulder and awakened me with a start.

A lean, loose-jointed Negro had commenced plunking a guitar beside
me ⋀while I slept⋀. His clothes were rags; his feet peeped out of his shoes.
His face had on it some of the sadness of the ages. As he played, he
pressed a knife on the strings of the guitar in a manner later popularized
by Hawaiian musicians who used steel bars. The effect was unforgetable
[*sic*]. His song, too, struck me instantly.

Goin' where the Southern cross the Dog.

The singer repeated the line three times, accompanying himself on the
guitar with the weirdest melody I had ever heard. The tune stayed in my
mind. (73–74)

20. Personal communication with Kirk West, 5 April 2006.

21. The whipping post was not a regional feature by any means. This particular
kind of corporal punishment had been brought to the New World early on, and virtually every town in New England had a whipping post. However, in the South the
whip was the master's preferred tool for enforcing his absolute power over his human
chattel, and so the whipping post became a symbol of the most inhuman cruelty
and injustice of the peculiar institution, as countless slave narratives attest. That
poor whites sometimes ended up tied to the whipping post was considered especially
effective punishment and deterrence in a region where flogging was associated with
the submission of unruly subhumans, the lowest of the low. The whipping post would
remain in use long past emancipation; in fact, southern states did not abolish it until
a few years after the end of Reconstruction (Franklin and Schweninger 42; Stampp
174; Woodward, *Origins* 94–96).

22. As a genre, southern rock at once resuscitated and revamped traditional
modes of southern masculinity (J. Butler 73–74; M. Butler 43–44; Ownby 371–74).
What Paul Wells calls the chivalric pattern of the plantation model "naturalises
hierarchies and the idea of an 'extended family' as a benevolent, self-evidently moral
construct. This enables southern rock bands to represent the South without reference
to the key issue of 'race'" (121). While the ABB was, and is, certainly complicit in
maintaining these southern gender hierarchies, the Allmans' racially integrated,
extended 'brotherhood' renders visible (and audible) the African American presence, something that sets the band apart from almost all the other acts in the genre.
See also Abernathy (14); Ostendorf (78–79).

23. On the original studio recording on the ABB's self-titled debut album, Gregg
Allman can be heard shouting off mic during the guitar-screams. And on the Fillmore tapes, Duane's announcement, "We got a little number from the first album
we're going to do for you; Berry [Oakley] starts her off," is followed a yell of recognition from the back of the hall, "Whipping Post!" which is picked up with joyful
anticipation by someone else closer to the stage, "'Whipping Post,' yeah!"

24. This kind of rhetorical minstrelsy has also seeped into the lyrics of Gov't
Mule, an offshoot of the ABB and mainstay on the jam band circuit since the mid-
1990s. Next to innovative covers—ABB-like reinventions really—of Son House or
Memphis Slim and leader Warren Haynes's tip of the hat to fellow North Carolinian

John Coltrane, the group's self-titled debut album also contains their theme song, "Mule." Ostensibly about social class, the chorus of "Mule" slips into discursive minstrelsy and asks

> Where's my mule,
> Where's my forty acres?
> Where's my dream,
> Mister Emancipator?

A more recent example of a full-length album of *sonic* minstrelsy is the 2002 *Me and Mr. Johnson* by Eric Clapton, that most prolific purveyor of the crossroads myth (Lipsitz 121).

25. And herein lies also a crucial difference: black minstrel shows such as Mahara's committed even more "significant crimes" simply by taking their show on the road. In an era when rituals of racial segregation pervaded every parcel of public space, the mere mobility alone of black minstrel troupes, not just crisscrossing the South, but sometimes venturing north of the Mason-Dixon line, even overseas, enacted recurrent transgressions of boundaries designed to keep Americans of African descent in their place (Gussow 88).

26. Brother Wynton explains in the liner notes to *Black Codes:*

> Black codes mean a lot of things. Anything that reduces potential, that pushes your taste down to an obvious, animal level, anything that makes you think less significance is *more* enjoyable. Anything that keeps you on the surface. The way they depict women in rock videos—black codes. People gobbling up junk food when they can afford something better—black codes. The argument that illiteracy is valid in a technological society—black codes. People who equate ignorance with soulfulness—definitely black codes. The overall quality of every true artist's work is a rebellion against black codes. (qtd. in Crouch 12–13)

That the ever-combative Stanley Crouch, Wynton's ideological amanuensis, (mis)quotes Rahsaan Roland Kirk's "Volunteered Slavery" in his liner notes speaks to yet another irony of the southern ritual ground, considering that it's this very tune that opens Derek Trucks's 2006 *Songlines* album (Crouch 7).

27. Coltrane's most famous recording in waltz time is his classic 1960 rendition of "My Favorite Things," and the tenorist returned again and again to this time signature. It was originally Jaimoe who spurred the ABB's interest in modern jazz: "Duane and Berry was very much into rhythm and blues, and I kind of turned them on to a lot of jazz things . . . John Coltrane and Miles Davis were Duane's favorite jazz people. 'My Favorite Things,' by Coltrane, he loved. And that Miles Davis thing, *Kind of Blue.* Duane's favorite song was 'All Blues'" (qtd. in Freeman, *Midnight* 63). Both "My Favorite Things" and "All Blues" are in waltz time, and both feature Coltrane. "Dreams," another early ABB classic, is in fact nothing else than a slightly spruced up "All Blues" with lyrics attached, as Oteil Burbridge likes to point out when he quotes the famous Paul Chambers bass line. Confirmed Duane Allman, "You know, that kind of playing [on *At Fillmore East*] comes from Miles and Coltrane, and particularly *Kind of Blue.* I've listened to that album so many times that for the past couple of years, I haven't hardly listened to anything else" (qtd. in Poe 182).

28. Pioneered by trumpeter Miles Davis, modal jazz requires the improviser to play over a mode or scale rather than over a chord progression. The borderline between chordal and modal improvisation is often somewhat blurry, but generally a modal jazz tune employs only one or two scales, whereas a chordal tune is harmonically much more complex; Davis's *Kind of Blue* and John Coltrane's 1960 "My Favorite Things" are the most influential examples of modal jazz. The shift from bebop's lightning-quick chord changes to merely one or two scales doesn't necessarily make the improviser's task any simpler, for modal jazz requires comparatively much greater melodic inventiveness. At the same time, neither Duane Allman's nor Dickey Betts's technical dexterity or their harmonic awareness match that of, say, a Barney Kessel, and so modal jazz offers a more accessible path than bebop (or standards for that matter) for blues-based instrumentalists seeking to exert their improvisational prowess. Almost all of the ABB's extended improvisations occur on tunes whose solo sections are either two-chord vamps ("High Falls") or entirely modal (Betts's homage to Charlie Parker, "Kind of Bird"—even though Bird, of course, never played modal jazz), but the heads are often harmonically and rhythmically advanced, certainly for rock.

29. The godfather of gypsy jazz recorded the tune six times under slightly different titles (Dregni 251; Vernon 166, 208, 214–15, 223, 229, 230–31). That Betts has Reinhardt in mind is evidenced by the fact that he quotes the eighth-note figure from the lullaby's bridge, which is also the part that Reinhardt borrowed note for note. That is also the same section that occurs in Grieg's op. 17, "Twenty-five Norwegian Dances and Folk Songs"—and in the third movement of Gustav Mahler's Symphony no. 1 (Benistad 76–82; Fischer 1–4, 181–90).

30. In this respect, "Mountain Jam" is fairly unusual in that most vehicles for extended improvisation in the ABB bandbook utilize a minor scale.

31. The oft-repeated comparisons between Gregg Allman and Jimmy Smith are desperately overhyped; in fact, Allman cites Booker T. Jones of Booker T. and the MGs as his biggest influence (Lynskey 17). Though he knows the music of Smith, King of the B3, very well, Allman is smart enough a musician to realize that he has neither Smith's fleet fingers nor Smith's harmonic sophistication; consequently, his solos are rare and always very short. His main task is to furnish the harmonic carpet for the guitarists and the bass player to float over. Also, it may sound as though Led Zeppelin initially forged a similar aesthetic approach as the ABB—their self-titled debut contains several blues covers—but rather than the mining of the southern groove continuum's (Afro)modernism, Zeppelin emphasized a parodic approach to the blues.

32. Tapings of several live performances allow tracing the evolution of the medley and corroborate that, other than a few signposts along the way, the structure of the extended performance could change virtually from day to day. At an April 11, 1970, performance in Cincinnati, the band was still relatively unknown and touring in support of their first studio album. At that performance, "Mountain Jam" had not yet joined "Whipping Post," but it lasted for over forty-four minutes and is particularly noteworthy for a funk section halfway through that eventually leads to fleet-fingered country and western, all of it merging into a Chuck Berry homage; also, the Zeppelin quote seems to have originated with Betts, who leads the ensemble here into the descending four-note riff from "Dazed and Confused." By July, a mere three months later, the medley had already gelled. Two performances of the conjoined "Whipping Post" and "Mountain Jam," only 48 hours apart, at the

second Atlanta International Pop Festival display the band's spontaneity: Friday's "Whipping Post" doesn't contain a rubato section until the very end, and, instead of the theme, "Mountain Jam" begins with Duane and Betts tossing back and forth a three-note motif the latter played around with in the first song. Gregg discards the Zeppelin quote from "Mountain Jam." The band's quick thinking and internal chemistry are on full display when the second half of the medley was interrupted for half an hour due to a severe thunderstorm; when the ABB resumed the set, Duane didn't even count off, simply started playing a funk lick, and the rest of the band fell in to continue "Whipping Post" where they had left off. On the Sunday version of "Mountain Jam," "Will the Circle Be Unbroken" makes its first appearance and is taken in tempo, to a shuffle beat to boot, before slowing to a statelier tempo. For a show in Washington, D.C., half a year later, the band played "Whipping Post" on its own again. From the very beginning of Duane's solo, the overall approach has decidedly shifted to modal (especially in Gregg's comping), even more so than later at the Fillmore, and there are now two lengthy free rubato sections. (And when Gregg Allman decided to record a stripped-down version of "Whipping Post" for a solo project, his arrangement remains chordal throughout, but he garners it with a "Spanish tinge" courtesy of maracas, timbales, and congas—missing is the sonic minstrelsy of the whip and cry.) By the final concert of the ABB's 2007 summer tour, "Whipping Post" closed out their performance and stood once again by itself, as it had in the very beginning. "Mountain Jam" did precede it in a truncated version, but it was now the closing bookend of a medley beginning with "In Memory of Elizabeth Reed" with a prolonged percussion-bass jam in between. The way the ABB navigates these frequently changing time signatures within an improvisational whole that bends, stretches, and contracts the underlying rhythmic pulse but never ruptures it abruptly also indicates why its music is modernist and not postmodernist like, say, the dizzying array of musical bric-a-brac of John Zorn's Naked City (Dombrowski 214–15).

33. Still, quite often—more often than not—American popular music has elevated 'blackness' as the emotional, expressive standard for white musicianship, a romanticization that lingers on in the new millennium, as David Grazian's study *Blue Chicago* shows. That negrophilia and negrophobia are not mutually exclusive, as Berndt Ostendorf has pointed out, is exemplified by the following exchange between Elvis Presley and his guitarist Scotty Moore in Sam Phillips's Sun Studios (Ostendorf 81):

> PHILLIPS: Fine, *fine*, man, hell, that's different! That's a *pop song* now, little guy! That's good!
> SCOTTY MOORE: Too much vaseline!
> (Elvis laughs, nervously, proudly.)
> MOORE: I had it too!
> ELVIS: Y'ain't just-a-*woofin'*!
> MOORE (imitating an eye-rolling black falsetto): Please, *please*, please—
> ELVIS: What?
> MOORE: *Damn*, nigger! (qtd. in Marcus 192)

34. The ABB was not nearly the first to stipulate racially integrated seating. A similar clause appeared in all of Roland Hayes's contracts following his 1923 return from a tour of Europe (P. Anderson 90–93).

35. All of Collier's quotes come from my interview with him, conducted on 14 April 2006, at the Georgia Music Hall of Fame's Zell Miller Center for Georgia Music Studies. In another bizarre niche of this particular southern ritual ground, Otis Redding's first recording was for producer Bobby Smith's Confederate Records Studio, whose offices were housed in Macon's Robert E. Lee building. Smith's first two signees were Redding and Redding's friend Wayne Cochran, "The White James Brown." Smith quickly realized the former's star potential and changed his label's name to Orbit Records in order to get more airplay (G. Brown 16–17; Freeman, *Otis!* 68–71)

36. Riffing along more contemporary revolutions of the southern groove continuum, historian William Jelani Cobb comes to the exact same conclusion when he adjudges that "[t]he legions of mic-grabbing rhyme-spitters in Germany, Japan, France, and Amsterdam are no more contrary to the black roots of hip hop than Leontyne Price was a threat to the Italian roots of opera" (7). Blues scholar Joel Rudinow locates the standard of authenticity in a performative stance marked not by ethnicity, but by the integrity and understanding with which an idiom is used that, historically, *did* originate with Americans of African descent (135–36). Extending the African American ritual of call and response, musicologist Samuel Floyd insists that "[t]rue dialogism requires that the composer, the performer, and the listener modulate effectively between black vernacular and European-derived voices in a way that keeps the cultural integrity of both intact and viable in a fused product" (266). It is my argument that, at its very best, the ABB's music exemplifies such "true dialogism" as it strains to give voice to (Afro-)modernism's historical conscience. Seconds sociologist Paul Gilroy, "I realise that the most important lesson music still has to teach us is that its inner secrets and ethnic rules can be taught and learned" (*Black* 109). Thus, as jazz scholar Jeffrey Magee summarizes it, "the phenomenon of Afro-modernism is at once both racially grounded and transcendent of race" (14).

Chapter 5

1. In hip-hop, a similar phenomenon occurs. There, the claim to authenticity is often accompanied by a militant territoriality, a fierce loyalty to the proverbial 'hood—East Coast, West Coast, the Dirty South, Nellyville, *et cetera*—framed as the incantatory ritual of 'keeping it real,' both a promise and an admonition. In hip-hop as *performance*, the ritual ground of the 'hood is usually under siege from a variety of threats: from the police, for example, or rival gangs, or simply just tragicomically unhip outsiders trying to crash the block party, and so on. At the same time, for hip-hop as *business*, the music, and all the defensive demarcations of its various ritual grounds that characterize much of it, has long since become a lucrative commodity in the global economy. And so, what Kembrew McLeod observes of black inner-city hip-hop applies equally to the white southern rock of the Drive-By Truckers: "Authenticity claims and their contestations are a part of a highly charged dialogic conversation that struggles to renegotiate what it means to be a participant in a culture threatened with assimilation" (147). And the Dirty South is no enclave in this regard, as Matt Miller points out: "The politically oppositional orientation of the Dirty South—expressive of the reclaiming of former sites and symbols of enslavement and segregation, and the legitimation and celebration of 'lowdown and

dirty' working-class African American culture—diminishes as the concept spreads outwards into global markets, and is often eclipsed by superficial notions of edginess afforded by the appropriation of contemporary southern urban blackness" ("Dirty").

2. Williams, convicted of three of the murders in 1982, has always proclaimed his innocence. Both the work of the Fulton County Task Force and that of the prosecution in Williams's trial has remained hotly debated over the decades, so much so that a quarter century later, DeKalb County Police Chief Louis Graham, a member of the Task Force at the time of the murders, felt compelled to reopen five of the cases falling under his current jurisdiction. Although that investigation was dropped a year later, alternate theories based on new or withheld evidence and witness statements keep resurfacing, most recently of involvement of the Ku Klux Klan or of a convicted child molester (Scott E3; Scott and Torpy A1; Suggs and Gentry A1; H. Weber). For in-depth accounts of the crimes, investigation, and trial, see Chet Dettlinger and Jeff Prugh's *The List* or Bernard Headley's *The Atlanta Youth Murders and the Politics of Race*. The entire case file is accessible on the Web site of the Federal Bureau of Investigation ("Atlanta").

3. The parental admonition here echoes the folk belief that thunder and lightning are signs of God being at work, which demand the respectful response of silence and rest (Lincoln, *Race* 54–55). The southern-gothic touches of the novel's opening scene also recall an earlier, very different Atlanta: W. E. B. Du Bois's poem "Litany of Atlanta," written in the wake of the bloody 1903 race riot, describes a city in the grips of an apocalyptic cataclysm: "A city lay in travail, God our Lord, and from her loins sprang twin Murder and Black Hate. Red was the midnight, clang, crack and cry of death and fury filled the air and trembled underneath the stars when church spires pointed silently to Thee" (line 11). And seven decades later, Dudley Randall asked,

> What desperate nightmare rapts me to this land
> Lit by a bloody moon, red on the hills,
> Red in the valleys? Why am I compelled
> To tread again where buried feet have trod,
> To shed my tears where blood and tears have flowed?
> Compulsion of the blood and of the moon
> Transports me. I was molded from this clay.
> My blood must ransom all the blood shed here,
> My tears redeem the tears. Cripples and monsters
> Are here. My flesh must make them whole and hale.
> I am the sacrifice. (lines 1–11)

Although "Legacy: My South" does not describe Atlanta directly, it acts nevertheless as a companion poem to "Litany of Atlanta" in terms of its postapocalyptic landscape. Setting these three ritual grounds side by side, this intertextuality thus points to one hallmark of the African American literary canon, namely its cyclical approach to time and history, because the opening scenes of "Magic Words" circumscribe a *pre*apocalyptic landscape.

4. Significantly, the novel recurrently depicts Tasha and her classmates as studying for a vocabulary test, doing spelling homework, or preparing a book report (33, 36, 54, 56, 70, 101, 164, 175, 188, 194). Not quite coincidentally, Rodney fails another spelling test in "The Direction Opposite of Home," and Octavia's spelling

book is stolen in "Sweet Pea" (109, 148). The unreliability of any kind of referential reporting also extends to physical acts and images: Tasha, for one, fails to grasp the import of her slightly older cousin Ayana's body language (61, 64). And all three of the major characters comment on the surreal disconnect between the images they see on the local evening news—usually introduced by WSB Channel 2's Monica Kaufman, the first black news anchor in Atlanta. To Tasha, the nine photographs of missing children broadcast by Channel 2 "looked like school pictures . . . arranged in three rows like a tic-tac-toe game waiting to be played" (24). And later, when Kaufman reports the discovery of Rodney's body, Octavia muses, "Kodak commercials say that a picture is worth a thousand words, but the one they showed of Rodney ain't worth more than three or four. Boy. Black. Dead" (155).

5. Befitting a city that displays a remarkable readiness to discard its past(s), the characters in Jones's follow-up novel, *The Untelling*, twentysomethings (and therefore of the same generation as Tasha, Rodney, and Octavia) negotiating the vagaries of love and marriage in the mid-1990s, have no memory of the Atlanta Child Murders—at least they don't display any awareness of them. Accordingly, the motif of the air freshener recurs, but it is divorced from its association with recent Atlanta history (143). The novel's narrator only remembers the janitor of her elementary school remarking darkly, "Wasn't even last year that someone was snatching kids right around here" (95). And while *Leaving Atlanta*, like *Cane*, isn't really a *roman à clef*, some of its characters resemble the actual victims. Jashante, for example, is a composite character of sorts: fourteen-year-old Edward Hope Smith, the first victim on the Task Force list of twenty-nine, was last seen in the evening of July 20, 1979, at Greenbriar Skating Rink; Lubie Geter, also age fourteen and the eighteenth name on the list, was hawking Zep Gel car deodorizers outside a shopping center in the afternoon of January 3, 1981, when he disappeared. Wayne Williams, though never even vaguely identified in Jones's novel, was known to have an uncanny ability to impersonate a police officer—he also liked to pose as a music producer and talent scout—and it is just such an impersonator who lures Rodney into his car ("Atlanta"; Headley 35, 81–83, 138–41).

6. For instance, the narrative voice knows that Leon, Rodney's classmate and an accomplished shoplifter, is lying to the candy store owner (105). The separation of the narrative voice from Rodney's mind, barely hinted at for most of "The Direction Opposite of Home," is perhaps most obvious at the very end, where the narrative voice identifies the serial killer only as "the driver" and foregoes any closer description, when Rodney himself remains, as usual, acutely aware and observant of everything else surrounding him at that moment (140).

7. At one point, the narrative voice coldly observes that "Monica Kaufman said that the missing children had been asphyxiated. Your children's dictionary (which you hate) does not include this important word, so you consulted the real one in the family room. Asphyxiate is to smother, which is almost the same as drowning" (113–14).

8. Jones herself has a different take on the nature of the second-person-singular point of view: drawing on Jim Grimsley's *Winter Birds*, she says that "[m]y idea for the second person in *Leaving Atlanta* is the idea of a guardian angel almost speaking to Rodney" ("(Un-)Telling" 74). Jones's insistence on the narrative voice as protector rather than stalker fails to explain, however, not only why it cannot protect him from a life already filled with terror and from a grisly, premature death, but why nothing is

ever really explained *to* Rodney. Either way, Jones's own interpretation of the voice as guardian angel still supports my reading of the disorienting nature of language because the voice, if it is an angelic one, after all still exists only as words.

9. Interestingly, the tangible "Terminus" surviving today—the Zero Mile Marker of the old Western & Atlantic Railroad from which in 1847 the city's original boundaries were drawn—is located approximately a quarter mile from the W&A's very first zero mile post. Where exactly that first marker's location was, no one knows today (Rutheiser 15–17). Once again, the southern ritual ground defies exact geographic circumscription.

10. Emphasizing again the chasm between the sign and its referent, both Tasha and Rodney discover that the school gossip on Octavia—her body odor, her intellectual deficiencies, and so on—is not accurate either (48–49, 89–90).

11. Accordingly, Octavia, prompted by her mentor Ms. Grier, expresses an interest in calligraphy: "I made sure that my penmanship was perfect, so somebody could know me for that" (165).

12. Octavia here remembers what Ms. Grier had told her earlier about her own childhood in an attempt to alleviate the fifth-grader's fear and anger. Orphaned at an early age, Ms. Grier tells Octavia that she was sent to live with an aunt and uncle. The first night in her new home, she wanted to share the bed with her cousin Twyla, who rebuked her: "'Not in here with me,' Twyla said, as though bed sharing was disgusting. I tucked my little head and went to the other twin bed. The pretty spread was butter colored and I was afraid that I might spoil it. I was as lonely that night as I have ever been in my life. But I didn't cry because I didn't want to wet the eyelet pillow slip" (235). Ms. Grier's anecdote here echoes the beginning of Toni Morrison's "Recitatif," in which the two main characters, Twyla and Roberta, meet as young girls at an orphanage and "changed beds every night . . . for the whole four months we were there" (1776). Other Morrisonian resonances in *Leaving Atlanta* include the recurring motif of marigolds—*The Bluest Eye,* also a story of a harrowing loss of innocence, begins with the observation that, "[q]uiet as it's kept, there were no marigolds in the fall of 1941"—and the dedication of Jones's novel, "Twenty-nine and more," points to the narrative's radically changed symbolic southern ritual grounds from those of *Beloved,* dedicated to "Sixty Million and more" (Morrison, *Bluest* 9).

13. The character of little Tayari in *Leaving Atlanta* therefore resembles Vladimir Nabokov's Vladimir Vladimirovich Nabokov in *Pnin* much more than the Man in the Macintosh in James Joyce's *Ulysses*—if, that is, one subscribes to Nabokov's own interpretation of the Bloomsday book (Nabokov, *Pnin* 185–91; Nabokov, *Lectures* 316–20; Joyce 90–91, 209, 273, 307–8, 348, 395–96, 529, 600). In *Ulysses,* the appearance of the author in disguise is but one of a myriad of puzzles Joyce proudly proclaimed to have hidden in the novel for generations of English professors to ponder over (Kenner, *Ulysses* 9). In both *Pnin* and *Leaving Atlanta,* neither author's alter ego is a Joycean "self-involved enigma," but serves to remind us that the images we form about each other are often less than truthful, and thus these images also have the dangerous potential of portraying the people behind them as less than human (J. Joyce 600; B. Boyd 278–79). Perhaps because both Jones and Nabokov are, ultimately, champions of the human imagination—if in very different ways, to be sure—*Pnin*'s hero, just like Octavia at the close of "Sweet Pea," is released at the end into a freedom that can only be imagined, not narrated: "Then [Pnin's] little sedan boldly swung past the front truck and, free at last, spurted up the shining road, which

one could make out narrowing to a thread of gold in the soft mist where hill after hill made beauty of distance, and where there was simply no saying what miracle might happen" (191). Tayari Jones's brother, Lumumba, also has a few cameo appearances of his own in *Leaving Atlanta*.

14. Rodney's father is also in many ways Jones's revision of the tragic hero in August Wilson's play *Fences*, Troy Maxson, who chastises his younger son, "A man got to take care of his family. You live in my house . . . sleep you behind on my bedclothes . . . fill you belly up with my food . . . cause you my son. You my flesh and blood. Not 'cause I like you! Cause it's my duty to take care of you. I owe a responsibility to you!" (2431). Claude Green imparts to his son that his brother Joe never amounted to anything because his father was already too old to give his youngest son "a good whipping when he needed it"; like Troy Maxson, Joe works as a garbage man for his city's sanitation department (132).

15. "Red Dog," the brief skit that precedes "Dirty South," mimics a drug raid gone bad. It begins with a character named Straight Shooter knocking on the door of a drug house. Immediately following the completion of the transaction, armed police storm the premises and subdue everyone with force. In an obvious distancing of referent from sign, the skit implies that Straight Shooter acts as an informant and is hence shooting anything but straight. The skit's title refers to a paramilitary antidrug police squad that was notorious, especially in Atlanta's black community, for its brutality and corruption (M. Miller, "Rap" 183–84). Although the squad has since dissolved, the Red Dogs' mystique continues to live on among the city's law enforcement and malefactors (Richard B. Lyle III, personal communication, Georgia State Board of Pardons and Paroles, Atlanta, Georgia, 20 May 2005).

16. Although the characters are, for the most part, not aware of it, the West End is also the location of The Wren's Nest, Joel Chandler Harris's home, a national historic landmark and perennial intimation of Harris's appropriation of the Uncle Remus stories. Furthermore, the name of the protagonist's sister, Hermione, Jones says she got not from Shakespeare's *The Winter's Tale*, but from a novel by H. D. entitled *HERmione*; there, the child bearing that name is constantly reminded by the mother that her name derives from the great playwright's work and therefore carries with it certain responsibilities of decorum (T. Jones, "(Un-)Telling" 73, 75). In *The Untelling*, the mother's favorite admonition is, "That is not what Dr. King died for" (1).

17. The time frame of the novel coincides with the very public debate surrounding the body of yet another Atlantan, the puzzling yet appropriately named mascot of the 1996 Olympics, the androgynous Whatizit? (Hiskey 14; Rutheiser 1–7).

18. Jones signifies here on Faulkner's famous pronouncement to his students at the University of Virginia that there was "no such thing really as was because the past is" (*Faulkner* 84).

Conclusion

1. To be sure, postmodernism is perhaps an even more hotly contested concept than modernism. Fittingly, the term itself eludes definition, or even consistent application. bell hooks, for example, appears to use it as a catchall term that includes the theoretical enterprises of deconstruction and poststructuralism. I use the terms

postmodernist to denote certain aspects of and trends in contemporary literary and mass culture, and *poststructuralist* or *deconstructionist* to denote the critical theories that accompany them.

2. The nexus between consumer capitalism and the commodification of culture Huyssen illuminates here brings to mind Robert Stepto's "'tribal' geography" that supplies "the currency of exchange, as it were, within the realm of *communitas*" (70, 77). Except that in Stepto's paradigm, this currency of the vernacular must resist capitalist cooption. This, then, also brings to mind Benedict Anderson's contention that "[c]ommunities are to be distinguished, not by their falsity/genuineness, but by the style in which they are imagined" (6).

3. Madhu Dubey's critique exposes an apparent self-contradiction in hooks's take on (black) postmodernism: elsewhere in *Yearning*, hooks's "cure for the fragmentation of black communal life in the post-Civil Rights era calls for a retrieval of the very conditions that she earlier admits to be irrevocably lost—the 'organic unity' and 'traditional black folk experience' of the days of racial segregation" (34). Nevertheless, hooks's "authority of experience" can remain a valuable concept for a critique of postmodern blackness if we remind ourselves that said experience is far from homogenous (as hooks herself insists repeatedly); nor is said authority always absolute (as the unresolved paradox in *Yearning* manifests).

4. See, for example, also K. Davis (242–44); Dubey (19–22); Hakutani (viii); Spaulding (1–4); and Werner (20). It is also worth pointing out here that elements of Christian Moraru's rereading of postmodernism as "memorious discourse" are based on bell hooks and on his readings of African American writers such as Ishmael Reed or Charles Johnson as well as on hip-hop (*Memorious* 118–24; *Postmodern* 83–125).

5. Postmodern neominstrelsy has also been satirized in feature-length films such as Robert Townsend's *Hollywood Shuffle* or Spike Lee's *Bamboozled* and is widespread enough that it has engendered a countermovement: the Internet-based "Stop Coonin Movement" consists of "an underground collective of educators and activists" whose slogan is "Hustlin Consciousness to the Hip Hop Community" (*Stop*).

SELECTED DISCOGRAPHY

Allman, Gregg. "Whippin' Post." *Searching for Simplicity*. 550 Music, 1997.
Allman Brothers Band. *The Allman Brothers Band. Beginnings*. Polygram, n.d.
———. *The Allman Brothers Band Live at the Atlanta International Pop Festival*. 2 CDs. Legacy, 2003.
———. *The Allman Brothers Band at Fillmore East*. Capricorn, n.d.
———. "Come On in My Kitchen." *Shades of Two Worlds*. Epic, 1991.
———. *Eat a Peach*. Capricorn/Polygram, n.d.
———. "High Falls." *Win, Lose or Draw*. Capricorn, n.d.
———. *Idlewild South*. Polygram, n.d.
———. *Instant Live: Alltel Pavilion at Walnut Creek—Raleigh, NC 8/10/03*. 2 CDs. Peach Records, 2003.
———. "Kind of Bird." *Shades of Two Worlds*. Epic, 1991.
———. "Mountain Jam." *Live at Ludlow Garage 1970*. 2 CDs. Polygram, 1990.

————. "Whippin' Post." *American University 12/13/70*. Sanctuary, 2005.

Basie, Count. "Gone With 'What' Wind?" *Charlie Christian: Genius of the Electric Guitar*. By Charlie Christian. Giants of Jazz, 1990.

————. "Gone With 'What' Wind?" *The Count Basie Story*. 4 CDs. Proper, 2006.

Bell, William. "I Forgot to Be Your Lover." *The Stax Story*. 4 CDs. Stax, 2000.

Charlie Daniels Band. "The Devil Went Down to Georgia." *The Essential Super Hits of the Charlie Daniels Band*. Koch, 2004.

————. "The South's Gonna Do It Again." *Fire on the Mountain*. Sony, 1990.

Clapton, Eric. *Me and Mr. Johnson*. Reprise/WEA, 2004.

Coltrane, John. "My Favorite Things." *My Favorite Things*. Atlantic, 1990.

————. *A Love Supreme*. Impulse!, 1995.

Davis, Miles. *Kind of Blue*. LP. CBS, 1962.

Derek and the Dominos. *Layla and Other Assorted Love Songs*. Polydor, 1990.

Derek Trucks Band. "Volunteered Slavery." *Songlines*. Columbia, 2006.

Dixon, Willie. "(I'm Your) Hoochie Coochie Man." *Willie Dixon: The Chess Box*. 2 CDs. MCA, 1989.

Drive-By Truckers. *The Dirty South*. New West, 2004.

Donovan. "There Is a Mountain." *Donovan's Greatest Hits*. Sony, 1999.

Edison Mixed Quartet. "When the Roll Is Called Up Yonder." By James M. Black. *Inventing Entertainment: The Motion Pictures and Sound Recordings of the Edison Companies*. Library of Congress. 17 Feb. 2005 http://memory.loc.gov/cgi-bin/query/r?ammem/papr:@filreq(@field(NUMBER+@band(edrs+80276r))+@field(COLLID+edison)).

Ellington, Duke. "Black and Tan Fantasy." *This Is Duke Ellington*. 2 LPs. RCA, 1971.

Goodie Mob. *Soul Food*. Arista, 1995.

Gov't Mule. "Mule." *Gov't Mule*. Capricorn, 1995.

Grieg, Edvard. *Grieg: Piano Music*, Vol. 2. Naxos, 1995.

Hooker, John Lee. "Boom Boom." *John Lee Hooker: Real Gold*. 2 CDs. Weton-Wesgram, 2003.

Johnson, Robert. "Cross Road Blues." *Robert Johnson: The Complete Recordings*. 2 CDs. CBS, 1990.

Kirk, Rahsaan Roland. "Volunteered Slavery." *Volunteered Slavery*. Atlantic, n.d.

Led Zeppelin. "Dazed and Confused." *Led Zeppelin*. Atlantic, 2000.

Little Brother. *The Minstrel Show*. Atlantic/Wea, 2005.

Ludacris. "Growing Pains." *Word of Mouf*. Def Jam, 2001.

Lynyrd Skynyrd. *Lynyrd Skynyrd*. 3 cassettes. MCA, 1991.

————. *Lynyrd Skynyrd (Pronounced 'leh-'nérd 'skin-'nérd)*. MCA, 2001.

————. *Second Helping*. MCA, 1997. ˇ

Mahal, Taj. "Statesboro Blues." *The Essential Taj Mahal*. Sony, 2005.

Mahler, Gustav. Symphony no. 1. *Mahler: Symphony No. 1*. Deutsche Grammophon, 1999.

Marsalis, Wynton. *Black Codes (From the Underground)*. Columbia, 1985.

McTell, Blind Willie. "Statesboro Blues." *Blind Willie McTell: The Classic Years, 1927-1940*. 4 CDs. JSP, 2003.

Mingus, Charles. "Fables of Faubus." *Fables of Faubus*. Jazz Time, 1998.

Nelson, Oliver. *The Blues and the Abstract Truth*. Impulse!, 1995.

Redman, Joshua. *Joshua Redman*. Warner Bros., 1993.

Reinhardt, Django. "Fantasie sur une danse Norvégienne." *Paris and London: 1937–1948, Vol. 2.* 4 CDs. JSP, 2001.

Shizzoe, Hank, and the Directors. *Out and About.* Sound Service, 2005.

Stravinsky, Igor, and Charles Ferdinand Ramuz. *L'histoire du soldat.* Nimbus, 1986.

Turner, Ike, and His Kings of Rhythm. "Rocket 88." *Rhythm Rockin' Blues.* Ace 2001.

Waters, Muddy. "Hoochie Coochie Man." *The Muddy Waters Story.* Déja Vu, 1989.

Zorn, John, and Naked City. *Naked City.* Elektra Nonesuch, 1990.

ABB 1971. Contracts Jan. to June. Folder. The Big House: The Allman Brothers Band Museum, Macon, GA.

Abbott, Lynn, and Doug Seroff. *Ragged but Right: Black Traveling Shows, "Coon Songs," and the Dark Pathway to Blues and Jazz.* Jackson: University Press of Mississippi, 2007.

Abernathy, Jeff. *To Hell and Back: Race and Betrayal in the Southern Novel.* Athens: University of Georgia Press, 2003.

Adell, Sandra. *Double-Consciousness/Double Bind: Theoretical Issues in Twentieth-Century Black Literature.* Urbana: University of Illinois Press, 1994.

Adorno, Theodor Wiesengrund. *Ästhetische Theorie.* Eds. Gretel Adorno et al. 1970. Frankfurt am Main: Suhrkamp, 1998.

Allen, William Francis, Charles Pickard Ware, and Lucy McKim Garrison, eds. *Slave Songs of the United States.* 1867. Bedford, MA: Applewood, 1995.

Allman Brothers Band. Concert. Piedmont Park, Atlanta, GA. 8 Sept. 2007.

Alridge, Derrick P. "From Civil Rights to Hip Hop: Toward a Nexus of Ideas." *Journal of African American History* 90.3 (2005): 227–53.

American Federation of Musicians of the United States and Canada Contract no. 524. Walden Artists Local no. 359. 10 Dec. 1970. Country Music Hall of Fame, Nashville, TN.

Anderson, Benedict. *Imagined Communities: Reflections on the Origin and Spread of Nationalism*. Rev. ed. London: Verso, 1991.

Anderson, Eric Gary. "Black Atlanta: An Ecosocial Approach to Narratives of the Atlanta Child Murders." *PMLA* 122.1 (2007): 194–209.

Anderson, Paul Allen. *Deep River: Music and Memory in Harlem Renaissance Thought*. Durham, NC: Duke University Press, 2001.

Andrews, William L., ed. *Critical Essays on Frederick Douglass*. Boston: G. K. Hall, 1991.

———. *To Tell a Free Story: The First Century of Afro-American Autobiography, 1760–1865*. Urbana: University of Illinois Press, 1986.

Appel, Alfred Jr. *Jazz Modernism: From Ellington and Armstrong to Matisse and Joyce*. New York: Knopf, 2002.

"Atlanta Child Murders." Federal Bureau of Investigation. 16 Dec. 2008 http://foia.fbi.gov/foiaindex/atlanta.htm.

Auerbach, Erich. *Mimesis: Dargestellte Wirklichkeit in der abendländischen Literatur*. 1946. Bern: Francke, 1988.

Baker, Houston A. Jr. *Blues, Ideology, and Afro-American Literature: A Vernacular Theory*. Chicago: University of Chicago Press, 1984.

———. *The Journey Back: Issues in Black Literature and Criticism*. Chicago: University of Chicago Press, 1980.

———. *Modernism and the Harlem Renaissance*. Chicago: University of Chicago Press, 1987.

Baldwin, James. *The Evidence of Things Not Seen*. New York: Holton, Rinehart, and Winston, 1985.

Bambara, Toni Cade. *Those Bones Are Not My Child*. Ed. Toni Morrison. New York: Vintage, 1999.

Bamboozled. Dir. Spike Lee. New Line Cinema, 2000.

Baraka, Amiri. *Blues People: The Negro Experience in America and the Music that Developed from It*. New York: Morrow Quill, 1963.

———. "The Great Music Robbery." *The Music: Reflections on Jazz and Blues*. By Amiri Baraka and Amina Baraka. New York: Morrow, 1987. 328–32.

Basie, Count. *Good Morning Blues: The Autobiography of Count Basie, as Told to Albert Murray*. Ed. Albert Murray. New York: Random House, 1985.

Bastin, Bruce. "Truckin' My Blues Away: East Coast Piedmont Styles." Cohn 205–31.

Baudelaire, Charles. *Les fleurs du mal*. 1857. Ed. Antoine Adam. Paris: Garnier, 1961.

Baugh, John. *Black Street Speech: Its History, Structure, and Survival*. Austin: University of Texas Press, 1983.

Benistad, Finn. "Grieg und der norwegische Volkston: Eine lebenslange Liebesgeschichte." *Edvard Grieg*. Ed. Ulrich Tadday. *Musik-Konzepte*. Vol. 127. Munich: Richard Boorberg, 2005. 67–82.

Benjamin, Walter. "Das Kunstwerk im Zeitalter seiner technischen Reproduzierbarkeit." 1935/36. *Illuminationen* 136–69.

————. *Illuminationen: Ausgewählte Schriften 1*. Ed. Siegfried Unseld. Frankfurt am Main: Suhrkamp, 1974.

————. "Kleine Geschichte der Photographie." 1931. *Walter Benjamin: Ein Lesebuch*. Ed. Michael Opitz. Fankfurt am Main: Suhrkamp, 1996. 287–312.

————. "Über einige Motive bei Baudelaire." 1939. *Illuminationen* 185–229.

Benston, Kimberly W. *Performing Blackness: Enactments of African-American Modernism*. London: Routledge, 2000.

Black, Les. "Out of Sight: Southern Music and the Coloring of Sound." *Out of Whiteness: Color, Politics, and Culture*. By Vron Ware and Les Black. Chicago: University of Chicago Press, 2002. 227–70.

Blackling, John. "The Problem of 'Ethnic' Perceptions in the Semiotics of Music." *The Sign in Music and Literature*. Ed. Wendy Steiner. Austin: University of Texas Press, 1981. 184–94.

Bleikasten, André. *The Ink of Melancholy: Faulkner's Novels from* The Sound and the Fury *to* Light in August. Bloomington: Indiana University Press, 1990.

Bontemps, Arna. "Letter to Langston Hughes." 14 Nov. 1939. Nichols 41–42.

————. "Letter to Langston Hughes." 26 Jan. 1940. Nichols 53–54.

————. "Letter to Langston Hughes." 7 Feb. 1941. Nichols 73–74.

————. "Letter to Langston Hughes." 2 July 1941. Nichols 84.

Boyd, Brian. *Vladimir Nabokov: The American Years*. Princeton, NJ: Princeton University Press, 1991.

Boyd, Eddie. "Eddie Boyd." 1977. *The Voice of the Blues: Classic Interviews from Living Blues Magazine*. Eds. Jim O'Neal and Amy van Singel. New York: Routledge, 2002. 226–79.

Brent, Marley. *Southern Rock: The Roots and Legacy of Southern Rock*. New York: Billboard, 1999.

Brown, Geoff. *Otis Redding: Try a Little Tenderness*. Edinburgh: Mojo, 2001.

Brown, James, and Bruce Tucker. *James Brown: The Godfather of Soul*. New York: Macmillan, 1986.

Butler, J. Michael. "'Lord, Have Mercy on My Soul': Sin, Salvation, and Southern Rock." *Southern Cultures* 9.4 (2003): 73–87.

Butler, Mike. "'Luther King Was a Good Ole Boy': The Southern Rock Movement and White Male Identity in the Post-Civil Rights South." *Popular Music and Society* 23.2 (1999): 41–61.

Butler, Robert. "The Postmodern City in Colson Whitehead's *The Colossus of New York* and Jeffrey Renard Allen's *Rails Under My Back*." *CLA Journal* 48.1 (2004): 71–87.

Campbell, Joseph L. *A Book of Tails: A Collection of "Tails"—My Life and Travels on the Road*. Private printing, 2001.

Cataliotti, Robert H. *The Music in African American Fiction*. New York: Garland, 1995.

Clapton, Eric. "Discovering Robert Johnson." *Robert Johnson: The Complete Recordings*. Booklet. 2 CDs. CBS, 1990. 22–23.

Cobb, William Jelani. *To the Break of Dawn: A Freestyle on the Hip Hop Aesthetic*. New York: New York University Press, 2007.

Cohn, Lawrence, ed. *Nothing But the Blues: The Music and the Musicians*. New York: Abbeville, 1993.

Crouch, Stanley. Liner notes. *Black Codes (From the Underground)*. By Wynton Marsalis. Columbia, 1985. 5–13.

Davis, Angela Y. *Blues Legacies and Black Feminism: Gertrude "Ma" Rainey, Bessie Smith, and Billie Holiday*. New York: Pantheon, 1988.

Davis, Kimberly Chabot. "'Postmodern Blackness': Toni Morrison's *Beloved* and the End of History." *Twentieth Century Literature* 44.2 (1998): 242–60.

de Man, Paul. "Autobiography as De-facement." *Modern Language Notes* 94.5 (1979): 919–30.

———. "The Resistance to Theory." *Contemporary Literary Criticism: Literary and Cultural Studies*. Eds. Robert Con Davis and Ronald Schleifer. New York: Longman, 1986. 94–108.

Decosta-Willis, Miriam. "Avenging Angels and Mute Mothers: Black Southern Women in Wright's Fictional World." *Callaloo* 9 (1986): 540–49.

Derrida, Jacques. *Of Grammatology*. 1967. Trans. Gayatri Chakravorty Spivak. Baltimore: Johns Hopkins University Press, 1976.

Dettlinger, Chet, and Jeff Prugh. *The List*. Atlanta: Philmay, 1984.

Dick, Bruce. "Richard Wright and the Blues Connection." *Mississippi Quarterly* 42.4 (1989): 393–408.

Dombrowski, Ralf. *Basis-Diskothek Jazz*. Stuttgart: Reclam, 2005.

Douglass, Frederick. *Frederick Douglass: Autobiographies*. Ed. Henry Louis Gates, Jr. New York: Library of America, 1994.

———. "The Proclamation and a Negro Army." *The Frederick Douglass Papers*. Eds. John W. Blassingame et al. New Haven, CT: Yale University Press, 1985. I.3: 549–69.

Doyle, Laura. *Bordering on the Body: The Racial Matrix of Modern Fiction and Culture*. New York: Oxford University Press, 1994.

Dregni, Michael. *Django: The Life and Music of a Gypsy Legend*. New York: Oxford University Press, 2004.

Du Bois, W. E. B. *The Autobiography of W. E. B. Du Bois: A Soliloquy on Viewing My Life from the Last Decade of Its First Century*. 1968. New York: International, 1997.

———. "A Litany of Atlanta." Hill et al. 754–56.

———. *The Souls of Black Folk*. 1903. New York: Dover, 1994.

Dubey, Madhu. *Signs and Cities: Black Literary Postmodernism*. Chicago: University of Chicago Press, 2003.

duCille, Ann. *The Coupling Convention: Sex, Text, and Tradition in Black Women's Fiction*. New York: Oxford University Press, 1993.

Dunbar, Paul Laurence. "We Wear the Mask." Hill et al. 615.

Duncan, Bowie. "Jean Toomer's *Cane*: A Modern Black Oracle." *CLA Journal* 15.3 (1972): 323–33.

Duvall, John N. *The Identifying Fictions of Toni Morrison: Modernist Authenticity and Postmodern Blackness*. New York: Palgrave, 2000.

Dyer, Geoff. "Tradition, Influence, and Innovation." *But Beautiful: A Book About Jazz*. New York: North Point, 1996. 181–216.

Eakin, Paul John. *Fictions in Autobiography: Studies in the Art of Self-Invention*. Princeton, NJ: Princeton University Press, 1985.

———. *Touching the World: Reference in Autobiography*. Princeton, NJ: Princeton University Press, 1992.

Ellison, Ralph. *The Collected Essays of Ralph Ellison*. Ed. John F. Callahan. New York: Modern Library, 1995.

————. *Going to the Territory*. 1986. Collected 487–781.

————. Introduction. *Invisible Man*. 1952. New York: Vintage, 1981. vii–xxiii.

————. *Invisible Man*. 1952. New York: Vintage, 1981.

————. *Shadow and Act*. 1964. Collected 47–340.

"Emancipation Day in Boston." *Liberator* 16 Jan. 1863: 12.

Evans, David. "Goin' up the Country: Blues in Texas and the Deep South." Cohn 33–85.

Fabre, Michel. *The Unfinished Quest of Richard Wright*. New York: William Morrow, 1973.

Faulkner, William. *Absalom, Absalom!* 1936. Ed. Noel Polk. New York: Vintage International, 1990.

————. *As I Lay Dying*. 1930. Ed. Noel Polk. New York: Vintage International, 1990.

————. *Faulkner in the University: Class Conferences at the University of Virginia, 1957–1958*. Eds. Frederick L. Gwynn and Joseph L. Blotner. New York: Vintage, 1967.

————. *The Reivers: A Reminiscence*. New York: Vintage, 1962.

————. *The Sound and the Fury*. 1929. Ed. David Minter. New York: Norton, 1987.

Favor, J. Martin. *Authentic Blackness: The Folk in the New Negro Renaissance*. Durham, NC: Duke University Press, 1999.

Floyd, Samuel A. Jr. *The Power of Black Music: Interpreting Its History from Africa to the United States*. New York: Oxford University Press, 1995.

Foley, Barbara. "'In the Land of Cotton': Economics and Violence in Jean Toomer's *Cane*." *African American Review* 32.2 (1998): 181–98.

————. "Jean Toomer's Sparta." *American Literature* 67.4 (1995): 747–75.

Foner, Eric. *Reconstruction: America's Unfinished Revolution, 1863–1877*. New York: Harper and Row, 1988.

Franklin, John Hope. *The Emancipation Proclamation*. Garden City, NY: Doubleday, 1963.

————, and Loren Schweninger. *Runaway Slaves: Rebels on the Plantation*. New York: Oxford University Press, 1999.

Freeman, Scott. *Midnight Riders: The Story of the Allman Brothers Band*. Boston: Little, Brown, 1995.

————. *Otis! The Otis Redding Story*. New York: St. Martin's, 2001.

Frow, George L. *The Edison Disc Phonographs and the Diamond Discs*. Rev. ed. Los Angeles: Mulholland, 2001.

Fulton, DoVeanna S. "Singing the Mississippi: New Directions from Black Women Gospel Singers." Stemming the Mississippi: Constructing/Deconstructing Myth and Reality. Centre Interdisciplinaire de Recherches Nord-Américaines CIRNA. Université Paris VII-Denis Diderot, Paris. 27 Feb. 2003.

————. *Speaking Power: Black Feminist Orality in Women's Narratives of Slavery*. Albany: State University of New York Press, 2006.

Gardner, Laurel J. "The Progression of Meaning in the Images of Violence in Richard Wright's *Uncle Tom's Children* and *Native Son*." *CLA Journal* 38.4 (1995): 420–40.

Gates, Henry Louis. *Figures in Black: Words, Signs, and the "Racial" Self*. New York: Oxford University Press, 1987.

————, et al., eds. *The Norton Anthology of African American Literature*. New York: Norton, 1997.

————. *The Signifying Monkey: A Theory of African-American Literary Criticism*. New York: Oxford University Press, 1988.

Gennari, John. *Blowin' Hot and Cool: Jazz and Its Critics*. Chicago: University of Chicago Press, 2006.

George, Nelson. *Buppies, B-Boys, Baps and Bobos: Notes on Post-Soul Black Culture*. New York: Harper Collins, 1992.

Gilroy, Paul. *The Black Atlantic: Modernity and Double Consciousness*. Cambridge, MA: Harvard University Press, 1993.

————. "Living Memory: A Meeting with Toni Morrison." *Small Acts: Thoughts on the Politics of Black Cultures*. London: Serpent's Tail, 1993. 175–82.

Grandt, Jürgen E. *Kinds of Blue: The Jazz Aesthetic in African American Narrative*. Columbus: The Ohio State University Press, 2004.

Grazian, David. *Blue Chicago: The Search for Authenticity in Urban Blues Clubs*. Chicago: University of Chicago Press, 2003.

Grimsley, Jim. *Winter Birds*. Chapel Hill, NC: Algonquin, 1994.

Gruver, Rod. "The Blues as Secular Religion." 1970. Tracy, *Write Me* 222–30.

Guralnick, Peter. *Sweet Soul Music: Rhythm and Blues and the Southern Dream of Freedom*. New York: Harper and Row, 1986.

Gussow, Adam. *Seems Like Murder Here: Southern Violence and the Blues Tradition*. Chicago: University of Chicago Press, 2002.

H. D. *HERmione*. 1927. New York: New Directions, 1981.

Hadley, Fank-John. "First Family of Modern Blues." *Down Beat* Feb. 2007: 27–33.

Hakutani, Yoshinobu. *Cross-Cultural Visions in African American Modernism: From Spatial Narrative to Jazz Haiku*. Columbus: The Ohio State University Press, 2006.

Handy, W. C. *Father of the Blues: An Autobiography*. Ed. Arna Bontemps. 1941. New York: Da Capo, 1991.

————. *Father of the Blues as Edited by Arna Bontemps*. Typescript, n.d. W. C. Handy Birthplace, Museum, and Library, Florence, AL.

————. *Fight It Out*. Typescript, n.d. Box marked "Handy Collection Box #3." W. C. Handy Birthplace, Museum, and Library, Florence, AL.

————. "Handy Explains the Origins of 'The Blues'!" *Florence Herald*. *W. C. Handy Memorial Edition* 1970: 16–17. Unmarked box. W. C. Handy Birthplace, Museum, and Library, Florence, AL.

————. Letter to Hank Patterson. 6 Sept. 1950. Unmarked box. File labeled "Correspondence with Mrs. Hubert Patterson, Taylor, TX." W. C. Handy Birthplace, Museum, and Library, Florence, AL.

————. Letter to Margaret Tubb. 30 Jan. 1930. Box marked "Miscellaneous donated items." File labeled "List of Handy's Recorded Music and Correspondence to Friends Donated by Roger Holtin." W. C. Handy Birthplace, Museum, and Library, Florence, AL.

Hay, Fred J., ed. *Goin' Back to Sweet Memphis: Conversations with the Blues*. Athens: University of Georgia Press, 2001.

Headley, Bernard D. *The Atlanta Youth Murders and the Politics of Race*. Rev. ed. Carbondale: Southern Illinois University Press, 2000.

Henderson, Stephen. *Understanding the New Black Poetry: Black Speech and Black Music as Poetic References*. New York: William Morrow, 1972.

Hewitt, Roger. "Black through White: Hoagy Carmichael and the Cultural Reproduction of Racism." *Popular Music 3: Producers and Markets.* Eds. Richard Middleton and David Horn. Cambridge: Cambridge University Press, 1983. 33–54.

Hill, Patricia Liggins, et al., eds. *Call and Response: The Riverside Anthology of the African American Literary Tradition.* Boston: Houghton Mifflin, 1998.

Hiskey, Michelle. "Where's Izzy? Blue Hot Potato Lives in Memories, but not in Public." *Atlanta Journal-Constitution* 22 July 2006: A1.

Hollywood Shuffle. Dir. Robert Townsend. Samuel Goldwyn, 1987.

Hood, Patterson. Interview. Nov. 2003. *Recoil.* 3 Nov. 2008 http://www.recoilmag.com/interviews/drive-by_truckers_1103.html.

———. Liner Notes. *The Dirty South.* By The Drive-By Truckers. CD. New West, 2004.

hooks, bell. *Yearning: Race, Gender, and Cultural Politics.* Boston: South End, 1990.

Hughes, Langston. "Daybreak in Alabama." *Selected Poems of Langston Hughes.* 1959. New York: Vintage Classics, 1990. 157.

Hurd, Myles Raymond. "Between Blackness and Bitonality: Wright's 'Long Black Song.'" *CLA Journal* 35.1 (1991): 42–56.

Hurston, Zora Neale. "The Gilded Six-Bits." Gates et al., *Norton* 1033–41.

———. "Sweat." 1926. Hill et al. 949–55.

———. *Their Eyes Were Watching God.* 1937. New York: Perennial, 1990.

Hutcheon, Linda. *A Theory of Parody: The Teachings of Twentieth-Century Art Forms.* New York: Methuen, 1985.

Hutchinson, George. *The Harlem Renaissance in Black and White.* Cambridge, MA: Belknap, 1995.

———. "Jean Toomer and American Racial Discourse." *Texas Studies in Literature and Language* 35.2 (1993): 226–50.

Huyssen, Andreas. *After the Great Divide: Modernism, Mass Culture, Postmodernism.* Bloomington: Indiana University Press, 1986.

Inventing Entertainment: The Motion Pictures and Sound Recordings of the Edison Companies. Library of Congress. 17 Feb. 2006 http://memory.loc.gov/cgi-bin/query/D?papr:1:./temp/~ammem_20Z3::.

Jennings, Derek. "*LB Weekly* Story of the Week: The Minstrel Show." *The Minstrel Show.* By Little Brother. Atlantic, 2005. 1–2.

Johnson, James Weldon. *The Autobiography of an Ex-Coloured Man.* 1912. New York: Vintage, 1989.

Jones, Kirkland C. *Renaissance Man from Louisiana: A Biography of Arna Wendell Bontemps.* Westport, CT: Greenwood, 1992.

Jones, Robert B. "Jean Toomer as Poet: A Phenomenology of the Spirit." *Black American Literature Forum* 21.3 (1987): 253–73.

———. *Jean Toomer and the Prison House of Thought: A Phenomenology of the Spirit.* Amherst: University of Massachusetts Press, 1993.

Jones, Tayari. *Leaving Atlanta.* New York: Time Warner, 2002.

———. "The Toxic Silence." *Atlanta Journal-Constitution* 22 May 2005: E1.

———. *The Untelling.* New York: Time Warner, 2005.

———. "(Un-)Telling Truth: An Interview with Tayari Jones." *Langston Hughes Review* 19 (2005): 70–81.

Joyce, James. *Ulysses.* 1922. Ed. Hans Walter Gabler. New York: Vintage, 1986.

Joyce, Joyce Ann. "Richard Wright's 'Long Black Song': A Moral Dilemma." *Mississippi Quarterly* 42.4 (1989): 379–85.

Jusdanis, Gregory. *Belated Modernity and Aesthetic Culture: Inventing National Literature*. Minneapolis: University of Minnesota Press, 1991.

Kemp, Mark. *Dixie Lullaby: A Story of Music, Race, and New Beginnings in a New South*. New York: Free Press, 2004.

Kenner, Hugh. *A Homemade World: The American Modernist Writers*. Baltimore: Johns Hopkins University Press, 1975.

———. "Poets at the Blackboard." 1982. *Historical Fictions: Essays by Hugh Kenner*. Athens: University of Georgia Press, 1995. 109–21.

———. *The Pound Era*. London: Faber and Faber, 1972.

———. *Ulysses*. Rev. ed. Baltimore: Johns Hopkins University Press, 1987.

Kenney, William. *Recorded Music in American Life: The Phonograph and Popular Memory, 1890–1945*. New York: Oxford University Press, 1999.

Kent, Drew. Liner Notes. *Blind Willie McTell: The Classic Years, 1927–1940*. 4 CDs. JSP, 2003.

Kent, George E. *Blackness and the Adventure of Western Culture*. Chicago: Third World, 1972.

Kerman, Cynthia Earl, and Richard Eldridge. *The Lives of Jean Toomer: A Hunger for Wholeness*. Baton Rouge: Louisiana State University Press, 1987.

Kibbey, Ann, and Michele Stepto. "The Antilanguage of Slavery: Frederick Douglass's 1845 *Narrative*." Andrews, *Critical Essays* 166–91.

Krims, Adam. *Rap Music and the Poetics of Identity*. Cambridge: Cambridge University Press, 2000.

Labov, William. *Language in the Inner City: Studies in the Black English Vernacular*. Philadelphia: University of Pennsylvania Press, 1972.

Leavell, Chuck, and J. Marshall Craig. *Between Rock and a Home Place*. Macon, GA: Mercer University Press, 2004.

Lehman, David. *Sign of the Times: Deconstruction and the Fall of Paul de Man*. New York: Poseidon, 1992.

Lesemann, Ballard. "Drive-By Truckers." 28 Feb. 2004. *AthensMusicNet*. 13 July 2006 http://athens music.net/newsdesk_info.php?newsPath=11&newsdesk_id=38.

Lewis, David Levering. *When Harlem Was in Vogue*. New York: Oxford University Press, 1989.

Lewis, George E. "Improvised Music After 1950: Afrological and Eurological Perspectives." *Black Music Research Journal* 16.1 (1996): 91–122.

Lhamon, W. T., Jr. *Raising Cain: Black Performance from Jim Crow to Hip Hop*. Cambridge, MA: Harvard University Press, 1998.

Lieb, Sandra R. *Mother of the Blues: A Study of Ma Rainey*. Amherst: University of Massachusetts Press, 1981.

Lincoln, C. Eric. *The Negro Pilgrimage in America: The Coming of Age of Blackamericans*. Rev. ed. New York: Praeger, 1969.

———. *Race, Religion, and the Continuing American Dilemma*. Rev. ed. New York: Hill and Wang, 1999.

Lindner, Burkhard. "Technische Reproduzierbarkeit und Kulturindustrie: Benjamin's 'Positives Barbarentum' im Kontext." *"Links hatte noch alles sich zu enträtseln . . .": Walter Benjamin im Kontext*. Ed. Burkhard Lindner. Frankfurt am Main: Syndikat, 1978. 180–223.

Lipsitz, George. *Dangerous Crossroads: Popular Music, Postmodernism, and the Poetics of Place*. London: Verso, 1994.

Little Brother. Booklet. *The Minstrel Show*. Atlantic, 2005.

"Little Brother: 'Getback.'" *The Hall of Justus Music Group*. Justus League. 7 May 2008 http://www. hallofjustus.com/littlebrother.php.

Locke, Alain. "The New Negro." 1926. *The Portable Harlem Renaissance Reader*. Ed. David Levering Lewis. New York: Penguin, 1994. 46–51.

Lott, Eric. *Love and Theft: Blackface Minstrelsy and the American Working Class*. New York: Oxford University Press, 1993.

Lynskey, John. "Gregg Allman: Simplicity Found." *Hittin' the Note* 19 (1998): 10–17.

Mackey, Nathaniel. *Discrepant Engagement: Dissonance, Cross-Culturality, and Experimental Writing*. New York: Cambridge University Press, 1993.

Magee, Jeffrey. "Kinds of Blue: Miles Davis, Afro-Modernism, and the Blues." *Jazz Perspectives* 1.1 (2007): 5–27.

Malone, Bill C., and David Stricklin. *Southern Music/American Music*. Rev. ed. Lexington: University of Kentucky Press, 2003.

Manis, Andrew M. *Macon Black and White: An Unutterable Separation in the American Century*. Macon, GA: Mercer University Press, 2004.

Marcus, Greil. *Mystery Train: Images of America in Rock 'n' Roll Music*. New York: E. P. Dutton, 1975.

Martin, Bruce K. "Music and Fiction: The Perils of Popularism." *Mosaic* 31.4 (1998): 21–39.

Martin, Waldo E., Jr. *The Mind of Frederick Douglass*. Chapel Hill: University of North Carolina Press, 1984.

Mattison, Mike. "Inside Looking In: The *Songlines* Story." *Hittin' the Note* 48 (2006): 38–43.

McCarthy, B. Eugene. "Models of History in Richard Wright's *Uncle Tom's Children*." *Black American Literature Forum* 25.4 (1991): 729–43.

McCole, John. *Walter Benjamin and the Antinomies of Tradition*. Ithaca, NY: Cornell University Press, 1993.

McDowell, Deborah E. *"The Changing Same": Black Women's Literature, Criticism, and Theory*. Bloomington: Indiana University Press, 1995.

———. "In the First Place: Making Frederick Douglass and the Afro-American Narrative Tradition." *African American Autobiography: A Collection of Critical Essays*. Ed. William L. Andrews. Englewood Cliffs, NJ: Prentice Hall, 1993. 36–58.

McFeely, William S. *Frederick Douglass*. New York: Norton, 1991.

McKay, Nellie Y. *Jean Toomer, Artist: A Study of His Literary Life and Work, 1894–1936*. Chapel Hill: University of North Carolina Press, 1984.

McLeod, Kembrew. "Authenticity within Hip-Hop and Other Cultures Threatened with Assimilation." *Journal of Communications* 49.4 (1999): 134–50.

McPherson, James M. *Battle Cry of Freedom: The American Civil War*. London: Penguin, 1990.

Michaels, Walter Benn. *Our America: Nativism, Modernism, and Pluralism*. Durham, NC: Duke University Press, 1995.

Millard, André J. *America on Record: A History of Recorded Sound*. Cambridge: Cambridge University Press, 2005.

Miller, Matt. "Dirty Decade: Rap Music and the U.S. South, 1997–2007." 10 June 2008. *Southern Spaces*. Emory University. 3 Nov. 2008 http://www. southernspaces. org/contents/2008/miller/1a.htm.

———. "Rap's Dirty South: From Subculture to Pop Culture." *Journal of Popular Music Studies* 16.2 (2004): 175–212.

Miller, R. Baxter. "Baptized Infidel: Play and Critical Legacy." *Black American Literature Forum* 21.4 (1987): 393–414.

———. "Blacks in His Cellar: The Personal Tragedy of Jean Toomer." *Langston Hughes Review* 11.1 (1992): 36–40.

———. "The Rewritten Self in African American Autobiography." *Alternative Identities: The Self in Literature, History, Theory*. Ed. Linda Marie Brooks. New York: Garland, 1995. 87–104.

Mitchell, Margaret. *Gone with the Wind*. 1936. New York: Warner, 1993.

Mitchell, W. J. T. "Representation." *Critical Terms for Literary Study*. 2nd ed. Eds. Frank Lentricchia and Thomas McLaughlin. Chicago: University of Chicago Press, 1995. 11–22.

Moraru, Christian. *Memorious Discourse: Reprise and Representation in Postmodernism*. Madison, NJ: Farleigh Dickinson University Press, 2005.

———. *Postmodern Narrative and Cultural Critique in the Age of Cloning*. Albany: State University of New York Press, 2001.

Morrison, Toni. Afterword. 1993. *The Bluest Eye*. By Toni Morrison. Rpt. in Hill et al. 1773–76.

———. *Beloved*. 1987. New York: Plume, 1988.

———. *The Bluest Eye*. 1970. New York: Washington Square, 1972.

———. "City Limits, Village Values: Concepts of the Neighborhood in Black Fiction." *Literature and the Urban Experience: Essays on the City and Literature*. Eds. Michael C. Jaye and Ann Chalmers Watts. New Brunswick, NJ: Rutgers University Press, 1980. 35–43.

———. Interview. *Black Women Writers at Work*. Ed. Claudia Tate. New York: Continuum, 1983. 117–31.

———. "'The Language Must Not Sweat': A Conversation with Toni Morrison." *New Republic* 21 March 1981. 25–29.

———. "Recitatif." Hill et al. 1776–86.

———. "The Seams Can't Show: An Interview with Toni Morrison." *Black American Literature Forum* 12.2 (1978): 56–60.

Morton, David. *Off the Record: The Technology and Culture of Sound Recording in America*. New Brunswick, NJ: Rutgers University Press, 2000.

———. *Sound Recording: The Life Story of a Technology*. Westport, CT: Greenwood, 2004.

Moses, Wilson J. "Writing Freely? Frederick Douglass and the Constraints of Racialized Writing." Sundquist, *Frederick Douglass* 66–83.

Murray, Sonia. "'Dirty South' Dominates the Hip-Hop Revolution." *Atlanta Journal-Constitution* 28 Sept. 2004: E1.

Myers, Mitch. "Extended Family: Allman Brothers Band Is as Influential as Ever as It Celebrates 35 Years Together." *Down Beat* October 2004: 54–59.

Nabokov, Vladimir. *Lectures on Literature*. Ed. Fredson Bowers. San Diego: Harcourt Brace, 1980.

———. *Pnin*. 1953. New York: Vintage International, 1989.

Naipaul, V. S. *A Turn in the South*. London: Penguin, 1989.

"National Recording Preservation Board: The National Recording Registry 2004." *National Recording Registry*. 2004. Library of Congress. 24 Sept. 2006 http://www.loc.gov/rr/record/nrpb/nrpb-2004reg.html.

Neal, Mark Anthony. *Soul Babies: Black Popular Culture and the Post-Soul Aesthetic*. New York: Routledge, 2002.

Nelson, Oliver. Liner Notes. *The Blues and the Abstract Truth*. 1961. Impulse!, 1995.

Nichols, Charles H., ed. *Arna Bontemps–Langston Hughes Letters: 1925–1967*. New York: Paragon House, 1990.

O'Brien, Ron, and Andy McKaie. "American by Birth . . . (Southern by the Grace of God)." Booklet. 3–25. *Lynyrd Skynyrd*. By Lynyrd Skynyrd. 3 cassettes. MCA, 1991.

O'Connor, John J. "The Trip to Dignity in 3 Short Stories." Rev. of "Long Black Song," "The Boy Who Painted Christ Black," and "The Reunion." *New York Times*. 16 Feb. 1996. 31 May 2008 http://query.nytimes.com/gst/fullpage.html?res= 990CE 5D81239F935A25751C0A960958260&sec=&spon=&pagewanted=all.

Odom, Gene, and Frank Dorman. *Lynyrd Skynyrd: Remembering the Free Birds of Southern Rock*. New York: Broadway, 2002.

Ogbar, Jeffrey O. G. *Hip-Hop Revolution: The Culture and Politics of Rap*. Lawrence: University Press of Kansas, 2007.

Oliver, Paul. *Blues Fell This Morning: Meaning in the Blues*. Cambridge: Cambridge University Press, 1960.

Olney, James. "Autobiography and the Cultural Moment: A Thematic, Historical, and Bibliographical Introduction." *Autobiography: Essays Theoretical and Critical*. Ed. James Olney. Princeton, NJ: Princeton University Press, 1980. 2–38.

———. *Memory and Narrative: The Weave of Life-Writing*. Chicago: University of Chicago Press, 1998.

O'Neal, Jim. "I Once Was Lost, But Now I'm Found: The Blues Revival of the 1960s." Cohn 347–87.

Ostendorf, Berndt. *Black Literature in White America*. Sussex: Harvester, 1982.

Ownby, Ted. "Freedom, Manhood, and White Male Tradition in 1970s Southern Rock Music." *Haunted Bodies: Gender and Southern Texts*. Eds. Anne Goodwyn Jones and Susan V. Donaldson. Charlotteville: The University of Virginia Press, 1998. 369–88.

Palmer, Robert. *Deep Blues*. New York: Viking, 1981.

———. *Rock and Roll: An Unruly History*. New York: Harmony, 1995.

Pavliç, Edward. *Crossroads Modernism: Descent and Emergence in African-American Literary Culture*. Minneapolis: University of Minnesota Press, 2002.

———. "'Papa Legba, ouvrier barriere por moi passer': Esu in *Their Eyes* and Zora Neale Hurston's Diasporic Modernism." *African American Review* 38.1 (2004): 61–85.

Pearson, Barry Lee, and Bill McCulloch. *Robert Johnson: Lost and Found*. Urbana: University of Illinois Press, 2003.

Perkins, Willie. *No Saints, No Saviors: My Years with the Allman Brothers Band*. Macon, GA: Mercer University Press, 2005.

Perlah, Jeff. "The Road Goes on Forever." *Electronic Musician*. 10 Jan. 2008. 30 May 2008 http://emusician.com/onstage/interviews/road-goes-forever/.

Petry, Ann. *The Street*. 1946. Boston: Houghton Mifflin, 1991.

Pitt, Barrie. *1918: The Last Act*. New York: Norton, 1963.

Poe, Randy. *Skydog: The Duane Allman Story*. San Francisco: Backbeat, 2006.

Potter, Russell A. *Spectacular Vernaculars: Hip-Hop and the Politics of Postmodernism*. Albany: State University of New York Press, 1995.

"Proclamation Day in Boston." *Liberator* 9 Jan. 1863: 7.

Quarles, Benjamin. *Frederick Douglass*. New York: Atheneum, 1968.

Raboteau, Albert J. *Slave Religion: The "Invisible Institution" in the Antebellum South.* New York: Oxford University Press, 1978.

Randall, Alice. *The Wind Done Gone*. New York: Mariner, 2002.

Randall, Dudley. "Legacy: My South." Hill et al. 1145–46.

Rankin, William. "Ineffability in the Fiction of Jean Toomer and Katherine Mansfield." *Renaissance and Modern: Essays in Honor of Edwin M. Moseley*. Ed. Murray J. Levith. Saratoga Springs, NY: Skidmore College, 1976. 160–76.

Rasula, Jed. "Jazzbandism." *Georgia Review* 60.1 (2006): 61–124.

Raybourn, Carole A. "The Black Aesthetic in Frederick Douglass's *Narrative*." *Postscript* 14 (1997): 29–41.

Reagon, Bernice Johnson. "Pioneering African American Gospel Music Composers: A Smithsonian Institution Research Project." *We'll Understand It Better By and By: Pioneering African American Gospel Composers*. Ed. Reagon. Washington, DC: Smithsonian, 1992. 3–18.

Redman, Joshua. Liner Notes. *Joshua Redman*. Warner, 1993.

Reed, Ishmael. "'I Feel Good': The Godfather of Everything." Rev. of *I Feel Good: A Memoir of a Life in Soul*. By James Brown. *New York Times*. 20 Feb. 2005. 31 May 2008 http://www.nytimes.com/2005/02/20/books/review/20REEDL. html?_r=1& sq=the%20godfather%20of%20everything%20reed&st=nyt&oref=slogin&scp= 1&pagewanted=all&position=.

Respect Yourself: The Stax Records Story. Dirs. Robert Gordon and Morgan Neville. Georgia Public Broadcasting Television. 6 Dec. 2007.

Richards, Keith. "Well, This Is It." *Robert Johnson: The Complete Recordings*. Booklet. 2 CDs. CBS, 1990. 21–22.

Ripley, Peter. "The Autobiographical Writings of Frederick Douglass." *Southern Studies: An Interdisciplinary Journal of the South* 24.1 (1985): 5–29.

Rochlitz, Rainer. *The Disenchantment of Art: The Philosophy of Walter Benjamin*. Trans. Jane Marie Todd. New York: Guilford, 1996.

Rosaldo, Renato. *Culture and Truth: The Remaking of Social Analysis*. Boston: Beacon, 1993.

Rosenbaum, Art. *Shout Because You're Free: The African American Ring Shout Tradition in Coastal Georgia*. Athens: University of Georgia Press, 1998.

Rothenberg, Kelly. "Frederick Douglass's *Narrative* and the Subtext of Folklore." *Griot* 14.1 (1995): 48–53.

Rowley, Hazel. *Richard Wright: The Life and Times*. New York: Henry Holt, 2001.

Rudinow, Joel. "Race, Ethnicity, Expressive Authenticity: Can White People Sing the Blues?" *Journal of Aesthetics and Art Criticism* 52.1 (1994): 127–37.

Rusch, Frederick L., ed. *A Jean Toomer Reader: Selected Unpublished Writings*. New York: Oxford University Press, 1993.

Rutheiser, Charles. *Imagineering Atlanta: The Politics of Place in the City of Dreams*. London: Verso, 1996.

Sanneh, Kelefa. "Lil John [sic] Crunks Up the Volume." *New York Times*. 28 Nov. 2004. 31 May 2008 http://www.nytimes.com/2004/11/28/arts/music/28sann.html? scp=1&sq=lil+john+crunks+up+the+volume&st=nyt#.

Schroeder, Patricia R. *Robert Johnson, Mythmaking, and Contemporary American Culture*. Urbana: University of Illinois Press, 2004.

Schuller, Gunther. *Early Jazz: Its Roots and Musical Development.* 1968. New York: Oxford University Press, 1986.

———. *The Swing Era: The Development of Jazz, 1930–1945.* New York: Oxford University Press, 1989.

Scott, Jeffry. "Attorney: Info Withheld in Williams Case." *Atlanta Journal-Constitution* 9 June 2006: E3.

———, and Bill Torpy. "Murders Made Atlanta Fear the Night." *Atlanta Journal Constitution* 15 May 2005: A1.

Scruggs, Charles. "The Mark of Cain and the Redemption of Art: A Study in the Theme and Structure of Jean Toomer's *Cane.*" *American Literature* 44.2 (1972): 276–91.

———, and Lee VanDemarr. *Jean Toomer and the Terrors of American History.* Philadelphia: University of Pennsylvania Press, 1998.

Sheridan, Chris. *Count Basie: A Bio-Discography.* New York: Greenwood, 1986.

Smith, William E. *Hip Hop as Performance and Ritual: Biography and Ethnography in Underground Hip Hop.* Washington, DC: CLS, 2005.

Smitherman, Geneva. *Talkin and Testifyin: The Language of Black America.* Detroit: Wayne State University Press, 1977.

Sollors, Werner. "Modernization as Adultery: Richard Wright, Zora Neale Hurston, and American Culture of the 1930s and 1940s." *Hebrew University Studies in Literature and the Arts* 18 (1990): 109–55.

"Southern Rock." *American Revolutions.* Prod. Ann Fentress. Country Music Television. 6 June 2005.

Spaulding, A. Timothy. *Re-Forming the Past: History, the Fantastic, and the Postmodern Slave Narrative.* Columbus: The Ohio State University Press, 2005.

Spielberg, Steven, dir. *The Color Purple.* 1985. DVD. Warner, 1997.

Spivak, Gayatri Chakravorty. "Translator's Preface." *Of Grammatology.* By Jacques Derrida. Baltimore: Johns Hopkins University Press, 1976. ix–lxxxvii.

Spottswood, Richard. Liner Notes. *The Slide Guitar: Bottles, Knives & Steel.* Columbia, 1990.

Stampp, Kenneth M. *The Peculiar Institution: Slavery in the Ante-Bellum South.* New York: Knopf, 1956.

Standing in the Shadows of Motown. Dir. Paul Justman. Bravo Television. 11 July 2005.

Stepto, Robert B. *From Behind the Veil: A Study of Afro-American Narrative.* Rev. ed. Urbana: University of Illinois Press, 1991.

Stewart-Baxter, Derrick. *Ma Rainey and the Classic Blues Singers.* New York: Stein and Day, 1970.

Stolle, Roger. "Standing at the Crossroads." *The Original Blues Festival Guide 2005.* Ed. Michele Lundeen. Reno, NV: RBL Publishing, 2005. 40+.

Stone, Albert E. "Identity and Art in Frederick Douglass's *Narrative.*" Andrews, *Critical Essays* 62–78.

Stop Coonin. 2007. Stop Coonin Movement. 11 May 2008 http://www. stopcoonin. com.

Stuckey, Sterling. *Slave Culture: Nationalist Theory and the Foundations of Black America.* New York: Oxford University Press, 1987.

Suarez, Ernest. "'Will You Hide the Dead Man's Ghost?': The Legacy of Duane Allman." *Five Points* 1.3 (1997): 85–105.

Suggs, Ernie, and Mae Gentry. "Skeptical Police Chief Resurrects 'Missing and Murdered' Cases." *Atlanta Journal-Constitution* 12 May 2005: A1.

Sundquist, Eric J., ed. *Frederick Douglass: New Literary and Historical Essays.* Cambridge: Cambridge University Press, 1990.

———. *To Wake the Nations: Race in the Making of American Literature.* Cambridge, MA: Belknap, 1993.

Swenson, John. Liner notes. *Dreams.* By the Allman Brothers Band. 2–23. 4 CDs. Island/Mercury, 1989.

Taylor, Carole Anne. "Postmodern Disconnection and the Archive of Bones: Toni Cade Bambara's Last Work." *Novel: A Forum on Fiction* 35/2–3 (2002): 258–81.

Taylor, Charles. *The Ethics of Authenticity.* Cambridge, MA: Harvard University Press, 1991.

Toomer, Jean. *Cane.* 1923. Ed. Darwin T. Turner. New York: Norton, 1988.

———. "Music." 1937. Rusch 276.

———. "The South." Rusch 233–34.

———. *The Wayward and the Seeking: A Collection of Writings by Jean Toomer.* Ed. Darwin T. Turner. Washington, DC: Howard University Press, 1982.

Tracy, Steven C. Introduction. *Write Me* 1–7.

———, ed. *Write Me a Few of Your Lines: A Blues Reader.* Amherst: University of Massachusetts Press, 1999.

Turner, Darwin T., ed. *Cane.* By Jean Toomer. New York: Norton, 1988.

———. Introduction. *Cane.* By Jean Toomer. New York: Liveright, 1975. ix–xxv.

———. "Jean Toomer and the South: Region and Race as Elements within a Literary Imagination." *The Harlem Renaissance Re-examined.* Ed. Victor A. Kramer. New York: AMS Press, 1987. 185–99.

Turner, Victor. *Dramas, Fields, and Metaphors: Symbolic Action in Human Society.* Ithaca, NY: Cornell University Press, 1994.

———. "Images of Anti-Temporality: An Essay in the Anthropology of Experience." *On the Edge* 227–46.

———. *On the Edge of the Bush: Anthropology as Experience.* Ed. Edith L. B. Turner. Tucson: University of Arizona Press, 1985.

———. "Process, System, and Symbol: A New Anthropological Synthesis." *On the Edge* 151–73.

Twain, Mark. *The Adventures of Huckleberry Finn.* 1884. Ed. Peter Coveney. London: Penguin, 1987.

Van Leer, David. "Reading Slavery: The Anxiety of Ethnicity in Douglass's *Narrative.*" Sundquist, *Frederick Douglass* 119–40.

Vernon, Paul. *Jean "Django" Reinhardt: A Contextual Bio-Discography 1910–1953.* Hampshire: Ashgate, 2003.

Von Fischer, Kurt. *Griegs Harmonik und die norwegische Folklore.* Berner Veröffentlichungen zur Musikforschung. Vol. 12. Ed. Ernst Kurth. Bern: Paul Haupt, 1938.

Von Schmidt, Eric, and Jim Rooney. "Fixin' to Die." Tracy, *Write Me* 531–39.

Wald, Elijah. *Escaping the Delta: Robert Johnson and the Invention of the Blues.* New York: Amistad, 2004.

Walker, Alice. *The Color Purple.* 1982. New York: Pocket, 1985.

Walker, David F. *Moral Choices: Memory, Desire, and Imagination in Nineteenth-Century American Abolition.* Baton Rouge: Louisiana State University Press, 1978.

Walker, Margaret. *Richard Wright: Daemonic Genius*. New York: Amistad, 1988.

Warren, Kenneth W. "Frederick Douglass's *Life and Times:* Progressive Rhetoric and the Problem of Constituency." Sundquist, *Frederick Douglass* 253–70.

Weber, Donald. "From Limen to Border: A Meditation on the Legacy of Victor Turner for American Cultural Studies." *American Quarterly* 47.3 (1995): 525–36.

Weber, Harry R. "New Test Can't Exclude Williams as Child Killer." *Atlanta Journal-Constitution*. 2 Aug. 2007. 22 Aug. 2007 http://www.ajc.com/search/content/metro/stories/2007/08/02/wayne.html.

Wells, Paul. "The Last Rebel: Southern Rock and Nostalgic Continuities." *Dixie Debates: Perspectives on Southern Cultures*. Eds. Richard King and Helen Taylor. New York: New York University Press, 1996. 115–29.

Welty, Eudora. "Place in Fiction." 1956. *The Eye of the Storm: Selected Essays and Reviews*. New York: Random House, 1977. 116–33.

Werner, Craig Hansen. *Playing the Changes: From Afro-Modernism to the Jazz Impulse*. Urbana: University of Illinois Press, 1994.

Westerfield, Hargis. "Jean Toomer's 'Fern': A Mythical Dimension." *Jean Toomer: A Critical Evaluation*. Ed. Therman B. O'Daniel. Washington, DC: Howard University Press, 1988. 269–72.

White, Booker T. "Bukka." "Blues Really Ringing Around There Like Birds: Bukka White at the Office." Hay 3–25.

Wilkins, Joe Willie, Houston Stackhouse, and Willis "Hillbilly" Kenibrew. "Why Don't You Cut Me Up Some Bream There: Beer Party at Joe Willie Wilkins's House with Houston Stackhouse and Willis "Hillbilly' Kenibrew." Hay 197–239.

Wilson, August. *Fences*. 1987. Gates et al. *Norton* 2411–62.

Woodward, C. Vann. *The Burden of Southern History*. Rev. ed. Baton Rouge: Louisiana State University Press, 1970.

———. *Origins of the New South, 1877–1913*. 1951. Baton Rouge: Louisiana State University Press, 1970.

Wright, Richard. *Black Boy*. 1944. Rev. ed. Ed. Arnold Rampersad. New York: Harper Perennial, 1993.

———. "Blueprint for Negro Writing." 1937. Gates et al. *Norton* 1380–88.

———. *Eight Men*. 1961. New York: Harper Perennial, 1996.

———. Foreword. *Blues Fell This Morning: Meaning in the Blues*. By Paul Oliver. Cambridge: Cambridge University Press, 1960.

———. "How Bigger Was Born." 1940. *Native Son* vii–xxxiv.

———. "Jazz and Desire." *Conversations with Richard Wright*. Eds. Kenneth Kinnamon and Michel Fabre. Jackson: University Press of Mississippi, 1993. 242–43.

———. *The Long Dream*. 1958. Boston: Northeastern University Press, 2000.

———. *Native Son*. 1940. New York: Perennial, 1989.

———. *Twelve Million Black Voices: A Folk History of the Negro in the United States*. 1941. New York: Thunder's Mouth, 2002.

———. *Uncle Tom's Children*. 1940. New York: Harper Perennial, 2004.

Young, Carlton E. *Companion to the United Methodist Hymnal*. Nashville: Abingdon, 1993.

Youngren, William H. "European Roots of Jazz." *The Oxford Companion to Jazz*. Ed. Bill Kirchner. New York: Oxford University Press, 2000. 17–28.